TOGETHER WE

Wellness and Resilience Framework

Tonya Hotchkin | Tanager

This book is offered as a resource for reflection, connection, and growth. It is not a substitute for professional medical, psychological, or therapeutic care. Healing and support often happen in relationship—if additional care is needed, seeking support from a qualified professional is an important part of that journey.

Published in the United States by
Tanager Press, LLC
Cedar Rapids, Iowa

Cover design by Mary Foreman
Original cover painting by Tonya Hotchkin

ISBN: 979-8-9951796-0-3 (paperback)
ISBN: 979-8-9951796-1-0 (e-book)

Printed in the United States of America

DEDICATION

To the children of my heart—

This role of mothering has been my greatest joy and my hardest journey—both blessed and exhausting, giving and humbling, fulfilling and painful. Nothing and no one can prepare you for what it means to hold so much love and so much letting go all at once. It has been the arena where I've stumbled the most, and the place where I've found the deepest purpose.

Bubba, Peanut, Journ, and Syd, thank you for letting me be in your life and for trusting me to be a safe place.

To my little brother, Skyler, the soul who first made me a mother—

You are one of the brightest rays I've ever felt. You made the sunshine warmer and the grass grow greener. Being called "Mom" by you carried my light forward through our darkest times, guiding me with a purpose I hadn't known I needed. Our souls have been intertwined since the day you were born. You left this earth far too soon. Thank you for teaching me the true meaning of unconditional love.

And to my three babies—

You will always be my North Star. You are the greatest gifts—to me, to this world. Keep shining. I am endlessly grateful to watch your stories unfold, loving you every step of the way. May you always know your light.

CONTENTS

INTRODUCTION

I am so glad you have picked up this book. It is an honor to share the RISE Framework and connect with others who believe in the greatness people bring to the world. The RISE Framework has a long history—and like most meaningful things, its evolution has not followed a straight path. It is difficult to pinpoint exactly how it came together because, in many ways, it has always lived in the hearts and experiences of those who care deeply about human growth (Hotchkin, 2020).

When I began my career, I wanted to be a therapist who specialized in trauma and attachment. I felt drawn to the parts of people that carried pain, but also to what was still possible for them. I trained extensively in neuroscience, attachment, and the impact of adversity. However, what I longed for most was the second half of the story—the part that asked what healing might look like. I wanted to know what helped people rise. Why did some move forward with strength and connection, even after hardship? What helped them live from a place of resilience and wholeness? And could we intentionally foster this in ourselves and others?

Those questions launched nearly a decade of listening, studying, reflecting, and learning from those who have borne the weight of life's greatest trials. The RISE Framework emerged from that work. It is a collection of ideas and practices shaped by consistent patterns in research, story, and lived experience. RISE is about seeing more deeply. It is about hope, connection, and the strength we find in our shared humanity. It embraces complexity and honors the full experience of being human. At its core, RISE represents light. Even in our darkest moments, the sun rises again. That light is in each of us. We all have the capacity to cultivate wellness and resilience—both for ourselves and for others.

The ideas you will explore here are rooted in four guiding beliefs that form the heart of this work:

Everyone has greatness within them.
Each person carries inherent value, gifts, and potential. With the right conditions, that core goodness within us can emerge, allowing what we bring to the world to be seen, felt, and needed.

We all long to be our best selves.
We all long to be our best selves, and when someone isn't doing well, it often reflects unmet needs or unresolved pain—because it is through safe, compassionate relationships that our capacity for healing and growth is supported.

The world is deeply connected.
Our lives are woven together in ways both visible and unseen, where what nurtures one of us nurtures us all—and through compassion and altruism, we strengthen the web of humanity that holds us.

Every moment offers a chance to build resilience and wellness.
Growth lives not in milestones but in the everyday moments when we show up with care, presence, and authenticity—honoring humans as whole beings: mind, body, and spirit.

While the RISE Framework can be applied to ourselves, our leadership, and the systems we create to support others, this book centers on youth. Here, we explore how the RISE domains and elements can be nurtured in the lives of young people, across the relationships and environments that shape their development.

The RISE Framework is used in many different settings where adults and youth engage with one another. By adult, I mean anyone parenting, caregiving, or walking alongside youth—birth parents, foster parents, relatives, educators, counselors, therapists, and others in supportive roles. By youth, I mean anyone from birth through age eighteen (or even into young adulthood, as our brains continue developing).

As you read this book, my hope is that you find inspiration and encouragement. Let these ideas meet you where you are, and notice what resonates in your own story. Throughout these pages, you will encounter *RISE Invitations*—gentle pauses meant to deepen reflection and connection. You are invited to engage with them in whatever way feels natural: to linger, to skip, to return later, or simply to notice what arises. There is no right way to move through this work—only your way.

RISE is not just a framework—it is an invitation to slow down, to see more deeply, and to nurture the light in yourself and others. May these pages remind you that you are a bright place in this world, that growth is always possible, and that together, we can rise toward greater wholeness and wellbeing.

RISE INVITATION

Arrive. Notice where you are right now—physically, mentally, and emotionally. There is no need to change anything. Just notice.

Reflect on your why. What drew you to this book? Let yourself lean into that as you explore these pages.

Notice your light. The RISE Framework wants you to begin this journey with a belief: You matter. The world needs you.

Set a gentle intention. As you move through these pages, you do not need to have all the answers. Instead, choose an intention grounded in self-love.

As you read, notice what resonates. Notice what stays with you. Notice what invites you to grow. What might it look like to meet yourself with curiosity as you begin?

You are already doing such beautiful work.

Thank you for being here.

RISE: WELLNESS & RESILIENCE FRAMEWORK

The RISE Framework is built around four interconnected domains that nurture both the inner and outer work of wellness and resilience. In this framework, RISE is used as an acronym. Each domain is introduced here and explored more deeply in the chapters ahead, reflecting how we relate, grow, and find balance within ourselves and with others.

Beneath these domains are the foundations that hold them steady—insights drawn from neuroscience, attachment, family systems, and restorative practices. Like roots beneath the surface, they shape how we understand human development, connection, and healing. Together, the foundations and each RISE domain form a living pathway—one that honors the whole person and guides us toward resilience and wellbeing in everyday life.

R — RELATIONSHIPS

The elements for engaging in authentic relationships rooted in emotional intelligence.

- **Experiences:** Understanding the influence of life experiences on human development
- **The You Intervention:** Cultivating personal insight to offer a centered expression of self
- **Characteristics:** Applying practices of intentional engagement

I — INDICATOR OF WELLBEING

The conditions for fostering a sense of psychological wellness and resilience.

- **Safety:** Establishing physical, emotional, and psychological security
- **Connection and Belonging:** Inviting inclusion, collaboration, and cooperation
- **Meaning and Purpose:** Creating fulfillment through contribution and significance
- **Efficacy:** Empowering capability through encouragement and perseverance

S — SOCIAL AND EMOTIONAL DEVELOPMENT

The skills for developing regulatory interactions with self, others and the world.

- **Awareness:** Developing and applying awareness and insight
- **Affect Management:** Responding to affective states and regulating emotions
- **Relational Rhythms:** Building and maintaining adaptive relationships
- **Healthy Choices:** Using whole brain integration to guide decision-making

E — ENHANCEMENTS

The experiences for integrating the whole person.

- **Body:** Nurturing one's physical vessel
- **Mind:** Maturing one's thoughts, feelings and beliefs
- **Spirit:** Connecting to higher energy

PART I: FOUNDATIONS

Theories informing the RISE: Wellness & Resilience Framework

Foundations is the starting point of the RISE Framework because it weaves together the science, theory, and deep wisdom of the human experience—the very elements that bring RISE to life. Before building the practical tools and applications that follow, I needed a solid base—one grounded in research and informed by experts who have spent decades studying what helps humans rise.

Much of what I intrinsically knew about RISE—the power of relationships, the role of wellness, and the potential for growth and healing—was affirmed and expanded by this research. The theories became the backbone of the framework, giving structure and validation to what I had long felt to be true.

This foundation sits at the crossroads of four interconnected disciplines: Neuroscience, Attachment theory, Family systems, and Restorative practices. Each of these fields has evolved significantly over time, offering rich insights into how our brains, relationships, and communities shape our capacity to feel safe, connected, and capable of greatness. In this section, you will explore four core components:

- **Neuroscience:** Understanding how the brain develops, manages stress, and adapts through relationships and experiences
- **Attachment Theory:** Recognizing how secure, trusting connections form the basis for resilience, identity, and emotional wellbeing.

- **Family Systems:** Exploring how internal and external families function as interconnected units, where patterns, roles, dynamics and relationships influence development and wellbeing.

- **Restorative Practices:** Honoring our deep interconnectedness and learning how intentional relationship-building, shared responsibility and repair strengthen conditions for healing and collective wellness.

Together, these theoretical constructs form the foundation for everything within the RISE Framework. They provide the lens through which we can better understand what youth—and all of us—need not only to survive, but also to truly flourish. This is where RISE begins: by grounding its practices in both science and wisdom, ensuring that every part of the framework that follows is deeply human and evidence-informed.

Before we go further, I want to offer you something important. This section is intentionally rich in science and theory. It is the scaffolding that holds the stories and practices together—but it is also more educational in tone than the chapters that follow it. If you find yourself craving story, heart, and lived experience, you are welcome to skip ahead to *Stories from the Cradle (0-6)* and then move into Part II: Relationships. You can always return here in smaller pieces, taking in one theory at a time. Think of this section as a reference point—something you can revisit when you want to understand why the work matters. There is no right way to move through this book. Follow your curiosity. Follow your energy. RISE will meet you wherever you begin.

CHAPTER ONE

Neuroscience

Every strong framework begins with understanding—and every understanding begins with curiosity. The science of resilience is not just about neurons or patterns; it is about the story of being human. These foundations remind us that resilience is not built overnight—it grows from the unseen systems that nourish us: the brain that adapts, the relationships that anchor us, the families that shape us, and the communities that restore us. To understand behavior, we must first understand the brain in action.

How the Brain Develops

The foundation of RISE is deeply rooted in neuroscience—the study of how the brain develops and responds to experience. Over the past several decades, this field has transformed how we understand behavior, particularly through the work of researchers like Dr. Bruce Perry, who helped shift the lens from punishment to understanding.

The human brain develops in a predictable sequence from the bottom up. The earliest structures to form are responsible for survival. As development continues, more complex systems emerge that support emotion, connection, and eventually reasoning. At the base is the brainstem, which regulates essential functions such as breathing, heart rate, and temperature. Above that sits the limbic system, where emotional processing lives, including the amygdala, which scans for safety and threat. The final layer to fully develop is the neocortex—the part of the brain responsible for reasoning, decision-making, impulse control, and abstract thinking. This region continues developing into early adulthood.

Because of this bottom-up sequence, early experiences matter deeply. When children grow up in environments that are predictable, safe, and nurturing, the brain builds strong, integrated pathways. When those early experiences are marked by stress or adversity, the brain adapts for survival.

Imagine a city built in layers over time. At its center are the oldest roads—simple, essential pathways that keep life moving. As the city expands, new roads form, buildings rise, and connections grow more complex. When the foundation is strong, communication flows easily throughout the system. But when early pathways are disrupted, the flow between regions becomes less efficient.

This is not a flaw in the brain—it is adaptation.

Research on Adverse Childhood Experiences (ACEs) has shown that early adversity is linked to long-term health and behavioral outcomes (Felitti et al., 1998). These findings are not predictions of a fixed future, but insights into how the brain organizes itself around experience—and how it can be reshaped through healing relationships and environments.

A Way to Understand the Brain: Upstairs and Downstairs

One helpful way to understand this layered development is through the concept of the "upstairs" and "downstairs" brain (Siegel & Bryson, 2020). The upstairs brain, located in the neocortex, supports reasoning, problem-solving, impulse control, and empathy. It allows us to pause, reflect, and make thoughtful decisions. The downstairs brain includes the limbic system and brainstem. This is where survival and emotional responses live. It is constantly scanning for safety, storing emotional memories, and preparing the body to respond to threat.

Picture a home with two floors. Upstairs is bright and open—this is where learning, connection, and thoughtful decision-making happen. Downstairs is more primitive and protective, designed to keep us alive. A staircase connects the two. When we feel safe, that staircase is open. Communication flows easily between emotion and reason. But when stress or threat is perceived, the connection weakens. The door between upstairs and downstairs can shut, and the brain shifts control to the systems designed for survival.

RISE INVITATION

Think of your own "city." When life feels stressful, which parts of your brain-city do you find yourself in?

What helps you return to the wider roads of calm and connection?

When Stress Takes Over

When the brain senses danger—whether real or perceived—it prioritizes protection over connection. The downstairs brain becomes more active, and access to the upstairs brain becomes limited. This is often described as "flipping our lid" (Siegel, 2020). In these moments, behavior is no longer driven by thoughtful decision-making. Instead, it is driven by survival responses. This is why individuals may react quickly, intensely, or in ways that seem disproportionate to the situation. These responses are not choices. They are the brain doing exactly what it is designed to do: keep us safe. Understanding this shifts how we respond to behavior. What may look like defiance, avoidance, or overreaction is often a nervous system working hard to manage stress.

The Window of Tolerance

Our ability to stay connected to both our upstairs and downstairs brain depends on something called the window of tolerance (Siegel, 2020). The window of tolerance describes the range in which we can experience stress while still remaining regulated, present, and connected. Within this window, we are able to think clearly, feel emotions without becoming overwhelmed, and engage with others in meaningful ways.

When stress moves beyond what our system can manage, we shift outside of this window. Sometimes we move into hyperarousal—where the system becomes activated. This can look like anxiety, anger, agitation, or over-functioning. At other times, we move into hypoarousal—where the system slows down. This can look like withdrawal, numbness, disconnection, or shutdown.

Imagine this as a river. When the current is steady, we float in the middle—aware, present, and able to navigate what comes our way. But when the current becomes too strong, we are pushed toward one bank—into overwhelm and reactivity. When it slows too much, we drift toward the other—into stillness and disconnection (Siegel, 2020).

Our window is shaped by both our biology and our experiences. Chronic stress and trauma can narrow this space, making it easier to be pushed outside of it. But the hopeful truth is that our window is not fixed. Through supportive relationships, consistent routines, and practices that promote regulation—like rest, movement, connection, and mindfulness—we can gradually expand this window. Over time, the nervous system becomes more flexible, and we are better able to return to a place of balance.

We cannot always control the storms. But we can strengthen our ability to move through them. And we can hold ourselves with compassion along the way.

RISE INVITATION

Take a slow, grounding breath. Inhale. Hold. Exhale. Hold. Notice how your body feels when the breath settles. This small act expands your window of tolerance.

Polyvagal Theory: Understanding the Body's Role

If the window of tolerance describes what we experience, polyvagal theory helps explain why it happens in the body. Developed by Dr. Stephen Porges, polyvagal theory focuses on the autonomic nervous system and the role of the vagus nerve in regulating safety and connection. The nervous system is constantly asking one central question: "Am I safe?" Based on that answer, it shifts between different states.

In a state of safety and connection—known as the ventral vagal state—we feel calm, engaged, and open to others. This is where learning, relationship, and growth happen. When the system detects threat, it moves into a sympathetic state. The body mobilizes for action—heart rate increases, muscles tense, and we prepare to fight or flee. If the threat feels overwhelming or inescapable, the system may shift into a dorsal vagal state. The body slows down, leading to shutdown, numbness, or disconnection.

These shifts can be imagined as moving up and down a ladder throughout the day (Dana, 2023). Safety and connection help us stay near the top. Stress and threat move us down. Regulation helps us climb back up. This is not a conscious process—it is automatic, protective, and deeply human.

RISE INVITATION

When you see someone in distress, notice your own breathing first. Slow it. Soften your voice. Let your calm presence become the ladder they can climb.

Safety is contagious; your regulated nervous system invites theirs to follow.

Bringing It All Together

These concepts are not separate—they are different ways of understanding the same system. The structure of the brain helps us understand how it develops. The upstairs and downstairs metaphor helps us understand how it functions. The window of tolerance helps us understand our capacity to stay regulated. Polyvagal theory helps us understand how the body shifts between states of safety and protection. Together, they offer a powerful lens: behavior is not simply a choice—it is a reflection of the nervous system's current state.

What This Means for Behavior

Every behavior communicates something about what the brain and body are experiencing. When a person lashes out, withdraws, or shuts down, they are not choosing disconnection—they are responding to what their nervous system perceives as necessary for safety.

Trauma is stored not just as a memory, but as a sensory experience. The brain does not always distinguish between past and present. A smell, a sound, or a tone of voice can activate a response that once served as protection. For example, if someone experienced harm connected to a specific scent, encountering that scent years later may trigger a strong reaction. The body responds as though the danger is happening again. This is why curiosity matters. When we approach behavior with understanding rather than judgment, we create space for connection. And it is within connection that regulation—and healing—becomes possible.

RISE INVITATION

When you notice yourself or someone else reacting strongly, pause and ask: What might the body remember that the mind has forgotten?

An Integrated Brain

As the brain and body become more integrated, individuals are better able to move between states, return to calm, and stay connected—even in the presence of stress. Integration allows emotion and reasoning to work together rather than in opposition, strengthening the pathways between the upstairs and downstairs brain and widening the window of tolerance.

This integration is not built through control—it is built through experience. Safe relationships, predictable environments, and moments of attuned connection all shape the developing brain. Each interaction has the potential to reinforce pathways of regulation, wellness, and resilience. We are not simply managing behavior. We are shaping brain architecture.

Neuroscience reminds us that the brain is always changing. That even in the face of hardships, the brain holds the capacity to grow, adapt, and reconnect. This is the heart of RISE. That within each of us is the potential—not just to survive—but to rise.

CHAPTER TWO

Attachment Theory

Attachment theory is a cornerstone of understanding and applying the RISE Framework in daily practice. Bowlby (1988) described attachment as a deep emotional bond that forms between an infant and their primary caregiver. This relationship becomes the blueprint for how we experience safety, connection, and love throughout our lives. Mary Ainsworth's research further demonstrated how early interactions—how caregivers respond to an infant's needs—shape a child's expectations of the world (Ainsworth & Bowlby, 1991; Allen, 2023). Attachment is a reciprocal process of emotional connection that influences not only relationships but also neurological, cognitive, and psychological development (Duschinsky, Granqvist & Forslund, 2023).

Attachment Patterns

A secure attachment provides a child with a safe base from which to explore the world. When caregivers are attuned and responsive, children internalize a sense of "The world is safe, and I am worthy." This sense of safety becomes the soil in which wellbeing and resilience grow. Secure attachment teaches children how to regulate emotions, trust others, and seek help when needed—all essential skills for navigating adversity later in life.

However, not all early relationships provide that foundation. When caregivers are inconsistent, emotionally unavailable, or frightening, children adapt in ways that help them survive. These adaptive responses become insecure attachment patterns—complex relational strategies that make sense in unsafe environments but can later interfere with connection and trust.

- **Anxious Attachment:** Formed when caregivers are inconsistent or unpredictable. The child learns that love is uncertain, so they cling tightly in an effort to keep it close. Imagine a child who follows their caregiver from room to room, seeking reassurance. Their body is often on high alert, scanning for signs of disconnection. Beneath the clinginess is fear—fear of being forgotten or left behind. Their need: "Please notice me. Please stay."

- **Avoidant Attachment:** Develops when caregivers are emotionally distant or dismissive. The child learns that showing need leads to rejection, so they turn inward, appearing self-sufficient. You might see a youth who shrugs off help, rarely cries, or seems overly independent. Their calm exterior often hides loneliness and longing. Their unspoken message: "It's safer not to need anyone."

- **Disorganized Attachment:** Emerges in the presence of fright or trauma, when a caregiver is both the source of comfort and fear. The child becomes confused and fearful about how to get their needs met. They may approach for safety, then withdraw in panic, unsure whether connection will soothe or harm. Imagine a youth whose eyes flicker between wanting closeness and pushing others away. Beneath the chaos lies profound vulnerability—the body's attempt to survive when love and danger live in the same person.

These patterns are not flaws; they are the brain's creative attempts to adapt to inconsistent or unsafe caregiving. They exist along a continuum of anxiety and avoidance, shaping how we approach closeness, dependence, and autonomy. The hopeful truth is that attachment is not fixed. Healing occurs when new experiences of safety, attunement, and reliability begin to reshape our internal maps of relationships.

Attachment and Resilience

Secure attachment does more than create emotional safety—it builds resilience. It is the original template for how humans manage stress and return to balance. Through secure bonds, children learn co-regulation: the experience of another person's calm nervous system helping their own body settle. Over time and experience, this repeated pattern becomes internalized self-regulation.

When attachment has been disrupted, secure patterns can still be cultivated later in life through new relational experiences. Healing begins with safety—when someone shows up again and again, with predictability and care. It deepens through connection; another person notices our signals and responds appropriately. And it expands through repaired relational rhythms, when ruptures in the relationship are acknowledged and mended rather than ignored.

These experiences teach the nervous system a new truth: Safety is possible here. Gradually, the body learns to soften, trust, and stay connected in moments of stress. That is the work of resilience—transforming survival patterns into pathways for growth.

RISE INVITATION

When a young person's behavior feels confusing—maybe clingy one moment and then distant the next or constantly shutting down or requiring frequent reassurance—pause and ask: What might this behavior be protecting? What might it be longing for?

When supporting youth, consistency is healing.

Choose one small, dependable act—greeting them by name, following through on a promise, or offering calm presence after big feelings.

Over time, these moments of reliability rebuild trust where uncertainty once lived.

The Power of Relationship and Perseverance

One of my most influential mentors, Dr. Randy Lyle, once taught me a lesson I have never forgotten. I asked him how to help a child struggling with self-esteem. I expected a list of strategies; perhaps what theoretical orientation could address this best in the therapeutic context. Instead, he asked one question: "Who is in their life?"

That question changed my understanding of healing. We exist in the context of attachment patterns and relationships; self-worth is born and sustained through secure attachment patterns. Our sense of value is reflected in the faces of those who see us and stay. The youth we encounter carry attachment patterns shaped by their earliest experiences—patterns that will echo in their relationships with us. Healing happens not through correction, but through connection: when we model security, reliability, and compassion. It is the patient, persistent rhythm of showing up—especially when it is hard—that reshapes attachment.

We often long to see behavioral change quickly, yet transformation is slow. Secure attachment is built through repetition, not perfection. When a child seeks attention, resists connection, or pushes boundaries, those behaviors are often bids for safety and connection. Our job is to stay steady—to be the calm in their storm. Over time, our reliability becomes their new internal rhythm. Connection and safety are foundational. New relational skills can only take root when a person feels secure enough to engage. Later in this book, we will explore how honoring boundaries and addressing harm are vital to healthy relational patterns—because resilience also grows when we teach that relationships are reciprocal, and everyone has a role in repairing them.

Attachment is not simply a theory—it is the living fabric of human resilience. It reminds us that healing does not happen in isolation but through the steady rhythm of safe relationships. Each moment of attunement, each act of repair, and every time we harness our own calm nervous system to offer predictability, we help rewire another's sense of safety and hope. Ultimately, attachment invites us into presence: the willingness to show up with steadiness, patience, and authenticity.

RISE INVITATION

Before responding to someone, you are supporting, pause and check in with your own body.

Is your breath calm? Is your voice gentle and steady? Can you offer predictability in this moment?

Your regulated, predictable presence is often the first lesson in safety.

CHAPTER THREE

Family Systems Theory

Every one of us is part of a living web—a system of relationships that shapes how we grow, adapt, and make meaning in the world. Over time, the messages and patterns of these early systems take root within us, forming—the network of beliefs and inner workings that guide how we relate to others and to ourselves. Family Systems Theory helps us see that we do not exist in isolation; we live within networks of connection that constantly influence our thoughts, emotions, and behaviors. From our earliest days, the family system teaches us what safety feels like and how love is given and received.

Think about the families you have known. Maybe your own is coming to mind, maybe ones you have worked with or observed. Every family has its own rhythm. Some talk loudly and tell stories around the table until long after dinner has ended. Some avoid hard conversations but show care through doing. Some rely on humor. Some walk on eggshells. Some wrap you in warmth the moment you step through the door.

Roles are important in families: some keep the peace while others confront, some lead while others follow. These everyday patterns become the lessons we carry into adulthood. And often, we don't realize we learned them until life presses on the places that hurt the most. These relational patterns become the templates through which we interpret the world. They guide our expectations, shape our identity, and influence how we show up—in conflict, in love, in caregiving, and in healing. To understand human resilience, we must first understand the systems that create us.

Seeing the System

Family Systems Theory reframes behavior as part of an ongoing pattern rather than an individual problem. Every action—even silence or resistance—is communication within the system's rhythm. When stress or change disrupts that rhythm, the system tries to regain balance. Sometimes it does this through a single member, often a child, whose behavior expresses what the family cannot say aloud.

Healthy systems adjust to stress. Rigid or chaotic systems cannot do this, so they fall back on old patterns that may have been protective in the past but are limiting in the present. These patterns become the unspoken rules of relationship: how we express emotion, how we handle conflict, how we define love and worth. We carry these rules into adulthood, and they quietly shape the way we parent, partner, and lead.

From Systems to Selves: Internal Family Systems

As we grow, the systems that once surrounded us begin to live inside us. The voices, patterns, and roles of our families become internalized, creating what psychologist Richard Schwartz (1995) describes as our Internal Family System (IFS). IFS reminds us that we are not one singular "Self" moving through the world, but a collection of parts—inner subpersonalities that carry our experiences, emotions, and protective strategies. Although IFS uses the word family, our "parts" are not our actual family members living inside the mind. They are aspects of ourselves—inner roles we created to stay safe, get needs met, or make sense of our experiences.

However, the families we grew up in strongly shape which parts we develop and how they learn to protect us. Families have patterns, roles, conflicts, alliances. Parts inside us behave in similar ways, and they carry patterns we learned from being a member of our particular family. These parts form naturally, as we develop. Each has a story and a role, and none are bad. They all emerged for good reason, often during times when we had little control or safety. However, over time, those once-helpful strategies can make it harder to connect and live vulnerably.

At the center of this internal system lives our Self—the calm, compassionate, and curious core of who we are. When the Self is leading, our parts can rest and cooperate. When the Self is overwhelmed or hidden, parts step in to protect and manage (Schwartz & Sweezy, 2020). In IFS, our protective parts often fall into two broad groups: Managers and Firefighters. These parts work tirelessly to shield us from pain held by Exiles (Schwartz, 1995), the parts that carry our most vulnerable emotions and memories.

- **Exiles:** The parts of us that carry deep pain, fear, or shame—often the echoes of childhood wounds and adversity. These are the tender, hidden aspects of ourselves that still hold memories of being hurt, abandoned, or neglected. Because their emotions can feel overwhelming, the rest of the system works hard to keep their pain contained. But when an exile's pain rises to the surface, the entire system can react with intensity.

- **Managers:** The parts that try to prevent that pain from being triggered in the first place. They work preemptively—organizing, controlling, pleasing, and perfecting—to keep life predictable and safe. A manager might be the voice that drives us to overachieve, the part that avoids conflict, or the one that always puts others' needs first. At their core, managers believe that if they can just maintain order or stay good enough, we won't have to feel the vulnerability of our exiles.

- **Firefighters:** The parts that rush in when the pain breaks through anyway. Their goal is immediate relief—putting out the emotional "fire" as quickly as possible. They often use distraction or intensity to numb the pain: bursts of anger, overeating, substance use, scrolling through social media, or overworking until exhaustion. In their own way, firefighters are trying to help us survive unbearable feelings. They may act impulsively, but their intent is protection.

Over time, these parts can become polarized—pushing and pulling against each other in an attempt to maintain balance. Managers tighten control, firefighter's rebel, and exiles cry out from underneath it all. Inside this internal struggle, the Self's voice can become quiet.

When we begin to approach our parts with curiosity and compassion rather than shame, the system starts to calm. Healing comes not from silencing or eliminating these parts, but from building relationship with them. When the Self leads with presence and empathy, our parts can soften their defenses and begin to trust that they no longer have to carry their burdens alone. Just as families heal through safety and connection, our internal systems heal through understanding and compassion.

RISE INVITATION

Think about a time you overreacted or withdrew and later wondered: Why did I do that?

What might that reaction have been trying to protect? Could there be a part of you that simply needed to feel safe?

Differentiation of Self

Family Systems Theory and Internal Family Systems intersect in a key concept: differentiation of self. Coined by Murray Bowen (1978), differentiation refers to the ability to maintain one's sense of identity while staying emotionally connected to others. It is the art of balancing autonomy and intimacy, individuality and belonging.

- **Fusion:** Absorbing others' emotions. Your perpetually stressed mother gives you a call and suddenly you are spiraling too—not because of anything that happened to you, but because you internalized her anxiety.
- **Cutoff:** Withdrawing completely. A difficult conversation with your partner ends, and you give the cold shoulder for days.
- **High Differentiation:** Your child's meltdown does not knock you off balance. You can stay calm and present without heightening your own emotions.

Youth who grow up in systems that nurture both connection and independence develop stronger differentiation. They learn that closeness does not erase individuality and that conflict does not mean abandonment. Adults with higher differentiation are more adaptable, self-aware, and emotionally regulated—the very qualities that help us rise when life becomes difficult.

Bringing It Together: Systems in Action

We are shaped by the systems around us and the systems within us—the families that raised us and the inner parts that continue their stories. When we begin to understand these dynamics, we stop seeing problems and start seeing patterns. This understanding changes everything: a child's anger, avoidance, or perfectionism is not defiance; it is protection. When we meet those reactions with curiosity instead of judgment, compassion instead of control, we become part of a new healing system—one that invites safety, trust, and growth.

Our task is not to fix the system but to bring calm awareness to it—to become the steady, regulated presence that helps restore balance. Healing begins when we can step back and see the whole dance: the patterns that move us, the parts that protect us, and the self that longs to lead. When we understand both the external families that shaped us and the internal families we carry within, we help ourselves and others build systems grounded in safety, compassion, and wholeness.

RISE INVITATION

Think of a young person whose behavior seems puzzling or extreme. Invite curiosity.

What patterns might they be repeating from their family system? What inner parts might be protecting them from pain or rejection?

CHAPTER FOUR

Restorative Practices

For generations, we have been conditioned to believe that change comes through control. From our earliest school days, we learned that good behavior earns reward and misbehavior earns punishment. We were taught compliance over curiosity, performance over play, and perfection over presence. These patterns were not accidental—they emerged from a westernized history that valued obedience, order, and productivity.

Our education, justice, and social systems evolved to meet the needs of an industrialized world—to shape people suitable for factory life, to keep things efficient and predictable. Yet as society has evolved, our systems have not. We continue to rely on old methods—fear, shame, and exclusion—as tools for change. When someone causes harm, we remove them. When a child struggles, we isolate them. When a rule is broken, we believe punishment will teach what compassion could not. But fear rarely transforms. It only hides what is hurting.

Restorative practices offer us another way—a way that challenges the westernized conditioning of "right or wrong," "good or bad," "us versus them." It invites us to replace control with collaboration, judgment with curiosity, and punishment with repair. Restorative practice is both a science and an art of belonging, rooted in the belief that humans are motivated not by fear of rejection but by the need for connection.

The Science of Interconnection

There is an African philosophy called Ubuntu—often expressed as, "I am because we are." It reflects the understanding that my wellbeing is bound to yours, that our humanity is intertwined. When one suffers, we all suffer; when one heals, we all rise. Restorative practices embody this worldview. It reminds us that harm does not happen in isolation, and neither does healing. The goal is not to punish wrongdoing but to restore relationships, repair trust, and rebuild community.

The research supports what many Indigenous and collectivist cultures have always known: people change not when they are shamed, but when they are seen. A Zulu greeting known as Sawubona literally means, "I see you," communicating recognition, respect, and value. In response, the person greeted replies, "Yebo, Sawubona." Meaning: "Yes, we see you too." We all long to be seen, respected, and valued.

To engage restoratively is to resist systems built on domination and fear. It is a quiet, radical act of humanity. It challenges the legacy of control that has shaped so much of Western culture—our schools, prisons, workplaces, and even families.

It is important to note, restorative practice does not reject accountability; it redefines it. Accountability is no longer something done to someone—it is something built with them. Human beings are happier, more cooperative, and more likely to make positive change when those in positions of authority work with them rather than to or for them (Boyes-Watson & Pranis, 2020; Bolton, 2022). It asks us to hold people capable, not broken; responsible, not disposable.

It also demands that we look inward. To practice restoration with others, we must unlearn the shame and fear we ourselves were taught. We must notice where control masquerades as care and where our own egos reach for power when we feel uncertain. Restoration begins with self-awareness—it is as much about how we show up as it is about what we do.

RISE INVITATION

Take a moment to notice the people in your life who make you feel seen. What do they do that communicates: I see you, I value you, I'm with you.

Now think of someone who may not always feel that way. What would it look like to offer them a moment of recognition—a pause, a smile, a question that says: You matter here.

Each time we truly see one another, we participate in the quiet revolution of restorative practice.

Beyond Punishment: The Path to Restoration

Science helps us understand why this works. The human brain is wired for connection. When we feel safe, our nervous system opens to learning, empathy, and growth. When we feel threatened—by exclusion, punishment, or shame—our stress systems take over. The amygdala activates, the body prepares for defense, and reasoning shuts down. Fear-based punishment triggers survival, not reflection. It teaches compliance, not conscience. Over time, it reinforces the very behaviors it hopes to control, because the brain begins to equate relationship with danger.

Restorative practices do the opposite. It creates environments where safety and accountability coexist. Instead of asking, "What rule was broken?" it asks, "Who was harmed, and what needs to be done to make it right?" These questions engage empathy, activate the social brain, and strengthen neural pathways for problem solving and compassion.

When harm happens, our instinct is often to retaliate—to demand consequence or revenge. We think punishment will make us feel better, but as Gandhi reminded us, "An eye for an eye leaves the whole world blind." Research on restorative justice shows that when people who cause harm have the opportunity to take accountability, make amends, and be reintegrated into community, both sides experience more healing and forgiveness. Victims report greater peace, and those who caused harm are less likely to reoffend.

The same is true for youth. When systems respond restoratively—inviting dialogue and repair instead of exclusion—young people build empathy, responsibility, and a sense of belonging. Rather than punishing, a child for acting out, restorative practice asks: What unmet need or unhealed pain is this behavior expressing? Who has been affected, and how can everyone be part of the repair? What support does this child need to do better next time?

The work of being human means that we will inevitably cause harm. What defines us is not the falling, but the rising. Restorative practices teach that there is always a path back to wholeness—a way to make things right through empathy, honesty, and repair. When we model repair, we teach youth that mistakes do not make them unworthy; they make them human. Every time we show up after rupture—listening, naming harm, and rebuilding trust—we widen their window for resilience. We show them that love and accountability can coexist.

Restorative practice says, "I believe in your capacity to grow." It holds high expectations and deep compassion at the same time. It creates communities where belonging is not conditional and where struggle is part of the learning, not the disqualification from it. Each time we choose connection over fear, we begin to rewire the systems—both societal and personal—that have long instilled shame and isolation into our DNA. Restorative practices are more than a tool for behavior management; it is a way of being in relationships. It asks us to move beyond compliance and toward cooperation, beyond correction and toward collaboration. It asks us to move toward connection. Toward community.

RISE: A Framework and Philosophy for Life

Every strong structure begins below the surface. The work you have just read—the science of the brain, the bonds of attachment, the patterns of systems, and the beauty of restoration—are not separate parts. They are threads of one tapestry, woven through the story of being human.

Neuroscience teaches us that our brains are built, not born. Attachment shows us that relational safety is the soil where wellbeing grows. Family systems remind us that we live and love within larger patterns, shaping and being shaped by those around us. And restorative practice invites us to bring it all together—to live what we know, to heal through relationships, and to hold one another accountable with compassion instead of fear. At their core, each of these foundations speaks the same truth: We are wired to love and belong. We are designed to grow through struggle, to repair what is broken, and to rise together.

Carry these truths with you and let them soften the way you see others and yourself. Every interaction has the power to heal—every moment of curiosity, patience, and presence is a seed of wellness and resilience. Trust that even the smallest shifts can open something new.

RISE INVITATION

Think of a time when you or someone you care for made a mistake that caused harm. Invite curiosity.

What might restoration have looked like instead of punishment?

Who could have been invited into dialogue, understanding, and repair?

How might the process have changed if the goal was of trying to understand instead of control?

INTERLUDE

Stories from the Cradle (0-5)

How do you ever really know if you were left to cry it out in the darkness, cold and alone? Maybe it's revealed in the way your body quivers when night falls. Maybe it's the quiet panic that hums through your nerves as the sun goes down. Maybe it's the terror that wakes you several times a night—haunted by dreams of being chased, falling, never escaping.

I was called a spirited child—too many feelings for one small body, too many needs for one weary home. A heart and soul searching from the moment I entered this world, longing to be held, to be loved, to belong. Born to two parents, both searching for love.

My baby book says I was easy—an infant with few needs. Slept through the night early. Independent with the bottle, eating young, toilet trained fast. Yet the murmur between those pages vibrates a different song. Entering toddlerhood, I've been told I clung to my mother so tightly that I cried whenever she left the room. Others encouraged her to let me cry, to toughen me up, to teach me that I could not always have what I wanted. She must have been torn between two loves—the love of being needed and the love of being free. I think she wanted to soothe me but also longed to rest from the weight of a lifetime of responsibility. Her own childlike parts needed tending too.

My parents married with me at their feet, whining and clinging. They tell the story often—how I cried through their wedding, begging to be held. It feels symbolic now: a child desperate for connection, sitting at the feet of love still tangled in its own trauma, trying to feel safe.

I remember waking at four years old from a nightmare, small feet padding down the hallway in search of comfort. We lived in a trailer near my dad's shop, where construction and community blended into late-night gatherings. I followed the sound of laughter and music, only to find the glow of lights and the smell of fear. I watched from the doorway—wanting warmth, finding chaos—and ran back to bed, crying myself to sleep.

That rhythm defined many nights: my parents with friends, the buzz of adult noise. The days were quieter, almost hollow—Dad gone and Mom searching. We struggled financially, and my dad worked endless hours, driven by equal parts pride and pain. I think he was trying to prove to himself that he was enough.

One summer, we lived in a pop-up camper and bathed in a pool. By fall, we moved into a shack-like house with rugs covering plywood floors and a small TV propped in the corner. We gathered around that flickering light, pretending the ghosts of our parents' unhealed stories were not shaping our own.

It was a childhood of contradiction: taught to want for nothing, yet filled with emotions that wanted love.

Even outside our home, belonging was slippery. After a playdate, a friend told me her grandmother said I could not come back because I had "run into her and spilled her coffee." I do not remember the spill. I only remember feeling joyful and free. That moment taught me I could be neither.

Preschool cultivated lessons of secrecy. My mom would take me to a relative's house to play with a cousin's son while they spent the afternoon upstairs engaged in extracurricular activities. In the basement, where adults could not hear, he asked me to do things I did not understand. He told me to be quiet, that we would get in trouble. Once, he hid me under his bed when footsteps came down the stairs. I remember the fear of being discovered and the shame of keeping a secret I couldn't name.

Kindergarten brought more lessons in isolation. One day on the bus, a classmate dared me to hold up my middle finger. I did not know what it meant, but I did it anyway. My father grounded me in my room for seven days, only leaving to go to school and the bathroom. I remember building a fort in my closet—hiding, trapped, confused—wondering if love could coexist with punishment. At least the spankings did not feel so lonely.

My little brain was trying to make sense of a world that felt unsafe and unpredictable. My father's discipline and avoidance tried to tame what he did not understand. He, too, was reacting from old wounds. My mother's addictions, the push and pull tried to tame what she did not understand. She, too, was reacting from old wounds.

I will never forget the day I was dropped off on the side of the interstate. I had been loud and melting down, my emotions too much for the moment—the threats, the storm. Then, before I knew it, I stood on the shoulder, five years old and shaking, watching the van drive away. The world went silent. I was cold. I was stone.

Each of these experiences became a layer—a message etched into my nervous system, whispering: you are too much; you are not enough.

A developing brain without co-regulation.

An attachment system that longed and feared at once.

A nervous system learning to brace instead of trust.

And yet, this story is not one of blame.

My parents were doing what they could with what they had, carrying their own traumas they never asked for. What they couldn't give wasn't from lack of love, but lack of healing and knowing. These early years shaped the framework that would one day become RISE—the longing for safety, the need for connection, the belief that even in struggle, there is always a path to repair.

Because behind every theory lives a heartbeat.

Behind every framework lives a story.

And mine began with a little girl who only ever wanted to feel safe and seen.

RISE INVITATION

As you read this story, notice what it stirs in you.

How did your early experiences teach you what love or safety meant?

What messages might still echo in your body today—and what new ones are you ready to write?

Every human has a story. Healing begins when we listen with compassion—to our own story, and to the stories of others.

PART II: RELATIONSHIPS

The "R" part of the RISE framework begins with the elements that open us, expand our awareness, and guide us toward authentic, emotionally attuned relationships.

For me, the Relationships piece of RISE was the easiest to comprehend, yet one of the hardest to journey through. The moments that shaped me most were those when I felt safe, seen, and cared for—connections that became my lifeline. Yet as my life evolved, relationships also demanded the most of me. They required honesty, healing and alignment with the person I wanted to be in this world.

Relationships are the soil where every part of RISE takes root. They make resilience possible. Some of the connections in my life lasted; others were brief. But each one—whether for a moment or a season—helped pull me learn and grow. This is why relationships matter so deeply. One person—one connection—can change the trajectory of a life.

In this section, we'll explore three foundational elements that shape and strengthen relationships:

- **Experiences:** Understanding the influence of life experiences on human development
- **The You Intervention:** Cultivating personal insight to offer a centered, grounded expression of self
- **Characteristics:** Applying practices of intentional, attuned engagement

These concepts form the building blocks for everything that follows in the RISE framework. When we show up with presence, awareness, and intention, we create the conditions for all other elements of RISE to take root.

CHAPTER FIVE

Experiences

The RISE framework emphasizes that our experiences directly shape how the brain develops: our distress tolerance and belief systems, and what we come to believe about ourselves, others, and the world around us. We all move through a range of experiences—some normative and nurturing, others stressful or traumatic. As we learned in Foundations, these experiences influence brain architecture and predict long-term emotional, social, and relational functioning.

Positive, safe, repeated, relational experiences lay the groundwork for wellbeing, emotional intelligence and the wholeness of self. Toxic stress, on the other hand, changes the developing brain in ways that lower stress tolerance, decrease integration, and limit a young person's capacity for regulation and connection. Understanding these patterns helps us stay curious and positions us to offer new, healing experiences that nurture wellbeing and resilience.

Experiences Shape Us

Brain research shows that early experiences shape how children make sense of themselves and the world. Every sound, facial expression, moment of soothing, moment of fear, moment of confusion, or moment of connection becomes part of the developing brain's architecture. Each experience affects the neural pathways being built, forming early blueprints for how a child understands life.

This shaping begins at birth. A baby cannot articulate hunger, fear, or loneliness. Their language is sensation—crying, arching, reaching. Thousands of experiences in the first year alone influence how their brain organizes itself. Each repeated moment becomes part of their internal wiring. In these earliest days, the caregivers and environment are the baby's world. Their presence or absence, predictability or inconsistency, attunement or dysregulation lays the foundation for how the child will interpret future experiences. As children grow, peers, teachers, community environments, and life events build on those early foundations, continuing to shape the story the brain writes about what life feels like.

Every child grows up with a mix of experiences. The research on Adverse Childhood Experiences (ACEs) illustrates this well. ACEs—such as physical or emotional abuse, neglect, domestic violence, parental mental illness, addiction, or chronic instability—act like repeated storms disrupting the developing brain. These experiences shape a brain geared toward survival: vigilant, guarded, and easily overwhelmed. Research shows us that these experiences have long-term implications (Felitti et al., 1998). A correlation to ACES and long-term health struggles demonstrate how being exposed to toxic adversity in our developing years can greatly influence wellbeing.

However, nurturing, predictable experiences shape the brain for regulation and resilience. They teach the brain that stress is survivable—not a threat that must be avoided or fought. When these experiences repeat, they expand a child's capacity for regulation, flexibility, and connection. The feeling of a caregiver's arms around you when you are afraid. The steady reassurance of a teacher who believes in you. The warmth of being comforted when you are sad.

Experiences like these create a different kind of wiring—pathways over time that have the ability to manage distress and build belief systems that say: "You are not alone. Your needs matter. People can be trusted. You are safe enough to grow." Over time, patterns of experience become pat-terns of wiring. Experiences are not passive events. They are sculptors—the architects of our internal world.

Experiences Shape Distress Tolerance

Some stress is necessary for development. Meeting new people, learning a skill, adjusting to a new routine or preparing for a test are examples of positive stressors that help the brain learn how to cope with challenges. When met with support, these experiences strengthen the nervous system.

Stress becomes harmful when it is overwhelming, chronic, or met without the buffering presence of caring, regulated adults. This is what neuroscience calls toxic stress—prolonged activation of the stress response without relief. Toxic stress disrupts developing neural pathways, making it harder for children to regulate emotions, tolerate frustration, or trust themselves and others.

As outlined in Maslow's hierarchy of needs (1943), children who lack basic consistency—stable sleep, predictable routines, adequate food, safe housing—face greater developmental risk. Emotional needs matter too: children need belonging, connection, and adults who reliably show up. These relational experiences provide the neurological fuel the brain depends on to organize itself effectively.

Regulation is key, and young children do not develop it alone—they learn it with someone. As they are held, soothed, mirrored, and comforted, their nervous system gradually internalizes the message: stress can be managed; feelings can be tolerated; connection is safe. When a child's early cries are met with consistency—feeding, rocking, soft voice, gentle presence—the nervous system begins associating stress with eventual relief.

But when cries are repeatedly ignored, unpredictably met, or responded to with tension, the nervous system adapts differently. It learns that stress does not reliably lead to comfort. The brain shifts toward vigilance, bracing, or shutdown. These early experiences often show up later as behaviors adults label difficult: arguing, aggression, withdrawing, avoiding, shutting down, or appearing disrespectful. These behaviors are not signs of defiance—they are signs of distress.

A moment from my own life illustrates this. My youngest child tugged at my leg, needing connection while I was distracted. After repeated attempts, she finally hit me—not out of malice, but out of distress. My first reaction was corrective: "Hands are not for hitting." She ran to her room in tears.

That moment revealed a pattern many children experience: escalating bids for connection, followed by distress, a big behavior, that finally gets an adult's attention—but in a way that leaves the child feeling ashamed and misunderstood. When I realized what had happened, I went to her room to repair the rupture. I reflected her feelings, acknowledged the frustration of not being heard, and offered comfort. Only then, once regulated, did we talk about other ways to get attention and practiced our "blowing the candle" breath together.

Her reaction was not unusual for a three-year-old. At that age, children have limited strategies for expressing frustration or handling unmet needs. When attempts at connection are overlooked, they escalate—not because they want to misbehave, but because escalation works. Unfortunately, by the time adults respond, the behavior has already crossed the line into something that gets a consequence instead of connection. The shame that follows starts to influence their internal narrative: "I'm bad," "I'm too much," "I get in trouble when I need something." Yet beneath these behaviors is often something very simple: a dysregulated child signaling, "I need you."

This understanding deepened for me during a Theraplay training while I was pregnant with my first child. At the time, I was reading about the "cry-it-out" method and trying to determine the best approach for sleep based on information from friends and the medical field. Theraplay offered a different perspective grounded in attachment science.

They explained that regulation does not begin at a specific age, nor does it unfold the same way for every child. Temperament, biology, and experience all matter. Nevertheless, one truth remained consistent: self-regulation develops through co-regulation—through steady, predictable relationships that model how to manage distress. One of the trainers shared findings from a longitudinal study measuring cortisol levels in mothers and babies during cry-it-out. Early in the process, both babies and mothers displayed high cortisol, signaling stress. As the days passed and the babies' crying subsided, the mothers' cortisol levels correspondingly decreased. However, the study showed that the babies' cortisol levels remained high, even though they were no longer crying.

The hypothesis was that the babies became quiet, not because they learned to regulate, but because they learned, crying no longer met their needs. This research challenges the belief that distress tolerance emerges from being left alone, requiring the baby to learn, independently, how to self-sooth. In reality, it reinforces what attachment theorists like Mary Ainsworth emphasized decades ago, children develop emotional regulation through responsive, attuned relationships—relationships that say, again and again, "I see you, and I'm here."

This does not mean parents who used this method harmed their child.

Parenting occurs under enormous pressure, with limited support and conflicting advice. The point here is about long-term relational patterns—not one-off moments or short periods of difficulty. Western culture pushes early independence. We fear "spoiling" babies. We worry if we do not "lay down the law," children will not be responsible adults. Yet research consistently shows that distress tolerance is built through repeated experiences of being soothed, supported, and having a sturdy relational base to rely on.

Frameworks like RISE recognize that this takes time—seeds of safety, connection, and consistency often must be planted again and again before they take root. Understanding this shifts our questions. Instead of asking, "What's wrong with this child?" we begin asking, "What has this child experienced—and what do they need right now?"

RISE INVITATION

For the next several days, simply observe how often a young person makes a bid for connection before a larger behavior emerges.

The first bid (often subtle—eye contact, proximity, a change in tone). The second bid (more direct—asking, tugging, interrupting). The third bid (the moment where frustration begins to show).

Do you tend to notice the first bid or only the last one?

What emotion surfaced in you when their bids escalated?

This practice helps you catch dysregulation while it is still a whisper rather than a roar.

Experiences Shape Beliefs and Behavior

Just as experiences shape how the brain learns to manage stress, they also shape our internal belief system—our private logic. Private logic refers to the beliefs we develop about ourselves, others, and the world—beliefs formed through our lived experiences. Over time, the brain organizes these experiences into patterns, which become our internal narratives and the stories we tell ourselves: "I'm capable" or "I'm unworthy." "People can be trusted" or "People leave."

The movie Inside Out illustrates this beautifully. Each of Riley's experiences becomes a glowing memory orb. When memories of a similar type repeat, they cluster, forming "islands of personality." These islands begin to shape Riley as a person, influencing her beliefs about herself and others and how she navigates her world.

Real life mirrors this. Our experiences—especially significant emotional ones or reoccurring ones—become the template through which we interpret our surroundings. Some frameworks, like Internal Family Systems (IFS), describe these patterns as different "parts" within us—each shaped by experience and organized around protection or connection. Whether we call them parts, patterns, or responses, the idea remains the same: our experiences shape how we interpret the world and how we behave within it.

And all behavior is communication. A tantrum, an outburst, a slammed door, a quiet withdrawal—each reflects something happening inside a young person's body and mind. When we understand behavior as communication, we stop reacting to the behavior itself and start listening to the need beneath it. Behaviors become signals—messages about how the brain is operating, how distress is being managed, and what beliefs may be activated.

When I work with teachers, I explain this through highlighting how our language, non-verbal's, and general approach, all influence the brain's stress response and belief system. For example, a teacher says, "Recess is in two minutes and you've only finished one problem. Try to get a few more done." This approach has neutral words, nothing outwardly harmful—yet for a child whose belief system includes "I'm not enough" or "I am dumb," the message can activate shame and trigger internal parts. A part may feel threatened, overwhelmed or ashamed. Contrast that with, "I see you've gotten started. You are working hard. Let us finish a few more before recess—you've got this. I believe in you." This message communicates capability, effort, and connection. It is less likely to activate protective parts and more likely to support the development of a resilient belief system.

Typically, youth are responding exactly as their experiences taught them to respond. The hopeful piece is this: when we offer experiences that cultivate distress tolerance and adaptive belief systems, we help them build new "islands"—ones grounded in resilience and wellbeing.

Offering Adaptive Experiences

Even when a child has experienced toxic stress or adversity, consistent and caring relationships can reduce that impact. One of the most meaningful ways we can support youth is by seeing them—not their behaviors or distress, but their hearts. Children do not need perfect adults. They need predictable, warm, willing adults who walk beside them as they face challenges.

And this is where we turn inward. If experiences shape children, they shape us too. The way we respond to distress, the beliefs we hold about behavior, the parts of us that seek control or avoid conflict—all influence the environment we create for youth. The next section, The You Intervention, explores this essential truth: to help young people rise, we must understand the lens through which we approach them.

When I train professionals, I illustrate this with a simple activity. Participants are divided into teams and given 90 seconds to draw a beautiful flower. Some teams receive only one or two crayons; others get a full box of colors. The imbalance is obvious—and so is the metaphor. Every child walks into our lives carrying a different set of "crayons"—their early experiences, resources, supports, and challenges. Some come with many colors: stability, encouragement, connection. Others arrive with only a few, but instead carry a backpack filled with adversity, fear, neglect. We cannot change what crayons they have. But we can offer more crayons.

When we stay regulated during conflict, model imperfection and repair, and respond with warmth even when behavior is difficult, we are offering new experiences their nervous system can learn from. When we notice effort instead of just outcomes, highlight strengths rather than only struggles, and allow room for mistakes as part of being human, we create small but powerful moments of connection and acceptance.

These everyday interactions provide youth with experiences and beliefs that counter past harm and help build a different understanding of themselves and the world around them. Each of these experiences helps strengthen new neural pathways—pathways that support regulation, resilience, and a healthier sense of self.

Experiences shape the brain. They shape belief systems. And they shape behavior. This is the heart of RISE: offering experiences that help youth feel safe enough, seen enough, and supported enough to grow.

RISE INVITATION

Take a quiet moment and reflect on your earliest experiences. What kinds of experiences shaped your sense of safety? Who were the people you turned to—or wished you could turn to—when you were distressed? When you were young, how did adults respond to your needs, your fears, your feelings? Which experiences expanded your world… and which constricted it? Gently notice without judging.

Now choose a person you support who struggles with regulation or challenging behaviors. What experiences might have shaped their distress tolerance? What beliefs (private logic) might have developed as a result? What do you think they need from you relationally? What experiences could offer opportunities to build a new "Island".

We don't need to show up perfect—only curious and open to offering warmth and kindness to ourselves and to others.

CHAPTER SIX

The You Intervention

The You Intervention is a central component of the RISE framework. It is the process of turning inward—of understanding how our own unhealed experiences, patterns, biases, and triggers shape our reactions. Self-awareness is essential because many challenges in supportive relationships do not arise solely from the other person's behavior. They come from our internal responses—the stories we tell ourselves, the expectations we carry, the parts of us still seeking healing. The You Intervention offers a path toward reflection, alignment, and intentional action.

I learned this lesson early in my training. In the final class of graduate school, after we had all written our position papers choosing the theory we believed would guide our professional work, my professor announced that he wanted to share the model that showed the greatest success in therapy. Given my slightly competitive spirit, I sat there hoping the model I had written about would be the "golden ticket"—the theory that proved I had chosen the right intervention.

Then came the reveal.

The largest predictor of therapeutic success—across all theories and techniques—was one thing: the relationship between the therapist and the client. I was annoyed—probably because my ego was bruised. I remember thinking, "Seriously? I spent all this money on a graduate degree for you to tell me to build a good relationship. No kidding. Duh."

But what my naïve, inexperienced self didn't yet understand was this: if I don't first nurture the relationship, none of the other interventions matter as much. Theories, practices, and skill sets are important—but only after safety and connection are established.

This hit me even harder during my first year as a therapist. I was working with a young child in play therapy, and I felt certain he did not like me. He told me as much—more than once. I felt anxious before each session and spent most of our time together collecting evidence that I was not the right fit. When I brought this to my supervisor, she kindly reminded me that therapists are not meant to succeed with every client, and she offered to transfer him. However, something in me knew the problem was not him—it was me. Something in me was being activated, and I needed to understand why.

That was when my professor's words and Lambert's Common Factors Model (Lambert, 1992) came full circle. It was in that moment that I understood: unless I addressed my own private logic—my patterns and insecurities—I would never be able to offer a grounded, centered, healing space. I had to do my own work if I ever expected to walk the journey of healing with others.

Many parents and helping professionals search for the perfect intervention—the strategy that will fix every behavior or work with every child. But there is no magic formula. The most effective intervention you will ever use is you. Your presence. Your attunement. Your awareness. Your willingness to look inward. This is the You Intervention: when we change the way we interact, the relationship shifts—and that shift helps the child change too.

The Ego

We cannot fully appreciate the purpose of the You Intervention without understanding the role the ego plays in shaping our perceptions and reactions. Holly Green (2013) describes the "Ladder of Inference," a process where we interpret experiences through our stories and assumptions. What we think happened is often very different from what actually happened. I didn't fully understand this until I watched an episode of Brain Games (Kralovansky et al. 2011) where a staged robbery was shown to a group of unsuspecting witnesses. Every person confidently described what they believed they saw—yet none of their accounts matched the recorded video. Their memories mixed, details blurred, and each mind filled in the gaps in a way that made sense to them.

That is the ego at work. It is a normal and inevitable part of the mind that helps us interpret experiences, even when our perception doesn't perfectly match reality. When we experience something, our brain assimilates information—crossing memories, pulling from old experiences, filling in missing pieces based on what we already believe to be true. Our biases surface. Our fears surface. And our past gets triggered. But here's the hard part: when we are busy trying to prove ourselves right, we often miss the other truths that also exist. And missing those truths keeps us from growing.

The ego isn't bad. It's trying to protect us. It wants us to feel safe by making us the expert, keeping us in control, and ensuring our perspective feels like the correct one. But when we rely only on what the ego notices, we shrink our capacity to see nuance, to hold curiosity, and to understand others. It's like the phenomenon that happens when you buy a new car. If I buy a black Corvette, suddenly I start seeing black Corvettes everywhere. Did the world change? No. My attention changed. And what we pay attention to grows.

This is the challenge at the heart of the You Intervention: "Can we be willing to tell ourselves we might be wrong? Can we allow space for more than one truth? Can we soften our certainty long enough to wonder what else might be possible?"During moments of stress, crisis, or overwhelm, the ego's grip tightens. It wants to be right. It wants control. It pushes us to react instead of reflect. However, humility—true self-awareness—comes from acknowledging our own story and being brave enough to explore perspectives beyond our own.

It invites us into relationships, both with ourselves and with the youth in our lives, with a spirit of curiosity and "not knowing." This is where connection grows. This is where healing begins. And this is where we begin being fully present in ways that truly transform lives.

RISE INVITATION

Think of a recent moment when you felt certain you were "right" about someone's behavior or intention. Invite curiosity. What story did your mind create? What else could be true?

You Can't Lead Others Past the Point of Your Own Healing

Just as experiences are shaping the youth we care about, our own experiences have shaped who we are. And we bring all of that into our expectations, interpretations, and interactions with a child. The most critical part of the You Intervention is learning to understand ourselves with honesty and compassion.

Think about the lifetime of experiences that have shaped you—how you were parented, what you learned about emotions, the patterns you absorbed from the adults around you, your culture, and the ways you were soothed or dismissed. The same way we are helping to shape the relationships youth will form in their future, our parents, caregivers, and environments shaped how we relate to others now. Some of those influences strengthened us; others left parts that still need tending.

We can begin to tap into this awareness by paying attention to our own sensations, thoughts, and reactions. Our bodies often speak before our words do. A tightening chest, a clenched jaw, a sudden irritation—these are signals worth noticing. Equally important are the stories we tell ourselves: "He's being lazy." "She doesn't care." "This kid is trying to push my buttons." These internal narratives often reveal more about our own belief systems than the child's actual intentions. When we become frustrated or irritated, that energy enters the space between us and the child. They feel it—even if we never say a word.

But when we notice our own activation early and pause long enough to breathe, refocus, or steady ourselves, the moment can shift. Our awareness becomes a bridge instead of a barrier. Instead of judging ourselves as "good" or "bad," we can soften into a more grounded, authentic presence. This kind of self-awareness takes vulnerability and courage. It asks us to meet ourselves with the same compassion we hope to offer others. Because the truth is simple but profound: we cannot lead a child into regulation, healing, or growth if we have not learned how to walk that path within ourselves.

The Spiral Metaphor

Many say the spiral is a metaphor for growth. Not linear, but looping—

revisiting lessons, deepening understanding, expanding capacity. This is how healing works. We revisit old wounds, but from a higher level of awareness each time. Everything good, wise, and necessary for your journey already lives within you (Boyes-Watson & Pranis, 2020). The You Intervention simply helps you access it. This work takes courage. When we begin unpacking our own story, feelings like anger, sadness, grief, or resentment often surface. That's normal. Healing is messy and nonlinear. It asks us to be honest without getting stuck, reflective without collapsing into shame and blame.

For me, healing meant sitting with hard emotions, then choosing to move toward acceptance and meaning. It meant believing that the adults in my life were doing the best they could with the resources they had. Not to excuse harm—but to release myself from the weight of carrying it. The sadness and grief still find me sometimes. Those tender parts of me are still alive. But now I know how to better care for them—how to offer love and leadership to myself, even when it's hard. I still struggle. Healing is never finished. Old patterns still tug at me. That is part of being human—beautiful and complicated. And instead of shaming myself for it, I aim to hold all of it with tenderness.

That shift offers me freedom. Freedom to forgive. Freedom to grow. Freedom to lead with love for myself and others. And that is the heart of the You Intervention: as we heal, we create the capacity to engage with more presence, curiosity, and compassion—for ourselves and for the youth we serve.

RISE INVITATION

Before you can help a young person regulate, connect, or grow, you must know what is happening inside you. Think of a recent moment when a child's behavior stirred something in you—irritation, anxiety, disappointment, helplessness, urgency.

Where did you feel that in your body? What emotion came up first? What story did your mind immediately tell about the child—or about yourself?

Follow the thread back. Gently explore. When have you felt this feeling before in your own life? Is there an earlier experience that might be shaping your response now?

Offer yourself compassion. What is one small thing you can try to stay present with youth when you feel activated? A breath. A pause. A softer tone. A quick internal check-in. Small shifts create new patterns—for you and for them.

Tools for Self-Discovery

There are many tools, reflections, and personality assessments that can help us cultivate curiosity about ourselves. Before beginning, there are two things worth remembering. First, assessments—whether evidence-informed or simply used for personal insight—reflect who we are in a moment of time. Our answers can shift depending on our mood, season of life, stress level, or level of self-awareness. Second, looking across different assessments can reveal patterns: the themes, tendencies, and traits that appear again and again and help us understand our inner landscape.

The most helpful way to approach any personality tool is with honesty—not by choosing the "right" answer or the "healthy" answer, but the truest one. We all have two versions of ourselves: the ideal self we strive toward, and the actual self we bring into daily life. The more honestly we can name the actual self, the more we can move toward growth and alignment with self.

When I first began taking these assessments, I did what many of us do: I tried to hide or minimize the parts of myself I did not like. I did not want to acknowledge traits that felt uncomfortable or shameful. The truth is, throughout my growth journey I have had tendencies toward being controlling, competitive, bossy, and a bit of a know-it-all. I interrupt. I over-analyze. I rush to fix instead of listen. I move too quickly. There are parts of me that lack patience and assume others' needs without asking. And for a long time, I didn't want to see any of that. Some parts brought shame. Some were in denial. Some were "shadow" parts I tried to keep tucked away.

But hiding them didn't make them go away—it only made me less honest with myself, less aware of what needed healing and nurturing. As I leaned into this process with more vulnerability, I began to see that these traits were simply parts, shaped by my history and experiences. Some parts emerged to help me survive difficult seasons. Some protected me. Some tried to keep me safe by staying in control. These parts were not the sum of who I am—and they were not my truest, wisest self. But they were invitations to deeper self-understanding.

This insight also helped me notice qualities I rarely showed but genuinely wanted to cultivate. Just like any skill, most traits can be developed with time, intention, and practice. We are not fixed beings. If you take these assessments again, a year from now, your results may look different—and that is okay. That is change and potential growth. That is the spiral metaphor in action.

Below is a guided pathway through the self-discovery tools woven into the You Intervention. Each tool offers a different lens for reflection and personal awareness. It can be especially helpful to share your results with someone you trust and ask, "Does this feel like me?" or name the parts that feel true, uncomfortable, confusing, or surprising. Sometimes self-awareness deepens most in the presence of another person who can lovingly mirror what we cannot always see in ourselves.

A Guided Pathway Through the Tools

What you will find in the back of the book is not just a list of assessments—it is a journey: a gentle unfolding of the inner world that shapes how we show up with youth, others, and ourselves. The order is intentional. Each tool builds upon the last, moving from early relational experiences, to internal beliefs, to protective parts, to conscious values, to personality tendencies, to biological wiring, and finally to strengths and wellbeing. Think of this section as a descent inward, and then a rise outward—mirroring the heart of RISE itself.

Where relationships began…

- **Adult Attachment Inventory:** Begins with our earliest relationships and the patterns that shape trust, regulation, and connection.

What beliefs formed…

- **Private Logic:** Explores the stories and beliefs we formed from those early experiences.

How we adapted internally…

- **Parts Mapping (IFS):** Identifies the internal parts that protect, react, or carry pain—and helps us understand how they influence our interactions.

What now guides us…

- **Values Inventory:** Clarifies the principles that guide our actions today and anchor our intention.

How we tend to behave interpersonally…

- **Personality Priorities:** Reveals the unconscious strategies we use to feel significant or safe (comfort, pleasing, control, superiority).

How we operate cognitively…

- **NERIS Type Explorer (16 Personalities):** Highlights how we take in information, make decisions, and move through the world.

How we behave under stress…

- **Enneagram:** Uncovers core motivations and stress responses, offering insight into relational dynamics.

What is biologically wired…

- **Temperament:** Honors the biologically based traits we were born with—intensity, adaptability, sensitivity, persistence, and more.

What strengths and resilience we can build upon…

- **Authentic Happiness / Positive Psychology Tools:** Focus on strengths, wellbeing, hope, grit, and flourishing—shifting the lens from "what needs healing" to "what is already strong."

You do not need to complete every tool at once. Move intentionally. Move gently. Let curiosity guide you more than urgency. Each tool offers a new perspective on your inner world—a doorway into growth, healing, and self-leadership.

The Ongoing Journey of Becoming

The You Intervention is not a one-time exercise—it is a lifelong practice of curiosity, reflection, and choosing to grow a little more each day. It rests on the belief that personal development is never "finished." The more we understand who we are, and the patterns we carry into our relationships, the more capable we become in offering safety, presence, and attunement.

This requires time and intention. It means slowing down enough to notice the unconscious patterns that drive us—our defenses, our family conditioning, our fears, our strengths. Most of us can look back on earlier versions of ourselves and realize how unaware we once were. That is not failure; that is the rhythm of being human. Growth requires spaciousness, honesty, and compassion. Along the way, we must give ourselves freedom to be learners—not perfect performers. Parenting, caregiving, teaching, or being a professional helper is profoundly difficult work. We are all human, and we are all still becoming. Grace for yourself is not optional; it is essential.

Part of this process means writing your own rules. It means loosening the grip of the "supposed to" messages you inherited—messages equating worth with productivity, or love with performance, or success with never making mistakes. Ask yourself gently: "Where did these beliefs come from? Do they still serve me? What do I want to carry forward? What can I lay down?" Letting go of others' expectations and living in alignment with your authentic self is an act of courage. It is an act of self-compassion. And it is an act of liberation.

And when you inevitably mess up—as every human does—that moment becomes part of the relationship too. Losing your patience, making a mistake, or raising your voice does not mean you have failed. It means you are human. What matters most is what comes next: pausing, breathing, repairing, reconnecting. This is the heart of the You Intervention.

Youth do not need perfect adults; they need adults who are willing to model honesty, humility, repair, and growth. When we show up imperfectly—but with awareness, curiosity, and care—we teach something invaluable: wellness, resilience, and healing are not destinations. They are journeys. Hard, nonlinear, courageous journeys. And they're journeys worth taking. And as we keep walking our own journey, we make it safer for young people to walk theirs.

CHAPTER SEVEN

Characteristics

By characteristics, we mean the traits that shape what we do in real life. It's where our understanding of human development and our own self-awareness turn into everyday interactions—how we respond on tough mornings, messy conversations, lingering hurts, small victories, and quiet moments of connection. These characteristics are not scripts or techniques. They are ways of being—rooted in presence, attunement, humility, and intentional engagement. They ask us not to perform connection, but to embody it.

We live in a culture obsessed with efficiency and quick fixes, and that pressure often shows up in our interactions. We want behavior to shift quickly, emotional regulation to appear on demand, and conflict to resolve neatly. Nevertheless, deep, authentic healing rarely happens in straight lines. It happens slowly, relationally, and often invisibly—through how youth feel in our presence long before they begin to show new skills. The RISE Framework asks us to step out of the rush for outcomes and be present with the young people in our lives.

Your Presence Matters

You have probably heard the familiar line often attributed to Maya Angelou: "People will forget what you said. People will forget what you did. But they will never forget how you made them feel." We spend so much time worrying about doing the right thing—choosing the perfect response, following the correct intervention, not messing things up. However, the truth is, what we do is rarely what shapes a young person's development. It is how our presence makes them feel: "Did they feel seen? Did they feel valued? Did they feel safe enough to be their messy, honest selves? Did they sense judgment or compassion? Pressure or possibility?"

Presence is not just about our words. It is the internal state we bring into each interaction—our tone, our expressions, our breath, our energy, our regulate-or-react tendencies, our ability to stay grounded when someone else is not. When we bring intention to our presence, it becomes a healing force.

The RISE framework offers a simple rhythm: Attunement, Assessment, and Action with intention. When used with care and flexibility, these processes help us transform everyday interactions into experiences that communicate safety, dignity, possibility, and hope. With our unwavering presence, even the smallest interaction becomes full of potential. A hallway greeting, a heavy sigh, a tear held back, an unexpected meltdown—all become rich sources of insight and opportunity. When we lean in with curiosity and presence, a moment stops being behavior to manage and instead becomes a relationship to nurture. Every interaction holds a spark of healing, and the Three A's help us fan that spark.

Attunement: Meeting Them Where They Are

Attunement is the heartbeat of intentional engagement—the moment we choose to step into their world rather than pulling them into ours. When we attune, we are not simply hearing words; we are listening with our whole body. We notice the tightness in a voice, the shift in posture, the bouncing foot, the eyes that avoid contact, the silence that speaks, and the energy that tells the truth long before words are found.

Attunement requires presence without agenda, curiosity without assumption, and connection without control. I once watched someone approach her 6th grade peer sitting alone on the bleachers, hood pulled low, knees tucked in, his heel bouncing rhythmically against the floor. She did not shout across the gym, "Come join us!" Instead, she walked over, sat beside him with respectful distance. After a minute, she whispered, "Long day?" He nodded. That was the turning point. Not a strategy. Attunement. Attunement is the quiet decision to enter the moment softly—listening, sensing, noticing what is emotionally there, and offering connection without pressure.

Assessment: Exploring What Lives Beneath Behavior

Assessment is not about diagnosing or analyzing behavior; it is the art of curiosity. It begins with humility: "I'm not here to prove anything. I'm here to explore." Assessment invites us to reflect rather than assume. Instead of concluding, "He's being disrespectful," "She just wants attention," or "They don't care," we ask ourselves: "What might they be feeling? What happened right before this? Which part of them might be activated? What does their nervous system need? What story are they telling themselves inside?"

Assessment is relational wondering—an invitation to slow down, get curious, and notice signals we may have overlooked. It also requires the humility to acknowledge our own filters: our experiences, insecurities, preferences, triggers, and biases. The You Intervention prepared us for this moment, reminding us that we cannot assess a young person clearly, if we are unaware of the lens we are using. Assessment is the bridge between attunement and action. It helps us hypothesize what we see and guides us toward questions rooted in compassion instead of control.

Action with Intention: Moving in Ways That Honor the Whole Person

Action comes last—not because it is least important, but because action without attunement and assessment is usually just reaction. Intentional action honors the young person's humanity. It is gentle, collaborative, flexible, and responsive to the moment. Sometimes action looks like conversation. Sometimes it looks like offering a break, co-regulating through breathing or movement, repairing a rupture, taking a walk, or simply staying close without demanding anything. What action is not is forcing change. Compliance is not transformation. A quiet child is not necessarily a regulated child. A child who holds it together may be shutting down, not growing. Real change grows slowly, through repetition, trust, and relationship.

The Three A's often blend and overlap, moving almost like a dance. When we attune, assess, and take action with intention, we honor the young person's wholeness.

The Three A's in Practice

A teacher once told me about a student who refused to begin her morning work. Every day she would put her head down, avoid eye contact, or mutter something under her breath. At first the teacher saw this as defiance, but one morning she tried something new. She sat quietly beside her.

Attunement began with noticing her hand trembling slightly around her pencil, her shoulders tight, her breath shallow. Assessment followed through curiosity instead of assumption. Instead of assuming she wouldn't work, she wondered whether she couldn't. She asked softly, "Is this one of those mornings where everything feels too big?" She nodded, tears barely forming. Action with intention came in the form of connection: "Let's just do the first one together. You don't have to do this alone." By the third problem, she whispered, "I think I can try the next one." Attunement created safety. Assessment created understanding. Action created possibility. This is the heart of the Three A's—meeting youth where they are and walking with them from that place, not from where we wish they would be.

RISE INVITATION

When a moment of challenge arises—a youth refusing expectations, rolling their eyes, shutting down, or escalating—slow the moment down internally.

Attunement: What are you noticing? What emotion do you sense? What is their body showing you?

Assessment: What might be underneath this behavior? What part of them might be activated? Is this "won't"... or "can't right now"?

Action: What is a compassionate next step?

Nurturing Intentional Engagement

Intentional engagement is not a technique; it is a way of being. Youth grow best in environments saturated with warmth, presence, honesty, steadiness, curiosity, and compassion. These characteristics create emotional climates where resilience can take root and grow. They are not skills we check off a list—they are commitments to act with humanity and dignity.

One of the biggest obstacles to intentional engagement is the set of expectations we quietly carry. We often define success through our own lenses—how fast we want a skill to develop, what we believe progress should look like, or how quickly a young person should adapt. However, young people cannot sustain thriving in environments where they feel constantly evaluated, stressed or pressured. They grow in environments where they feel whole.

Intentional engagement requires us to release the idea of perfection—both in others and in ourselves. It redefines success as cooperation, not compliance; presence, not performance; growth, not perfection. People cannot become their best selves in environments where they feel judged or misunderstood. They flourish in relationships where all parts of them—the shining parts and the struggling parts—are welcomed with gentleness.

We get to redefine success not only in how we see youth, but also in how we see ourselves. We are invited to let go of who we think we are supposed to be as helpers, caregivers, or professionals, and instead lean into authenticity, compassion, curiosity, and tenderness. Progress is winding. Healing is nonlinear. Nevertheless, the relationship is steady.

As parents, caregivers, educators, mentors, and helping professionals, you already hold the most powerful intervention available: your presence. Your steadiness. Your belief in them. Your love.

Love that listens.

Love that sees beyond behavior.

Love that repairs instead of withdraws.

Love that stays.

Love that says, "You don't have to figure this out alone."

You cannot fix a hurting child by adding more hurt. However, you can offer something far stronger: a relationship that communicates, "You are safe. You matter. I'm here." Our approach begins with relationships because they are the foundation of everything else—every skill, every intervention, every moment of growth. Relationships water the seeds of hope. And hope is where healing begins.

INTERLUDE

Stories from the Backyard (6-10)

How do you ever really know if safety is something you've felt, if love is something you've ever known? How quickly things slip away between heartbeats—gone by the next exhale.

When I was six, I was terrified of storms. Of darkness. Of wind. Of the way everything familiar could be lifted without warning. Dorothy tangled in a tornado. Lost. Carried somewhere far from home. No family in sight as she followed the yellow brick road—scared and brave at the same time, afraid to lose it all, desperate to be free of it all.

When the sirens screamed, the wind snapped branches in half. Rain slammed the house like fists. I was placed in the bathtub, pillows stacked on top of me, a body pressed over mine, as if weight could quiet what raged both outside and in. My screams matched the storm. My fear had a weather system of its own.

How did Dorothy land in Oz? Was she terrified she'd never see her family again? Did she miss home while learning how to walk forward? How did she let go of the sky that broke her and step onto the road anyway?

I wonder now—what if I had landed somewhere else? I fantasized daily about a hidden road, waiting for the tornado that might finally take me away. But instead, that wicked witch learned my address and took up permanent residence.

Darkness brought dreams of being chased, falling, never escaping. Night has a way of rehearsing the same demons, over and over, in the unconscious. I'd wake alone and slip from my bedroom, finding the kitchen alive—parents and friends laughing, music humming, cards slapped onto tables dusted with white lines. Go to bed. Don't come out. There was nowhere safe to hide.

The monsters were inside. The monsters were outside. And there was no one I could confide.

Sometimes I woke up sick, scared, searching for comfort. Connection came through screams and tears. A sister held my hair back while panic danced among the stars, untamed, unnamed. I quickly learned how to clean my own wet bed. The moon seemed to know how to wait patiently.

No matter how much time I spent awake, I could never find comfort in darkness. I learned that darkness was for secrets. For hiding. When the sun sets, bad things happen.

The lessons continued as I grew, and not through bedtime stories.

A bowling league in a town too far away. Smoke. Alcohol. Neon lights and motion. Adults teaching us what being grown meant: flirting, gambling, naked women on playing cards. A guidebook to connection written in beer and bets. Fights spilled easily. Rounds of shots followed. Kids invisible—afterthoughts in a world rehearsing adulthood. We drove home with wobbling tires, a shaking steering wheel, arguments echoing louder than the engine.

Under the influence, my mom was chaos. Uncontrolled. Unattached. One night she stayed after bowling to spend the night with a girlfriend. That was when I noticed I had to start seeing past the seeming—not as a concept, but as something I felt in my body.

The touch. The energy. The dynamic. The knowing.

I did not understand. What was love? What was marriage? Right and wrong had no compass—grownups made rules for children and none for themselves.

Those late Saturday nights meant we returned home at a time when the television glowed while the world slept peacefully—as if other houses could rest. Porn at nine years old. Sexuality entered my life again and again—without knocking, without consent, without a name for what it was taking.

Innocence disappearing, thinning, fabric pulled too many times.

I walked in on my parents once when I was six—two adults wrestling naked. I was yelled at. I ran out crying, escaping into the hallway like it could hold me, I found my sister who said to just leave them alone. But why didn't she realize—bad things happened when I left them alone.

Sex. Intimacy. Boundaries—was it violence? Was it care? Hurting? Loving?

Pleasure? Escape? A split current in my body. And that confusion leaked outward, into friendships, into kissing, touching, experimenting—trying to understand closeness without a map, without a compass, without anyone teaching me where the key was.

My body learned lessons it could not translate. Dirty. Confused. Shame-soaked.

Who still had those perfect Barbie's and their innocence intact? What did it take to be one of those girls? Ones whose bodies and minds did not confuse them, betray them. Ones whose parents knew how to protect them. To let them play in innocence. That world was not in reach.

Camping weekends sharpened my skills—a village without boundaries. Boats. Bars. Bonfires. Adults lived freely. Fought loudly. Drank endlessly.

I tried to save us once—mixing ketchup and mustard in a bar bathroom stall, pouring it into a toilet, pretending to be sick, begging to leave.

By then, I understood: safety was never found in rest. It lived in vigilance.

Grounded in my bunk for feelings and needs that interfered with adult leisure, I tucked a doll into my place and wandered the dark for hours, watching grownups laugh under string lights and loud music. No one noticed I was gone. Invisible. Too much. Roaming around, young and vulnerable, for hours and hours under the stars. Was I the one who owned the night, or the thing that lived in it, unseen and unmissed?

Lessons continued to unfold, stories continued to be untold. At sunset, I could hear the hum of the storms brewing, so I begged my mom to come inside. I knew what tomorrow would be like if she did not. But another adult stepped forward—beer breath, salt and authority—telling me she was a grown woman and I needed to stop begging, to go inside and let them be. The same mouths that sang hymns Sunday morning. Sin washed clean by dawn. The only ones tired were the only ones who remembered what happened in the darkness come daylight.

I learned my oldest sister was not my real sister—my friend had overheard it around the campfire. Two other kids by my dad, forever unknown. Foreign goodbyes. Broken beginnings. To know things and talk about nothing was a constant lesson. Look. Listen. Hear what isn't said. Learning that even my own thoughts were not always safe inside my head.

So many of those camping mornings found me making coffee, telling my dad it was from my mom. Cleaning what unsteady legs had broken before the rest of the world would wake. Protecting siblings. Studying patterns. Learning the rhythms of conflict—cold, chaotic, pursuit, withdrawal.

Parentification gave me connection. Purpose. Efficacy. Safety was not a feeling. It was a task. One I tried so hard to master. Predictable unpredictability. Sand like knives beneath my feet. The waves and tides were starting to take me away.

One summer we visited family distanced by state lines—a lineage whose DNA was prison and self-medication. Trauma passed down like heirlooms.

I watched my mom drink through the night, tried to get her inside, tried to put up a fight. I needed her to go to sleep, to not give herself to the men that seek. At five in the morning I found her in the backyard, pants down, peeing, nowhere to hide. On the drive home, she slept in the backseat. For the first time, I talked to my dad—meeting a man, I did not know. Who was he in the midst of the storm? Why did he escape through every door?

One of those nights when he was away, I watched a group of younger kids while all the parents played. They left to have fun, my heart started to drum. I put everyone on a pallet, soft and cozy, yet when I woke hours later and found them gone, panic reached my tummy. I looked for my mother, her bed empty. Morning arrived before answers. I was patiently in panic, waiting. The screen door opened. Relief surged. She made good choices; she was up walking the dog. Stepping up the entry door—falling hard onto the floor. Relief shattered on the welcome mat. She slept the day away with my sister in bed. Later, my dad called to talk. I told him she was grocery shopping.

I learned the truth was a privilege. Hope became something you rationed. I grew fluent in survival rhythms. Here is the thing; I was learning that love was not something you just received. It was something you earned by doing enough to be allowed to stay.

So it should be no surprise that I found friendship in a home like mine—chaos familiar, scarcity predictable. They taught me beauty had hiding places, that drugs lived where I thought sparkle belonged. They taught me loyalty through tests, initiation through secrets. Parking lot cigarettes and stolen wine coolers. Little did they know—I came into the relationship prepared.

Connection lived in backseats after long drives, watching for the midnight affairs, waiting for the fights.

Hypervigilance followed me everywhere. Belonging came with a price.

School taught me similar complexities. Wanting to be seen and invisible, loved and alone. I skipped recess to clean classrooms. To organize. To be helpful. The nurse's office became a refuge. Warm. Quiet. Hidden. School gave me things I never had. I stole small things to know their warm lies. When I was caught, I learned how to manage perception. Deception a curriculum. One lesson at a time.

Identity formed not in being—but in doing. Anticipating. Watching. Managing. Calculating. Air traffic control for broken systems.

A weekend away at my godparents, a barn party and a band. A role for me, that special girl. Charge for keg cups. One drink for them, one for me. Money in my pocket. Head spinning. Two truths and a lie. Or maybe all a lie. I learned morality from empty glasses and communion plates. Dreamed of being saved. Dreamed of disappearing. Dignity slipping away. Am I them or who am I? Relationships required payment. And I paid in pieces of myself.

By ten, I knew shame had a long sentence.

Each day I walked home from school replaying memories, conversations, rewriting myself, planning contingencies. Plan A. Plan B. Plan C. I dreamed of a house at sea, of Dorothy, of Pippi, of breaking the shackles of PTSD.

Throughout these years, the backyard became my lookout. Not for play—but to prepare for storms. So I could see them coming. Feel the wind before it took me.

By eleven, I stopped being afraid of storms. I said I loved them. What did I know about love anyway?

The backyard is where becoming began. And unbecoming too.

RISE INVITATION

As you step out of these stories, pause for a moment. Let your body catch up with what your mind has just traveled through. Invite curiosity. How did your younger self learn what safety meant? What were close relationships like for you? What parts of yourself did you learn to hide, sharpen, or silence in order to stay connected?

Now, gently, bring a hand to your chest or rest it somewhere grounding. Take one slow breath in—and a longer breath out.

If it feels right, imagine the child you once were. Let your older self-step closer now, offering love, light, grace, and compassion—reminding them they no longer have to carry this alone.

PART III:

INDICATORS OF WELLBEING

The "I" part of the RISE framework focuses on the Indicators of Wellbeing—the conditions that help young people feel safe, connected, and ready to grow. These are more than protective factors; they are the everyday experiences that support a youth's wellness and build the inner resilience needed to navigate life's challenges over time.

This section became one of the most meaningful pieces of RISE for me. It felt like the bridge between hardships, stressors, and adversity—and the possibility of true wellness. As I began researching the elements that help people feel well and build resilience, I found myself untangling pieces of my own story. I needed a way to make sense of the things that had quietly shaped me, even when I did not fully understand their power at the time. "Why did sports steady me? How did trusted adults make such a profound difference? Why did the wilderness—water, fresh air, the safety of green space—bring me so much peace? How did having any sense of personal control give me agency? Why did discovering my passions at a young age propel me forward? How did creativity, optimism, and hope open doors to wellness, even in the midst of toxic stress?"

These questions did not just lead me into research; they led me into reflection. I realized I had always carried a list in my heart—things that felt good, that supported me, that helped me stay grounded despite the challenges I faced. I just never had the language or the structure for them. Naming these elements gave shape and meaning to experiences I had long held but never fully articulated.

As I began organizing my own story, I could steadily see what I had been doing intuitively with the youth I worked with: being curious about the elements that foster wellbeing, noticing where those elements were missing, where they existed, and then building experiences where they could grow.

From that place, and into my leadership journey, the Indicators of Wellbeing began to take form—a template for the conditions that nurture wellbeing and resilience. What began as my personal search for understanding evolved into a set of conditions that seemed to embrace all that I had come to know through experience and training.

When these conditions are present and consistent, young people begin to feel seen, valued, and capable. This part of the framework includes four key indicators:

- **Safety:** Establishing physical, emotional, and psychological security
- **Connection and Belonging:** Inviting inclusion, collaboration, community, and cooperation
- **Meaning and Purpose:** Creating fulfillment through contribution and significance
- **Efficacy:** Empowering capability through encouragement and perseverance

Together, these elements remind us that wellbeing is not something we arrive at alone. It is something we help make possible—through the environments we shape, the relationships we cultivate, and the experiences we intentionally nurture. This section is an invitation to notice what strengthens a young person's inner landscape, and to imagine what becomes possible when those conditions are firmly in place.

CHAPTER EIGHT

Safety

Safety is the first Indicator of Wellbeing—and perhaps the most foundational. Yet it is also the one most often misunderstood. When adults think about safety, we tend to think of physical protection first: keeping a child out of harm's way, preventing injury, creating environments free from danger. Physical safety matters deeply. However, for young people, the experience of feeling safe expands far beyond the physical. Before anything else, safety begins with honoring the young person's dignity.

A child is not a problem to manage but a human being with agency, identity, culture, emotions, preferences, dreams, and a nervous system that tells the truth long before their words do. Feeling safe begins when being seen is felt. When their humanity is acknowledged—not corrected, minimized, or overridden—they experience a deeper sense of security. It is the set of conditions that shift a young person's brain out of survival and into possibility.

When youth feel safe, they can learn, explore, try, fail, wonder, regulate, connect, and grow. When I talk with young people, they rarely describe safety in technical terms. They describe it relationally. They talk about adults who listen without rushing. Adults who explain instead of intimidate. Adults who follow through, who don't shame them for their mistakes, who allow them to be imperfect without withdrawing affection or respect. They talk about people who speak to them with dignity, even in conflict, and spaces where they do not have to brace for humiliation, unpredictability, or emotional whiplash.

When we honor a young person's humanity, the dimensions of safety begin to reveal themselves. Safety is emotional, physical, psychological, physiological, and social—a sense of being emotionally held, physically secure, psychologically understood, physiologically supported, and socially protected. These layers do not operate in isolation. They braid together, telling a young person—often long before words—"You are safe." Safety is deeply felt. It lives in the nervous system, not just in the rules. Safety is the quieting of vigilance. The softening of breath. The moment a young person realizes, "I don't have to protect myself right now. I can be myself here."

This is why restorative practices matter—a way of being with youth that creates consistency, equity, transparency, and shared humanity. Predictable responses. Clear pathways to repair. A tone that signals respect, even when boundaries are firm. When youth know what to expect—not only in routines, but also in an adult's emotional presence—they begin to relax. Safety allows them to make mistakes without fear of character judgment. It frees them to try, fail, reflect, repair, and grow. When safety takes root, the brain loosens its grip on survival. Curiosity awakens. Connection becomes possible. The body settles. The spirit steadies.

A young person, feeling safe, is able to discover who they are and who they are becoming. A young person who feels safe takes the risks necessary for growth—asking for help, naming their boundaries, trying something new, and letting someone in. Safety is the bedrock of wellbeing. It is the soil from which connection, meaning and purpose, and efficacy start to rise.

Trust and Respect

Safety grows through the presence of trust and respect. These are not abstract ideals—they are lived experiences, communicated through the way adults speak, listen, and respond. These concepts are a two-way street. Youth want to feel trusted and respected, but they also want to know they can trust and respect the adults in their lives. When young people feel trusted, they feel capable.

When they feel respected, they feel worthy. When young people feel trust and respect, they describe it in small, everyday moments: When an adult keeps a promise, even when it would be easier not to. When my teacher asks me if it is okay to share something I disclosed to another teacher. When changes are explained ahead of time instead of sprung on them. When a difficult moment is followed by a gentle check-in rather than withdrawal.

Over time, these piggy banks of trust begin to fill, and respect is felt. Together, trust and respect become the practices that allow safety to flow within a relationship. Trust and respect are often felt before they are consciously known.

They show up in tone, presence, and the willingness to honor boundaries. They appear when adults acknowledge emotions without minimizing them, when they offer guidance without humiliation, and when they make space for a young person's preferences, perspectives, and pace.

They show up in transparency. This happens through open and honest communication. When adults explain expectations, decisions, and reasons, young people sense clarity instead of hidden agendas. Transparency quiets the fear of being controlled. It invites mutual understanding. It communicates; I respect you enough to be real with you.

They show up through confidentiality. Just as adults feel hurt when something personal is shared without their consent, young people experience the same rupture. When their fears, mistakes, or private struggles are repeated casually to others, something in the relationship shifts. Trust becomes thinner. Vulnerability retreats.

Trust shows up through humility and authenticity. When adults admit mistakes, apologize sincerely, and repair without defensiveness, young people learn that relationships do not collapse under imperfection. They learn that accountability is safe. Restoration is possible. Connection can bend and return. They learn that they, too, can show up as their whole selves.

And it shows up through predictability in our presence. Children build internal schemas—mental templates—based on how adults show up. For example, if a young person makes a mistake and consistently experiences support, guidance, and opportunities to repair, they begin to expect that mistakes are part of life, safe to talk about, and can lead to growth. Their internal message becomes something like: "It's okay to be imperfect here. I won't be shamed for getting it wrong."

On the other hand, if mistakes are usually met with harshness or unpredictable reactions, they may develop a fear of being honest. They learn to hide, to people-please, or to shut down. The way we respond in these moments either fosters safety and learning or creates anxiety and avoidance. Our consistency—in tone, boundaries, and emotional presence—is the quiet structure we create within the relationship, the kind that allows young people to soften into trust. None of these gestures are dramatic. They accumulate quietly, becoming a felt message in a young person's body. Trust and respect are the everyday relational practices that turn safety from a concept into a lived experience.

RISE INVITATION

Set aside a few minutes to reflect on your recent interactions with a young person. Invite curiosity. What did your presence communicate?

Think about the tone of your voice, your facial expressions, the way you listened.

How did you respond to their emotions? Did you respect their pace, their preferences? How transparent were you? What did you model with your own imperfections? Did you apologize when you missed the mark?

After reflecting, choose one small practice to grow your trust and respect "bank" this week.

It might be something like following through on one small promise. Asking a young person, "Is it okay if I share this with another adult?" It could be naming your own emotion before it spills into tone. It could be offering a brief explanation behind a decision. Or maybe checking in gently after a hard moment.

These actions are quiet, but they land loudly in the nervous system of a young person.

Structure, Routines, and the Safety of "Knowing What Comes Next"

Safety is not only felt in relationships; it is also felt in the rhythm of the day. Predictability is one of the most powerful builders of safety. Children thrive when they have some sense of what is coming next—when the world feels organized enough for their bodies and brains to relax.

A bedtime routine is a simple example. A child who knows that pajamas come before brushing teeth, and teeth brushing is followed by reading with a caregiver, settles more easily. Morning routines do the same work: getting dressed, eating breakfast, finding shoes and backpacks. These patterns aren't about control; they are about orientation. They help a child's nervous system say, I know this. I can handle this. I'm not alone here.

Rituals add another layer of safety. A two-minute dance party before lunch in a classroom, a silly song before bedtime, a shared phrase on the way out the door—these small, repeated moments become habit. They signal predictability and give children a familiar rhythm to ground them. For some children, predictability needs to be visual. Schedules on the wall, picture charts, or simple checklists can become anchors in the day. Countdown warnings before transitions help sensitive nervous systems stay regulated: "Five more minutes... two more minutes... one more minute, and then it's time to clean up." Some children need several warnings; others need fewer. The goal is not rigidity—it is generosity. We are making the invisible visible so that their bodies are not constantly bracing for surprise.

Of course, life does not always follow the plan. A routine is disrupted, dinner is delayed, and bedtime is late. Children who thrive on structure often struggle in those moments, not because they are difficult, but because their internal map has suddenly shifted.

This is where preparation and clear communication become an extension of safety. Simple phrases like, "When we get home, it will be time to get ready for bed right away," or, "Dinner is going to be late today, so we'll have a snack to help our bodies," act like a future social story. They orient a child to what is coming, even when the usual pattern isn't possible.

In group settings, like residential care or classrooms, pausing to name changes out loud, inviting input where appropriate, and offering small adjustments (a snack, a quiet activity, a shorter routine) communicates: I see what this change might feel like for you. I am with you in it.

Being intentional about routines and transitions—while modeling flexibility when things shift—helps children feel they can trust both the adults and the process. It also teaches a powerful message: life does not always go according to plan, and we can still manage and be successful.

RISE INVITATION

Think about a part of your day that consistently feels rushed, chaotic, or difficult for young people. Invite curiosity. What do you think the child's nervous system is experiencing? What would help them know what is coming next? What cue or ritual could make this moment predictable and kind?

Now create a simple plan.

A structure: What happens first, next, last? Who is involved? Does it need to be visual? Does it need to be practiced?

A cue or transition plan moving to and from the activity: A countdown, a song, a phrase, a visual reminder.

A connection point: A smile, a touchpoint, a shared moment, a check in, a shared "word" or "thumbs up."

Keep it gentle. Keep it consistent. Then try it for a week.

Norms and Expectations: Clarity as a Form of Care

Safety also requires clarity. Young people need to know what is expected of them, how to communicate when something does not feel right, and what happens when norms are broken—not through fear, but through guidance. Norms are simply the shared agreements, rules, and values that shape how a family, classroom, or program functions. They are most powerful when they are created with young people, not just handed down to them.

When my children were younger, we created a simple family chart rooted in our values: kindness, caring, and respect. We even had a family motto—"We can do hard things." Those values became the heart of our shared expectations.

Our chart was not fancy; it was handwritten and taped to the wall. But it was ours. It reflected who we wanted to be together. We used kid-friendly norms like: Kind hands. Walking feet. Calm voices. Caring words. Safe Bodies. Oops is ok—and make things right. These expectations changed with age, because norms should grow with the child. What "kind hands" means to a four-year-old looks different for a fourteen-year-old. But the value underneath stayed the same.

Norms are essentially the gold standard of behavior you hope to see—clear, explicit, observable. Instead of, "Don't climb on the counter," a norm might be, "We sit at the table during meals." Instead of, "Stop yelling," a norm might be, "We use a calm voice to communicate." This matters because of how the nervous system processes language. The word "no" usually activates a defensive reaction—fight, flight, freeze, or fawn. And the brain tends to latch onto the last thing it hears. Therefore, "No hitting" leaves the nervous system centered on "hitting," whereas "Kind hands" directs it toward the behavior you want to see.

This does not mean we never say "no." There are moments when "no" is necessary and protective. And being intentional with language is hard work, especially when we are tired, stressed, or overstimulated. Nevertheless, whenever possible, shifting from "don't" language to explicit, positive norms can reduce power struggles and support a deeper sense of safety.

Norms work best when they are taught and modeled, not simply stated. A child asked to mop the floor cannot be expected to succeed unless someone shows them how. Just like teaching a child to ride a bike or tie a shoe, we have to take the same patient, hands-on approach with teaching norms: how to have calm communication, how to keep a safe body, how to make things right after harm.

Children also follow expectations more consistently when they understand the why behind them. A rule without meaning can feel arbitrary or controlling. A rule connected to safety, care, or shared values begins to make sense. And sometimes, the why is developmental, contextual, or relational—our job is to make that understandable.

When my children were little, I spent a lot of time saying phrases that feel almost universal in caregiving, "Don't climb that", "Get down from there "or "Stop leaning back in your chair." I said them automatically, as if the rule itself should be obvious simply because I was the adult. However, one afternoon at the park, I watched my son climb up the slide instead of using the ladder. My instinct was to call out, "Slides are for going down!" But I paused. He was not being defiant—he was exploring. Testing his strength. Learning how his body moved in the world. When he was younger, there was no conversation about climbing up the slide—we simply went down. His body was not ready yet, and the boundary was clear.

As he grew, so did his capacity. Now he was strong enough to try something new, but not able to fully consider the impact on others. I walked over and said, "I know climbing up the slide feels fun. And your body is getting strong enough to do it safely. The only reason I am asking you to wait is that other kids are trying to come down, and I do not want anyone to get hurt. When the slide is empty, you can climb up it. When other kids are waiting, we take turns."He looked at the slide, looked at the kids at the top, and said, "Okay. I'll wait till it's empty." And he did.

That moment changed something in me. He was not resisting the rule—he did not yet understand the why behind it. We continued to build on that understanding. When the park was empty, I allowed him to climb up the slide. When other children were present, we talked about taking turns and being aware of others. We also added another layer: different places have different expectations. At school, a teacher might say no to climbing up the slide, and we respect that—even if the rule feels different from what we do at home or the park.

The expectation was not fixed—it evolved with his development, his awareness, and the context around him. This is how children learn discernment. Not through rigid rules alone, but through guidance that grows with them—helping them build awareness, impulse control, and the ability to navigate day to day expectations. The norm changed with development and context. He could only understand that if I explained it. We are also modeling; the world is grey and complex. Rarely are people harmonizing in a world of only black and white.

A similar moment happened at home with one of my kids who loved leaning back in his chair. After several reminders, I finally said, "I'm worried the chair could tip and you might hit your head. I don't want you to get hurt." He froze, set the chair down gently, and said, "Oh... that makes sense." Understanding shifted the dynamic. The rule wasn't about obedience—it was about care. And when he reads this book someday, I hope he giggles, because this kind reminder had to happen a lot... and sometimes it wasn't all that kind. I am an imperfect human, after all. Little bodies love to move, and big bodies can sometimes feel annoyed.

Explaining the reason behind expectations gives young people the dignity of clarity. It turns correction into connection, frustration into cooperation, and rules into shared agreements rooted in safety rather than power. When youth understand the why, they are far more likely to follow through—not because they fear consequences, but because the expectation finally has meaning. When we take time to explain the purpose behind norms—why we clean up toys, why we use quiet voices inside, why we don't climb certain structures, why we pause during transitions—children begin to internalize the expectation. They understand the reasoning, not just the rule.

This matters because there will be moments when we are not physically present to enforce the rules. Do our practices teach kids to meet expectations only when watched? Are we cultivating an understanding of what is good for the brain, body, and relationships? We don't want children who blindly comply when we are around and become secretive and risk-taking when we are away. We want kids who grow into adults who can think critically, perspective-take, and have empathy for others—people who make choices rooted in values, not fear.

When norms are connected to meaning, youth do not simply comply—they understand. And understanding is what empowers them long after childhood.

RISE INVITATION

Take a quiet moment to reflect on the values you feel are important for youth to cultivate. Write down three to five core values—such as kindness, respect, courage, curiosity, or responsibility.

From these values, create a simple motto or grounding phrase you and the youth can use together such as, "we are kind, caring and respectful."

Once your values and motto feel right, list three to five norms that make those values visible. Keep them clear, concrete, and teachable.

Now think about explicit ways you could teach or model those norms. Make a list.

Your norms become the daily language of safety. They tell young people what to not only do, but also who we are together.

The Social Discipline Window: Living in the "With" Space

One helpful way to visualize the balance between structure and care is the Social Discipline Window (Wachtel & McCold, 2000). This framework looks at two key elements: expectations and support. It explores how much is being asked of a young person and how much encouragement, teaching, and support are they receiving as they try to meet those expectations. The window describes four patterns to create a quadrant:

- **High expectations + Low support = "TO" window:** Adults do things to youth. This is the punitive space—a lot of control, little guidance. Youth may comply on the surface, but often feel fearful, resentful, confused, or unseen. They learn to avoid, hide, or rebel rather than engage honestly.

- **Low expectations + High support = "FOR" window:** Adults do things for youth. This is the permissive or rescuing space. There is warmth and nurturance, but few boundaries or challenges. The unintended message can be, "You can't handle hard things." Over time, youth may feel incapable, dependent, or unsure of their own strength.

- **Low expectations + Low support = "NOT" window:** Little is done with, for, or to youth. This is the neglectful space. There are no clear rules and little emotional backing. The message becomes, "You don't matter. No one is really paying attention." This is the most harmful window for safety.

- **High expectations + High support = "WITH" window:** Adults work with youth. This is the restorative space. Boundaries are clear, individualized expectations are high, and so is the level of care, teaching, and encouragement. Youth are held accountable in a way that communicates, "I'm on your side. I believe you can do this, and I won't leave you alone in it."

The WITH window is where resilience and wellbeing live. When youth are guided, encouraged, and held accountable within a supportive relationship, they learn that challenges are not threats—they are opportunities. They experience themselves as capable, and they experience adults as dependable partners in their growth.

Of course, no adult lives in the WITH window all the time. There are moments when safety concerns require a quick TO response, like scooping up a toddler running into the street. There are moments when time or capacity constraints pull us into the FOR window, like putting a child's shoes on for them when you're late. What matters is not perfection, but awareness.This framework invites reflection on the very human reasons we drift into the TO or FOR windows. I have lived in every window at different points in my parenting and professional life. I have found myself in the TO window when I was overwhelmed, overstimulated, or afraid of being judged—fearful that a rowdy group or a child melting down in public reflected poorly on me. In those moments, my responses were more about control than connection.

I have also lived in the FOR window—especially when my kids were very young or early in my social work career. It felt good to be needed. Being the one kids reached for. It gave me purpose. However, if I was not paying attention that instinct could slip into doing too much for them; shielding them from struggle, or rescuing them from challenges they were fully capable of managing. And while it felt loving, it unintentionally limited their agency. Both patterns make sense. Both come from human places. And both require self-awareness—because neither leads to long-term wellbeing for youth.

Structure, norms, and the WITH window all point toward the same truth: Young people feel safest when life is coherent, expectations are clear and connected to values, and the adults around them combine boundaries with warmth. High expectations with high support communicate: "You are capable. You are not alone. And we will grow through this together." That is safety—not the absence of struggle, but the presence of someone who stays with you in it.

RISE INVITATION

Take a moment to sketch your own version of the Social Discipline Window. Draw the four quadrants—To, For, Not, and With—and begin filling them in with real moments from your recent interactions with youth.

When did you find myself moving into "To"—leading with control, urgency, or fear?

When did you shift into "For"—rescuing, over helping, or cushioning every challenge?

Were there moments you slipped into "Not"—checked out, exhausted, or emotionally unavailable?

When did you operate in "With"—holding boundaries and offering support at the same time?

As you reflect, resist the temptation to judge or evaluate yourself. This is not a scorecard; it is a map. Every quadrant reveals something about your nervous system, your beliefs, and your needs.

Once you've filled in your map, gently explore these questions.

Where could you build in more support while still holding high expectations? Where might clarity help—clearer norms, explicit teaching, or quieter pacing? Where are you tightening too much out of fear or control? Where are you disappearing because you feel overwhelmed? What would help you return to the "With" window more often?

RISE doesn't ask you to be perfect—it asks you to be aware. This practice helps you understand your own patterns so you can meet young people with the steadiness, compassion, and predictability that cultivates a felt sense of safety.

When Things Get Messy: Responding, Repairing, and Restoring Safety

Even in the most connected relationships, things get messy. Youth break rules, test boundaries, argue, shut down, or act in ways that feel impulsive or unsafe. Adults get overwhelmed, overstimulated, or afraid. Safety is not measured by the absence of these moments—but by what happens next. How adults respond in moments of rupture becomes one of the most powerful shapers of a young person's felt sense of safety. These responses teach them what relationships can hold, whether mistakes are survivable, and whether honesty is worth the risk.

In many western contexts, discipline has long been rooted in punishment. Time-outs. Isolation. Removal of connection. Forced apologies. Public consequences. Even our language reflects a cultural belief that fear motivates change. But punishment rarely teaches what we hope it will teach. Punishment tends to activate shame—and shame does not create responsibility. Shame creates defense. As Brene Brown (2012) describes: Guilt says,

"I did something bad." Shame says, "I am bad."

When a young person lands in shame, their nervous system moves into survival. They do not lean into repair—they retreat from it. They are not learning accountability—they are learning protection. And protection can take many forms: resistance, defensiveness, blaming others, attacking themselves, shutting down, or even exploding outward in anger. In those moments, the child is no longer focused on learning or growing—they are focused on escaping the emotional danger they feel.

Imagine a coach who calls a time-out, gathers three players, and—voice sharp, brows tight—asks, "Who was guarding that guy? How did you let him drive to the hoop like that?" The tone is accusatory, aggressive, and overflowing with frustration. What do the players learn in that moment? Not that mistakes are part of the game. Not that they can problem-solve together. Not that learning happens through struggle. They learn a different lesson: Get out of this mess however, you can.

Some will blame their teammates. Some will blame the referee. Some will turn inward, whispering, "I'm terrible. I blew it." Some will get angry and push back, "Why don't you get out there and guard him?" Some will shut down completely. None of these reactions builds teamwork, curiosity, openness, or growth. They are not signs of a child who is being difficult—they are signs of a nervous system trying to survive shame. When punishment pushes a child into self-protection, the opportunity for learning slips away. When discipline protects dignity and preserves connection, the opportunity for growth expands.

The Compass of Shame, developed by Nathanson (1992), helps us understand the patterns that show up when shame is triggered. Some young people direct their shame outward, attacking others through criticism, sarcasm, or explosive reactions. Others turn inward and withdraw, shutting down emotionally, isolating, or disappearing from connection. Some attack themselves, slipping into harsh self-judgment or statements like "I'm so stupid," or "I shouldn't even be here," revealing how deeply shame has pierced their sense of worth. And others try to escape it altogether, avoiding responsibility, lying, numbing, or distracting themselves with risky behaviors or denial.

None of these responses are signs of a "bad kid." They are signs of a young person trying desperately to survive an internal experience that feels overwhelming or unbearable. They are indicators—not of defiance—but of pain. When we shift our posture from control to curiosity, we begin to ask: "What is this reaction protecting? What story is this young person telling themselves? Where are they feeling unsafe—inside or outside?" This is the doorway to safety-based responding.

Safety-based responses do not let harm slide. They simply refuse to use fear, humiliation, or power-over tactics to teach lessons. Instead, they combine four essential elements:

- **Curiosity:** What skill is missing?
- **Compassion:** What support is needed?
- **Clarity:** What boundary needs to be addressed, and what consequence—if one is appropriate—best supports long-term development?
- **Connection:** How do we stay in relationship while addressing the behavior?

When these elements come together, moments of misbehavior become opportunities—not punishments. Opportunities to teach a missing skill. Opportunities to understand the root of a behavior. Opportunities to reconnect instead of disconnect. Opportunities to practice making things right. This is the living heart of the WITH window—where accountability meets support, where limits meet love, where teaching meets trust.

I deeply believe in consequences. Consequences are not the enemy; misaligned consequences are. Language matters here. When I talk about consequences, I am not talking about punishment, revenge, or control. I am not talking about responses driven by anger or heightened emotion. I am talking about responses that are grounded, relational, and oriented toward growth. The most effective consequences—those that truly support development—are often natural when possible, rooted in love, and shaped with a young person's developmental capacity in mind. Another word for consequence is discipline, rooted in the Latin meaning 'to teach.' For example, if my child is in middle school and chooses not to wear a coat on a cold day, he will feel the natural consequence of being cold—the cold becomes the teacher.

Consequences are not meant to overpower, but to guide. Not to shame, but to teach. Not to disconnect, but to stay in relationship while holding a boundary. These kinds of consequences are most effective when they are established long before anything goes wrong, through the shared creation of norms and expectations.

In my playroom, that usually sounds like a reminder of the norm, a clear boundary, and then—if needed—the consistent follow-through of that boundary. For example, if the sand stays in the sand tray, we keep playing. If sand is thrown, we pause and review the expectation. If it happens again, I state the boundary: "If sand is thrown again, we will be done with the sand today." If it happens a third time, I follow through—not with anger or shame, but with steadiness and warmth, and with validation of whatever emotion comes up: "It is so hard to be done with the sand when you love it so much."

The consequence isn't punishment; it's a pathway back into harmony. It is a moment to learn and grow. And for my own children—one day you will read this—I know this is an area where I have struggled the most. I get dysregulated and I use consequences out of a desire for felt control. I will keep working to do better.

Many adults confide in me that they struggle to be both loving and accountable. They say when they feel frustrated by a broken expectation they go into drill sergeant mode and feel the need to take over control. In these moments, they feel they need law and order and go into "do" and "fix" mode. They don't know how to enforce norms without an element of power and control. Others tell me they feel too much empathy to hold limits. They lower expectations to accommodate a child's struggles, but sometimes this slips into permissiveness or enabling.

What children need is stewardship. A steady base where young people can learn, grow, and know what to expect. And it is profoundly loving to give a child the gift of boundaries they can count on. RISE believes that boundaries honor a child's strength, not their weakness. It believes that consequences are natural parts of living in a community, and that young people deserve the dignity of learning how to exist in society—not through shame, but through guidance.

Safety-based consequences are designed to teach. They are not about activating survival responses. They are not about fear, punishment, or control. They do not require a child to shrink in order to learn. Instead, they are designed to help a child return to regulation, to relationship, and to responsibility. The consequence becomes a guiding tool—a gentle reorientation back into healthy rhythms. There is an art to being both steady and loving. It often sounds like: "You're right, this feels hard—and I also know you can do hard things." "You're frustrated and saying the rules don't matter. And I know you're a kid who wants to make things right." "You're calling this dumb. And I also know you know what's expected of you." Boundaries do not break connection when they are held with warmth. In fact, they strengthen it.

Of course, adults have nervous systems, too. We have histories, triggers, parts, and worries. We carry beliefs about what "good" kids should do, what "good" parents, teachers, therapists should look like, and what other adults might think. And when our own shame or fear is activated, we often respond with the very same patterns—just in grown-up form. Sometimes it comes out as snapping or irritation, a quick flare of anger that masks the deeper feeling underneath. Other times we shut down completely, pulling away from the moment or disengaging emotionally because it feels too overwhelming to stay present. We may turn inward and spiral into self-blame, convinced we've failed or ruined everything, even when the situation is repairable. And sometimes we avoid the moment altogether—changing the subject, getting busy, walking away, or numbing ourselves rather than facing the discomfort.

These reactions don't make us bad adults. They make us human. Becoming aware of them gives us the power to pause, to re-center, and to choose a response rooted in intention rather than instinct. This is when the You Intervention becomes essential: "What part of me is reacting right now? What fear is beneath this reaction? Am I regulated enough to respond with intention? Is this about the child—or about me? What story am I making up about this moment?" Triggered parts responding to triggered parts do not cultivate safety. But the moment we pause—even for a breath—we interrupt that cycle. We create just enough space for clarity, care, and alignment to return. And even when we don't respond the way we hoped—and we won't—there is an incredible gift waiting on the other side: repair.

Repair is one of the most powerful builders of safety. It communicates: relationships can withstand hard moments. Imperfection does not equal rejection. Accountability is safe. Adults take responsibility for their impact. When an adult says, "I'm sorry I yelled. I was overwhelmed. I should not have handled it that way. Next time, I'm going to take a breath before I respond." Several things happen simultaneously: shame dissipates. Trust strengthens. Modeling occurs. The relationship deepens. Repair does not erase harm. Repair restores connection. It teaches youth that struggles—both theirs and ours—do not end relationships.

Safety is not the absence of conflict or missteps—it is built in how we respond to them. Because the reality is, teenagers do not suddenly become open, honest, and vulnerable if childhood taught them that mistakes lead to shame or disconnection. Trust is built slowly, through years of responses that say: your humanity is safe with me. Your mistakes do not threaten our relationship. Your struggles do not define you.

RISE INVITATION

Think back to a recent moment when you felt overwhelmed, impatient, or reactive with a young person—maybe you spoke sharply, shut down, withdrew, or moved into control and punishment.

Instead of judging yourself, approach this memory with curiosity and gentleness. What was happening in your body at that moment? Were you tired, overstimulated, frustrated, or feeling out of control? What response did you move toward? Did you lash out? Did you shut down? Did you turn inward with self-blame? Did you try to escape the moment? Just noticing this is the first step toward responding differently next time.

Now imagine returning to that moment—not to fix the past, but to practice repair. What would it sound like to take responsibility without self-shaming? What message do you want the young person to carry forward from this interaction? What is one small practice you can use next time you feel myself slipping?

Finally, offer yourself the same compassion you are learning to offer. Repair is not a sign of failure—it is evidence of courage.

Safety as a Shared Experience

A crucial part of cultivating safety is explicitly teaching young people how to recognize unsafe situations and trust their own internal alarms. Many children ignore discomfort to avoid seeming rude or disappointing others—something adults do, too. Gavin de Becker, in The Gift of Fear, (de Becker, 1997) describes how people often silence their instincts out of politeness, sometimes with devastating consequences.

Youth deserve a different lesson. They deserve to know that the tightening in their stomach, the urge to pull away, the sense that something is off, is not overreaction—it is information. Teaching safety begins with helping them notice those signals, trust what their body is saying, and name their discomfort openly. When a young person says, "I don't like this," or "Something about this feels wrong," our job is not to correct them but to welcome the awareness. We slow down. We get curious. We help them explore what their nervous system is trying to tell them. Boundaries become not an act of defiance but an act of self-protection.

Young people also need guidance in identifying the adults and environments where they feel safe. Sometimes the people they instinctively trust surprise us, and that is okay. What matters is giving them language for why someone feels safe in their body—the softness of a voice, the steadiness of a presence, the consistency of follow-through. Safety grows when their internal experience is honored rather than overridden. Teaching and integrating safety means helping young people understand their own signals, assert their boundaries, recognize safe adults, and access support. Yet, safety is not only about helping young people understand danger; it is also about creating a climate where truth can live. Where questions can be asked without fear. Where adults are steady enough to hold curiosity, confusion, and even discomfort.

One of the most overlooked elements of safety is honest, age-appropriate transparency. Young people deserve truthful information—about their bodies, their boundaries, their experiences, and the world around them. When adults avoid hard topics, minimize concerns, or offer half-answers, children learn two things very quickly: This adult can't handle my questions, and I must look elsewhere for information. And they will. If we do not become our children's primary and trusted source of information, the internet will step in. Peers will step in. The older kid on the bus will step in. Safety means setting the stage early—long before adolescence—for young people to turn toward us, not away from us.

One of the earliest places safety breaks down is around bodies. Even toddlers learn quickly which topics make adults uncomfortable. "Don't touch that. Don't say that word. That's gross. That's embarrassing." We slap nicknames on body parts, we redirect curiosity, and we unintentionally teach shame long before children even understand what they are feeling. But bodies are not shameful. Curiosity is not dangerous. Sexuality is not dirty. These are human experiences—sacred, natural, and deserving of clarity and respect.

Developmentally appropriate conversations about body parts (using correct anatomical names), privacy, consent, and bodily autonomy should start early—not in middle school when hormones arrive, peers are already exchanging information, and the internet has been whispering long before we realized it. Young people deserve to hear: "All bodies have private parts, and we use real names because your body is important." "Curiosity about bodies is normal." "If you ever see or hear something that confuses you, come tell me. You will never be in trouble."

Being open also prepares youth for real-life situations long before they encounter them: what to do at a sleepover if something feels uncomfortable, how to exit a situation that doesn't feel right, what to do at a party if pressure builds, how to assert boundaries with peers or adults, and how to recognize the internal signal that says, "This doesn't feel safe." These conversations do not create fear; they create agency. They give children clarity, voice, and options.

Over time, transparency, attunement, and steady conversations create a relationship where youth feel safe not because nothing difficult will ever happen, but because they know exactly where to come when something does. Safety becomes not only an external environment we shape together, but also a felt sense they can eventually carry within themselves, wherever they go. Safety is not something youth achieve alone, and it is not something adults simply provide. It is something we cultivate together. When adults offer trust, respect, predictability, open communication and shared humanity, youth begin to believe they are safe. And when they believe they are safe, something profound happens: they take more risks, explore more freely, connect more deeply, and learn more courageously.

Integrating Safety: When the "Safer Place" Doesn't Feel Safe

One of the most misunderstood truths about safety is that new environments—even healthier, stable ones—feel more safe than the environments that caused harm. Trauma conditions the nervous system to survive chaos, and the familiar often feels more tolerable than the unknown.

When I was fifteen, a friend's family invited me to live with them after witnessing something painful in my home. They provided warmth and stability I had rarely known: predictable rhythms, quiet evenings, gentle conversations. They were kind. Their home was peaceful. And yet my body didn't rest. The quiet felt loud. The calm felt foreign. I found myself lying awake, wondering what was happening at home and feeling responsible for anything happening while not being there. Within ten days, I moved back—not because my home was safer, but because it was familiar.

For fifteen years, I had learned how to survive in that home. I understood it in my bones. Returning home was not a rejection of the kindness offered to me; it was a reflection of how deeply my nervous system equated familiarity with safety. This is why simply removing a child from danger is not enough. Safety cannot be imposed. It must be built thoughtfully, collaboratively, and with respect for the child's internal world. When we intervene, we must be careful not to take away the agency that helped them navigate their lives. Instead, we walk with them, honoring their pace and their voice.

Around that same time, my volleyball coach offered me a different kind of safety. She learned I was struggling, and she quietly handed me the keys to the gym. "Come in anytime you need," she said. Before school. After practice. Late at night. She did not ask questions, didn't require me to disclose anything. She did not rescue me or demand explanations. She simply created access to something steady and let me choose when, how, and why to use it.

Looking back, I see how profound that gesture was. She provided safety without control, support without intrusion, and guidance without ownership. She gave me a tool and trusted me to use it. That is what integrating safety looks like: not doing things to young people, and not always doing things for them, but creating a path we walk with them.

RISE INVITATION

Take a quiet moment to reflect on your own relationship with safety—both the safety you try to create for young people, and the safety you learned to navigate in your own life.

Bring to mind one young person. Let them sit in your imagination for a moment. Invite curiosity. What does this young person's nervous system need in order to feel safe?

Not the safety you think they "should" feel— but the safety their body actually registers.

Do they need more predictability? More voice? More softness? More clarity? More space? How do they show you they feel unsafe? Is it withdrawal? Big emotions? People pleasing? Anger? What might those signals be trying to protect? What would it look like to build safety with them, rather than for them? Are there choices you can offer? Access you can create? Rituals you can share? Predictability you can strengthen?

And then, turn inward with the same compassion. What supports you in showing up as a steady presence? Is it rest? Clarity? Boundaries? A moment to breathe? A connection?

Finally, choose one small, meaningful practice you will carry into the week ahead to cultivate safety.

CHAPTER NINE

Connection and Belonging

Every young person longs to feel accepted, loved, and worthy. They long to know they belong. All of us are wired for connection, but for youth in particular, relationships are formative. A child's sense of connection and belonging shape their identity, their emotional wellbeing, and their fundamental belief about who they are in the world.

There is a saying often attributed to an African proverb—though its exact origin is unknown—that captures this truth: "The child who is not embraced by the village will burn it down to feel its warmth." The message is not about destruction; it is about longing. When children do not feel a sense of belonging, they reach for connection wherever they can find it. Not because they want to cause harm, but because they are aching to feel held, valued, and seen—and may not yet have the skills to find those feelings in safe or prosocial ways.

Young people will choose the path of least resistance to get their needs met. If they cannot find belonging through healthy channels, they may seek it in ways adults find confusing: becoming the loud one, the funny one, the angry one, the difficult one. These identities—however imperfect—offer something predictable: attention, acknowledgment, a feeling of mattering. For many youth, negative attention feels safer than invisibility. It gives them a role. It gives them a place. It gives them a way of existing in the world. Which is why isolation—intentional or unintentional—can be so harmful.

Yet we use exclusion constantly: suspensions, expulsions, sending a child to their room, planned ignoring. Often, we do these things out of fear of what might happen if we don't, or because we hope it will teach accountability. But exclusion often widens the very gap that created the behavior in the first place. A child who is already struggling with belonging may interpret exclusion as confirmation: "You don't fit. You're too much. You're not wanted."

Another force that fuels disconnection is our cultural preference for quick fixes. True connection takes time. Belonging takes intention. Changing neural pathways takes repetition and relational consistency. This is why RISE is a long-term relational practice. It does not aim for instant compliance; it aims for integrated wellbeing.

A school professional once discovered this truth firsthand while working to improve middle school attendance. His school had embraced restorative practices and eliminated exclusionary discipline, yet attendance issues persisted. Many students skipped school to be with friends around town. After weeks of frustration, he reframed the problem with one transformative question: "How can we create an environment that offers as deep of a sense of connection and belonging as the peer groups they're choosing instead?" It shifted everything. Instead of trying to stop youth from avoiding school, the staff began imagining how school could become a place youth wanted to be—a place where belonging was felt, not forced.

That question stayed with me because connection and belonging were essential pieces of my own resilience story. When I was in fifth grade, I was invited to join a club basketball team. I was a girl from a tiny town of 250 people. I did not have money, a recognizable last name, or a clear place among my peers. Much of my school day was spent in the nurse's office or cleaning the classroom during recess—subtle signs of a child searching for purpose and connection.

I still don't know exactly why those adults asked me to join, but their invitation became a turning point. Being part of a team gave me something I had been missing: belonging. It gave me friendships, taught me how to be part of something larger than myself. I wanted to show up. I wanted to practice, to sweat, to lose and win alongside others—because it made me feel wanted. It made me feel special. It made me feel included. During a time when much of my life felt heavy and isolating, being part of that team helped me feel like I belonged somewhere.

I have countless memories of coaches, teachers, and adults who offered me moments of connection just when I needed them most—people who saw me, who invited me in, who let me, matter. Each invitation became a seed of wellbeing. Each sense of belonging reminded me that even in the darkest seasons of my childhood, there were places where I could feel connected, supported, and held. And those places helped me rise again and again.

So I often ask adults the same questions I ask myself: "What helps you feel connected?" Is it being included? Being asked for your opinion? Someone remembering a detail about you? A warm greeting? A sense that your presence shifts the room in a meaningful way? Whatever connection looks like for us, we can assume young people long for something similar. Connection is not a mystery—it's a mirror. When we understand what helps us feel valued, we can begin offering those same relational openings to the youth in our lives.

Connection grows through small invitations. Belonging deepens through consistent presence. Both begin with knowing that humans do not rise in isolation—we rise in each other's care.

RISE INVITATION

Take a few quiet minutes to reflect on your own story of connection and belonging. Before we can meaningfully support young people, we must understand the pathways—and barriers—that shaped our own sense of being welcomed in the world.

Remember a time you felt you truly belonged. Where were you? Who created that feeling? What did they do—specifically—that helped you feel wanted, seen, or included?

Pay attention to the small gestures; they are often the ones that mattered most.

Now recall a time you felt excluded or invisible. What messages—spoken or unspoken—shaped that experience? How did you respond? Withdraw. Perform. Act out. Try harder. Shut down.

Notice the parallels to what young people often do when they feel they don't fit. Now invite curiosity. What conditions helped belonging grow? What conditions made it harder? Which of those conditions do you have the power to create for young people today?

Choose one small, consistent practice that you can offer this week to help a young person feel they matter.

Seeing What Shapes Us: Understanding How Bias Affects Belonging

If connection and belonging are essential to a young person's wellbeing, then we must also be honest about the forces that can interrupt or distort those experiences. One of the most impactful—and often invisible—barriers to connection is our own bias. Bias is not a character flaw. It is a human experience. It is the collection of messages we have absorbed across our lives—through family, school, media, culture, faith communities, neighborhoods, books, and the unspoken rules of the places we grew up. Bias is the lens we inherited long before we knew we were looking through one. Every adult has biases. Every young person has biases. None of us escape them, because all of us are shaped by the narratives around us. Bias becomes harmful only when they go unexamined.

When left unacknowledged, bias subtly shapes how we interpret youth behavior, how quickly we offer patience, how warmly we respond, whose mistakes we forgive, and whose we judge. It influences who we lean toward and who we pull away from without ever saying a word. And young people feel these differences immediately—in tone, in presence, in body language, in the quiet cues that tell them whether they are welcomed or merely tolerated.

Sometimes bias shows up in ways we can see—like avoiding someone, stereotyping them, being harsher with certain groups, or dismissing someone's feelings because they do not match our expectations. However, most often, bias shows up in unspoken places: who gets a softer voice, who gets the benefit of the doubt, whose expression is interpreted as attitude, whose is interpreted as anxiety, who is seen as capable, who is seen as a problem. And youth notice. Even if we never say the words out loud, they feel the story underneath.

Because bias is learned, it can also be unlearned. But unlearning requires awareness. Becoming aware of our biases is not about shame or judgment. It is about curiosity. It is about asking ourselves: "Where did this belief come from? Who taught it to me, directly or indirectly? Is this belief aligned with the adult I want to be? Does this belief help or hurt the young people in my care?"

Bias is not dismantled through self-criticism. Bias is transformed through self-compassion, honesty, humility and intentional practice. When we bring a bias into consciousness, we reclaim the ability to choose differently. We can pause before responding. We can soften our assumptions. We can widen our understanding. We can build relationships rooted in equity and dignity rather than inherited prejudices.

And just as adults carry biases, young people do too. Sometimes they absorb them from caregivers, peers, media, or cultural narratives. Bias can make youth feel insecure, ashamed, superior, inferior, confused, or angry. It can influence who they befriend, who they exclude, and how they see themselves within their community. This is why adults play a crucial role. We model what it looks like to question the stories we have inherited. We show how to replace judgment with curiosity. We create environments where difference is not a threat, but an opportunity to learn.

Helping youth recognize bias—with gentleness, without shame—builds empathy and emotional intelligence. It teaches them to slow down, to wonder about others' perspectives, and to question the narratives that divide instead of unite. It supports their ability to form deeper, more meaningful relationships. Most importantly, it expands their capacity for compassion—for themselves and for others.

Belonging cannot flourish where bias goes unchecked. But when adults are willing to see themselves clearly, to soften the stories they've inherited, and to approach youth with open-hearted curiosity, something shifts. We create spaces where every young person—no matter their identity, culture, neuro-type, background, or way of being—can feel valued and included.

RISE INVITATION

This reflection helps you trace a single bias back to its roots—not to judge yourself, but to understand the stories you inherited and how they may shape your relationships with youth.

Start with one honest observation. Identify a moment when you felt more frustrated, less patient, more affectionate, or more distant with a young person. Invite curiosity. "Where did you first learn that reaction? Who taught you—directly or indirectly—to see this behavior, characteristic, or trait this way?"

Consider what messages from childhood, school, media, faith, or culture may be woven into it. Let the answers be gentle and evolving. The goal is awareness, not certainty.

Notice how the bias shows up in relationship. Reflect on how it may influence your tone, warmth, expectations, assumptions, the grace you offer, and the story you tell yourself about this young person. Rewrite the story—on purpose.

Choose one belief that better aligns with widening the doorway of acceptance—for the youth and for yourself.

Inclusion: Creating Spaces That Say, "There Is Room for You Here."

Once we begin to see our biases with clarity and compassion, we gain the capacity to build something intentional in their place: inclusion. Inclusion is the moment-by-moment practice of ensuring that every young person can answer fundamental belonging questions with a steady yes. "Is there space for me here? Do I matter here? Do people want me here?"

Inclusion is not the result of a poster, policy, or slogan. It is the lived experience of entering a space and feeling the atmosphere shift—as if the room itself is saying, "We asked for you. You belong." It often begins in the smallest relational moments. Inclusion grows when a child is greeted warmly, when their name is spoken with care, when adults make room for their stories and identities without assumptions. It shows up in the way we widen our attention to include the young person who hovers at the edges, or the one who doesn't quite know how to step in. These gestures signal: "You are welcome to take up space here."

Inclusion deepens when every young person's voice matters. Restorative circles are a powerful way to structure this. Rooted in Indigenous community practices and relational accountability, circles create a shape where no one sits at the head and no one is left outside the conversation. A talking piece moves from person to person, granting each youth the right to speak and the right to pass. The norms—listening without interruption, speaking honestly, holding the group with respect—help cultivate an atmosphere where dignity is shared.

Circles reveal what young people carry with them into the room. They help adults notice who is hurting, who is joyful, who feels unsettled, who feels ready to connect. They weave inclusion into daily practice not simply because everyone speaks, but because everyone is held within a shared container of care.

Inclusion becomes meaningful when every young person has opportunities to participate and contribute. Some express belonging through leadership, others through creativity, service, humor, or quiet consistency. When adults intentionally create roles, responsibilities, and moments that honor each young person's strengths, inclusion shifts from: "You may join us" to "We need what you bring."

And inclusion does not happen by accident. It is a choice we make repeatedly: to invite rather than assume, to slow down rather than overlook, to enter cultural and personal differences with curiosity rather than assumptions. It shows up when adults intervene gently but firmly in moments of exclusion, and when they model what it looks like to welcome others with openness. When adults practice inclusion intentionally, they create the foundation upon which true belonging can grow. It is not about perfection. It is about presence. It is the steady work of making sure no young person has to search for a place at the table.

Engagement: The Heartbeat of Belonging

If inclusion answers the question, "Is there space for me here?" Engagement answers a deeper one, "Do you want to know me?" Engagement is where belonging comes alive. It is the moment a young person feels not just welcomed but wanted. It is not participation for participation's sake—it is the felt sense of being seen, understood, and emotionally held by the adults in their world.

Authentic engagement happens when adults go beyond surface-level exchanges and choose to connect with each young person as a whole human being. It grows when we notice the small details: the way their face lights up when they talk about drawing, how they always hum while working, the story they told last week that we remember and ask about again. These moments accumulate into a powerful message: "You matter enough to be remembered."

I once heard a story about a camp counselor who discovered a boy's love for green Life Savers. A full year after camp ended, she mailed him a pack. That simple act left a lifelong imprint—not because of the candy, but because it said, "I still think of you. You matter to me, even when you aren't here." Belonging is built from gestures like that.

Engagement deepens when adults show up with presence instead of preoccupation. It is in the way we sit down rather than stand over a child, the way we soften our voice when they are overwhelmed, the way we stay curious about their inner world rather than rushing to correct or fix. It is woven into the small rituals of relationship—laughter, shared stories, inside jokes, predictable check-ins, and moments where we pause long enough to ask a question that invites more than a one-word answer.

At home, this might sound like shifting from "How was your day?" to questions that open a door into their experience: "What was something that made you smile today? What felt hard? What is something you're proud of? What's one thing you wish adults understood about today?" Little games—"Would you rather?", "highs and lows," "rose and thorn"—can turn ordinary transitions into moments of engagement. They teach youth that their thoughts and feelings matter, not just their behavior.

Engagement is also how the brain learns belonging. When children reflect on their experiences, talk about their emotions, and feel genuinely listened to, the neural pathways for regulation, resilience, and motivation strengthen. Dopamine systems activate. The brain begins associating relational connection with safety and reward. Engagement literally supports healthier brain development and overall wellbeing.

Engagement is not grand or dramatic. It is the slow, steady accumulation of intentional presence. It is the adult who keeps asking, keeps noticing, keeps showing up. Over time, these moments tell a young person, in deeply embodied ways: "You matter. I see you. You belong."

Collaboration: The Integration of Belonging

If inclusion says, "You're welcome here," and engagement says, "Come closer—I want to know you," then collaboration communicates, "Your voice shapes this space." Collaboration is belonging, in its most active form. It moves young people from the edges of community life into true partnership. It shifts the dynamic from adults doing things for youth to adults doing things with youth.

Belonging cannot be passive. Youth must have a sense that their ideas, feelings, and perspectives matter—that they are not simply guests in a world adults built, but co-creators of the environment and relationships around them. Collaboration is how we make that real.

It begins with an attitude of un-knowing. Adults often assume expertise because of age, training, or role. But young people are the experts of their own lives; they hold the only firsthand knowledge of what it feels like to inhabit their internal and external worlds. When adults position themselves as learners—curious, open, willing to be shaped by youth perspectives—they communicate something transformative: "Your lived experience is real, it is valid, and it has a place here."

Collaboration takes root when adults create judgment-free spaces for ideas, questions, and emotions. In these spaces, youth can speak without fear of being dismissed or coerced. They can share creatively, honestly, imperfectly—knowing the goal is not compliance but connection. When adults respond with openness, even when youth feedback is difficult to hear, they demonstrate that disagreement does not rupture the relationship. Instead, it becomes part of how the relationship grows.

Through collaboration, youth learn essential relational skills: how to negotiate, compromise, share power, express needs, navigate conflict, and take responsibility for shared outcomes. These skills not only strengthen their sense of belonging—they shape the foundations of future friendships, partnerships, work environments, and communities.

For young people with trauma histories, collaboration is especially healing. Trauma can push youth toward extremes: controlling others to feel safe or disappearing into submission to avoid conflict. Collaboration offers a middle path. It models a healthier relational rhythm—we can figure this out together—and teaches that power does not have to be taken or surrendered; it can be shared.

This is why the RISE framework emphasizes cooperation, not compliance, as the path to true collaboration. Compliance may produce quiet classrooms or perceived order, but it does not build connection. It does not cultivate belonging. Cooperation, on the other hand, invites youth into meaning making. It explains the why behind boundaries. It gives them roles in decision-making. It encourages them to practice voice and agency within safe, supportive structures.

In collaborative environments, adults intentionally offer opportunities for shared leadership—taking turns, proposing solutions, solving problems together, reflecting on what works and what doesn't. Youth begin to understand themselves not as passive recipients of adult rules but as contributors to the community's wellbeing.

Collaboration also reinforces identity. When young people are encouraged to explore their strengths, cultural backgrounds, interests, and values—and when those expressions influence the community—the message becomes clear: "Who you are enriches us." Shared rituals, group decisions, and co-created norms reinforce that every person has a role and every voice has weight.

In these co-created spaces, adults and youth grow side by side. They build communities that are steadier, kinder, more flexible, and more resilient—because they are built with many hands and many voices. Collaboration is where belonging moves from a feeling to a practice, from something youth receive to something they help sustain.

Feeling Valued: The Emotional Root of Belonging

If inclusion says, "You're welcome here," and engagement says, "Come closer—I want to know you," and collaboration says, "Your voice shapes this space," then feeling valued offers the quiet, anchoring truth beneath them all, "Your presence makes a difference." Belonging becomes transformative only when a young person begins to believe they matter—not for how well they perform, not for how easy they are to love, but for who they are.

Feeling valued is the deep internal knowing that moves beyond someone noticing when you walk into a room, it is when someone notices when you do not. It is the belief that the community and relationships around you need your unique qualities.

Young people feel valued when adults take the time to affirm their strengths, acknowledge their efforts, and recognize the parts of them that might otherwise go unseen—their persistence, their sense of humor, their creativity, their kindness, their discernment, their ability to bounce back after disappointment. When adults notice these things consistently, youth learn that value is not something they have to earn through perfection, pleasing, or performance. It is something they carry simply by being themselves.

Feeling valued also deepens when youth are invited to contribute in meaningful ways. When a child is given a role that matters—helping lead a routine, contributing ideas to a project, supporting a peer, sharing cultural traditions, or using a personal strength to help the community—it communicates that their presence shapes the collective good. They are not just participants in the group; they are contributors to it.

These experiences, small as they may seem, accumulate over time. A sincere "Thanks for sharing that opinion," a moment of undivided attention, a warm acknowledgment of cooperation, an invitation to speak, a thoughtful follow-up on something they shared earlier—these moments reinforce an internal message many young people desperately need: "I am valued here."

Feeling valued is inseparable from healthy identity development. When youth feel valued, they are less likely to retreat into isolation or internalize the belief that they are invisible. Instead, they develop stronger, more resilient self-concepts. They become more willing to take healthy risks, to seek help when needed, to engage more fully in relationships, and to trust that their voice has impact.

Belonging may open the door, but feeling valued is what helps a young person stay. It roots them in community, strengthens their sense of identity, and nurtures the courage required to grow. And perhaps most importantly, feeling valued teaches them a lesson that shifts the trajectory of their life: "My existence has worth, and the world is better because I am in it."

RISE INVITATION

Belonging is created through the daily decisions we make about how we see, engage with, collaborate with, and value the young people in our lives. This reflection will help you create your own Belonging Blueprint.

Inclusion: Who is not fully in the room? Think of one young person who may not feel welcomed or understood. What might be getting in the way of their belonging? What is one small act of invitation you could offer?

Engagement: How well do you truly know them? Choose one youth and write what you know. What lights them up? What shuts them down? What do you still not know? What could you learn by asking one more question?

Collaboration: Where can you offer shared power? Where could you invite this young person into decision-making? What part could you co-create?

Feeling Valued: What message do you want them to carry? Imagine this youth years from now, recalling your connection. Write one sentence: "Through our relationship, I want you to know..." What is one thing you can do this week to bring that message to life?

You now have a simple, relational map—your blueprint for cultivating belonging.

Creating Pathways to Connection and Belonging

Connection and belonging do not unfold automatically for every young person. For some, the road to belonging is layered with rejection, disappointment, or relational wounds that make vulnerability feel risky. After enough hurt, even the most connection-hungry youth may appear closed off, distant, or uninterested. But beneath that protective shell is almost always a longing: "Please show me that I still have a place."

This is where our role becomes sacred. We cannot force belonging—but we can create the conditions in which it becomes possible. We can offer steady invitations into community, moments of shared laughter, and gentle opportunities for youth to participate, contribute, and simply be with others. Group activities, team projects, rituals, and shared responsibilities all become small bridges toward connection. They teach young people how to listen, how to take turns, how to share space with others, how to repair after conflict, and how to trust that their presence matters.

These opportunities do not need to be elaborate. They can be built into everyday routines—conversations on the way home from school, cooking together, reading side by side, joining a child in an activity they love, or offering a simple, "Do you want to sit with me for a minute?" Belonging is strengthened not by grand efforts, but by the accumulation of small moments where a young person feels chosen.

Sometimes connection is best nurtured through thoughtful pairing with peers who share similar interests. Other times, it grows through one-on-one conversations with the adult who feels safest to the child. What matters most is the message we send with our presence: "You don't have to do life alone. I'm willing to walk with you."

At its core, the RISE Framework invites us to notice a young person's greatness and reflect it back to them—to celebrate who they are in our world. When we do this consistently, we help shape the internal narratives youth carry about their worth. We help them internalize these messages: "You are needed. You are wanted. You belong here—exactly as you are."

RISE INVITATION

One tool for intentionally connecting with youth is to understand and know their love language—whether it is gifts, words of affirmation, acts of service, quality time, or physical touch. Knowing this provides insight into how they best receive care and feel valued.

https://5lovelanguages.com/quizzes/love-language

Choose one young person and spend time simply noticing. When do they light up? What gestures soften them? What do they do to show affection or appreciation toward others? Do they seek closeness or hugs? Do they bring you little drawings or objects? Do they ask you to play with them? Beam when you praise them? Do they appreciate when you help them with tasks?

Once you know a child's love language, you can offer intentional ways to engage. Choose the love language and try one small act tailored to it.

Words of Affirmation: "I noticed how hard you worked on that puzzle. Your effort really stood out."

Quality Time: "Do you want to choose a game for us to play together?"

Acts of Service: "I saw you were frustrated. Want me to help you get started?"

Gifts: "I saved this sticker for you because it reminded me of how much you love dogs."

Physical Touch: "You look like you need a high-five. Or two."

Notice your own love language filter. Invite curiosity. How do you naturally show care? How might that limit or enhance your ability to communicate love in ways this child can truly receive?

When we understand our own love language, we become more intentional.

CHAPTER TEN

Meaning and Purpose

Meaning and purpose are the quiet sparks that light our inner world—small at first, but powerful enough to guide us through the hardest parts of being human. They help us feel that our lives matter, that our experiences have weight, that we are part of something larger than the moment we are standing in. When we carry purpose, even the ordinary decisions of our day begin to feel like steps toward something greater, something deeply human and profoundly fulfilling.

It can be hard to describe what a felt sense of meaning is in words. It often lives more in the heart than in the intellect—felt long before it is understood. But for me, meaning and purpose have always been essential parts of rising. It helped me survive what I could not make sense of. It gave shape to experiences that once left me angry, jealous, resentful, and asking a question many young people ask in their hardest moments: "Why me?" That question can trap us. It can freeze us in place. It can make us feel powerless, invisible, without options or direction. What helped me move forward was not an answer—but a shift.

At some point, I began asking a different set of questions: "What can I do with what I've lived through? How can I give these experiences purpose? How can I turn them into something that helps rather than harms—something that becomes my superpower rather than my burden?" That shift changed the trajectory of my life.

People often ask why I chose this path, why I became a social worker, therapist—why I care so deeply about the wellbeing of youth. And I tell them that the seed was planted when I was just nine years old. I was watching a television show where a kind woman—who I now realize was a social worker—comforted a frightened boy who called her in the middle of the night. She listened. She held space. She made him feel safe. And at nine years old, something inside me whispered, "I want to be her."

Perhaps I longed for that same steady presence in my own life. Perhaps I recognized myself in that child's fear. Perhaps I already understood, in a way only children can, what it feels like to need someone who won't turn away. But I also knew something else: "I wanted to be different." Different in my being—steady where there had been unpredictability, presence where there had been absence, gentle where there had been hurt.

That shift became my meaning. It became my purpose. It became the direction I walked toward, even when the path wasn't clear. It became the hope I held onto—the hope that allowed me to rise.

Meaning, Purpose, and the Stories We Live

Meaning does not arrive all at once. It takes shape slowly, through a young person's inner world and through the models around them. It is less a definition and more a feeling—a quiet awareness that my life matters, my experiences mean something, and I am connected to something larger than myself.

Meaning is not only cognitive; it is physical, emotional, and relational. It is the spark of curiosity when something resonates. It is the grounding that comes with the realization, "This aligns with who I am." Meaning begins in the body long before it becomes a sentence.

Purpose, then, is the movement born from that awareness—the direction we choose, the actions we take, the ways we use our gifts, struggles, and stories to shape the world. It is the inner pull that says, I want to move toward this. Youth act with purpose when they persist through challenges, take risks, protect what they love, or pour themselves into something that feels aligned and joyful. When we help young people understand the difference, we help them understand themselves.

Meaning is what. Purpose is how. Meaning roots them. Purpose moves them. Even before youth can name these ideas, they begin forming them.

Children discover meaning in the small moments that tell them who they are and what they bring to the world. Adolescents shape meaning through questions—sometimes spoken, often silent: "Do I matter? Does my life mean anything? What is my place? What am I becoming?" These questions are not signs of insecurity—they are signs of becoming.

Meaning and purpose don't grow in a vacuum. They grow out of what we have been building all along. When a young person feels safe—truly safe—their nervous system finally has room for reflection. When they feel connected and experience belonging, they begin to believe their life has weight and value. Safety steadies the ground. Belonging warms it. On that foundation, meaning and purpose have space to breathe.

In addition, whether we realize it or not, young people watch how we answer these same questions in our own lives. They watch how we respond to stress, what we celebrate, how we recover from mistakes, how we treat others, how we talk about meaning and regret and hope. They watch how we hold joy. They watch how we survive pain. They watch how we find purpose when life feels uncertain.

Adults often underestimate how closely youth study the emotional landscapes of adults. Young people learn meaning through the stories we tell—and the stories we live. When we narrate our reflections aloud—"This mattered because…" "Here's what this taught me…" "This helped me understand something about myself…"—youth learn to ask these questions themselves. Meaning is contagious when adults are intentional.

We also model purpose in the way we show up: our passions, our commitments, and the things we consistently return to. Young people notice when adults follow the pull of their heart with sincerity. When we trust our own inner wisdom, we show them how to listen to their own.

Meaning-making is a natural extension of this modeling. It is the process of asking deeper questions about our experiences and giving them a place in our larger life story. Not through forced positivity or minimizing pain—but by approaching life with honesty, curiosity, and courage. Meaning-making asks: "What can this experience teach me? What strength did I not know I had? How might this shape who I am becoming?"

This is where Viktor Frankl's wisdom becomes so relevant. Frankl wrote that suffering ceases to be suffering at the moment it finds meaning (Frankl, 1959). He did not mean that hardship becomes easy or that pain disappears. His insight was far more profound. Frankl believed that meaning is a fundamental human drive—that even in the darkest circumstances, people search for something that helps them hold onto their humanity. While imprisoned in Nazi concentration camps, he observed that those who survived longest were not necessarily the strongest, but those who had something to live for: a loved one, a dream unfinished, a contribution yet to be made.

He wrote, "Everything can be taken from a man but one thing: the last of the human freedoms—to choose one's attitude in any given set of circumstances, to choose one's own way." This was not denial of brutality. It was the recognition that meaning cannot be taken from us. It is our internal anchor—the orientation that remains when the external world collapses. Frankl's lesson is not that young people should find meaning in suffering. It is that meaning can transform suffering—not by erasing it but by giving it context and direction.

Meaning helps youth understand that hardship is not the final word. It is one chapter in a much larger story still unfolding. Meaning making can keep young people from collapsing into shame or rigid narratives like "I'm broken. I am alone. I'll never be okay." It widens their identity. It softens the nervous system. It steadies the spirit. When a young person senses meaning—even faintly—something opens.

- **Meaning builds curiosity:** They begin to explore and wonder. Adults can foster this by inviting experimentation—"Let's try something totally new today and see what we discover together"—signaling that curiosity is welcomed, not judged.

- **Meaning deepens learning:** They try harder and pay attention because something matters. Adults can nurture this by connecting learning to a child's inner world: "You care about animals so much—I wonder what else we could learn that would help you understand them even better?" When adults link effort to passion, learning becomes personal.

- **Meaning strengthens identity:** They understand their values and begin choosing in alignment with them. Adults cultivate this by naming what they see—"I notice how kind you were to your friend today. That tells me kindness is important to you"—helping youth recognize the threads of who they are becoming.
- **Meaning fuels hope:** They begin to see futures that feel possible. Adults can model this by voicing hope aloud—"I don't know exactly how this will turn out, but I believe in what's possible"—offering a steady, hopeful voice when a young person's own hope feels thin.
- **Meaning awakens motivation:** They push through challenges because the goal feels connected to who they are. Adults can show this in real time: "I can't figure this out yet, so I'm going to research it and try again. When something matters, we keep going." Youth learn motivation by watching motivation.
- **Meaning organizes direction:** Choices make more sense when connected to a larger story. Adults support this by helping youth pause and reflect—"How does this choice fit with who you want to be?"—guiding them toward alignment rather than impulse.
- **Meaning reduces stress:** Purpose reframes obstacles as stepping stones rather than dead ends. Adults model this by normalizing struggle—"This is hard, and that's okay. Hard things often mean we're growing." Stress softens when struggle is framed as purposeful rather than shameful.
- **Meaning expands resilience:** They begin to believe, I can rise through this. Adults strengthen this belief by naming resilience in the moment—"You kept trying. You didn't give up. That tells me something powerful about you." When youth hear their strength reflected back, they begin to recognize it inside themselves.

Purpose is what moves all of this into motion—turning meaning into action, identity into effort, curiosity into exploration, hope into goal-setting, resilience into direction. When a young person begins to feel both meaning and purpose their internal world shifts.

Experiencing Mattering: Contribution + Significance = Fulfillment

Meaning and purpose deepen when young people begin to experience themselves as someone who matters. This happens long before adulthood, long before a job title, long before they can name concepts like contribution or significance. It begins in the subtle ways they feel themselves making a difference—in their families, in their classrooms, in their communities, in the tiny ecosystems where their presence shifts something for the better.

For many youth, contribution does not come naturally. Especially for those who are frequently on the receiving end of care—children in support systems, in therapy, in foster care, or in families navigating hardship. When a child is constantly positioned as the one who needs help, they may quietly form the belief: "I don't have anything to give. I'm the one people fix, not the one who makes things better." This is why contribution is so powerful. It begins to rewrite the story.

I grew up attending a small youth group. We took a mission trip one summer, and something inside me cracked open, in the best way. I deeply felt what it was like to contribute to something bigger than myself—to care for strangers, to work alongside peers, to see that my hands and my effort could make a difference. It was life-changing. It pulled me out of the small world I often felt trapped in and allowed me to see the ripple effect of my existence.

That is the quiet magic of contribution: it awakens the belief; "I can make a difference here." And once youth begin to experience contribution, something else begins to grow—significance. Significance is the emotional imprint that settles into the heart when a young person realizes: "I am needed here."

Significance is rarely born from grand gestures. In my life, it came from the smallest moments—the moment's adults might not even remember. I felt significant when my coach asked me to lead the team in a drill. When my teacher wrote a note on my paper that was not about the assignment at all, but about me—something she noticed that was unique about my perspective—it stayed with me. I felt significant when a friend's mom asked me to babysit because she saw me as capable and trustworthy. These weren't awards. They weren't spotlights. They were invitations into mattering.

Feeling special is deeply connected to feeling significant. And for many youth—especially those who often feel invisible or overlooked—these micro-moments become anchors in their identity. They whisper the truth: "You bring something important into the world. You are not just here—you are needed."

When contribution and significance begin to weave together, something profound emerges— fulfillment. Fulfillment is the quiet, deep satisfaction a young person feels when they realize their presence creates good in the world. It's not pleasure. It's not temporary happiness. It's the internal glow that comes from living in alignment with their values, strengths, and purpose—even if they cannot yet name them.

I felt this in a powerful way at sixteen, just a week after getting my driver's license. I started volunteering at a community program called HD Youth Center—a safe place where young kids gathered after school. The man who ran it, Henry Davidson, was one of those rare adults whose presence made young people stand a little taller. He was admired, respected, and trusted. Kids felt safe with him.

Somehow, he trusted me. He handed me responsibilities: running a clothing program, organizing a holiday food giveaway, helping coordinate events. He saw something in me I did not yet see in myself. He believed in me. He counted on me. And that belief shaped me.

What I did not realize then—what I only understand now—is that fulfillment is what happens when a young person experiences contribution and significance in the same breath. I was not just helping. I was not just needed. I was part of something meaningful. Fulfillment is the fuel that helps youth imagine a future they influence. It builds internal direction. It strengthens identity. It nurtures hope. It anchors purpose. And it is one of the most powerful protective factors for mental health.

- **Contribution:** Shows youth, I can make a difference.
- **Significance:** Shows youth, I am needed here.
- **Fulfillment:** Shows youth, my existence has meaning.

And from that place, purpose begins to bloom. Every time we invite youth to help, notice their impact, reflect their strengths back to them, give them real responsibility, or express belief in their ability to shape the world around them—we water that soil. We help them see and feel they are someone who matters, not because of what they produce, but because of who they are.

RISE INVITATION

Take a moment to reflect on your own experiences of mattering. Think back to a time when you felt like you made a difference—no matter how small. What happened? What did that moment teach you about yourself?

Now remember a time when someone saw something in you that you did not yet see in yourself. What did they do or say that stayed with you?

Turn your attention to a young person in your life—especially one who is often on the receiving end of help. When do they get to contribute? How might you create a small opportunity for them to feel capable, helpful, or needed?

When they do, name it. "That made a difference." Or, "I'm glad you're here." Choose one moment today to help a young person feel seen in a specific, genuine way.

You might also ask, "What's one way you helped something go better today?" The goal is: help them experience that they matter.

And remember—someone once did this for you.

Awakening Hope, Expanding Possibility, and Opening the Heart to Awe and Gratitude

Meaning and purpose do not need to grow from hardship. They can grow from the light—from small, breathtaking moments that remind us the world is bigger, softer, kinder, and gentler than the news will ever portray. Meaning and purpose can shine when we cultivate experiences of awe, hope, and possibility. These are not extras at the edge of wellbeing; they are essential nutrients for the soul.

Hope, at its core, is not wishful thinking. It is not pretending things are okay when they are not. Hope is the belief—grounded in evidence, experience, and resilience—that tomorrow can be shaped, that the future holds openings that life can expand in ways we cannot yet imagine. Researchers have found that hope predicts thriving more reliably than intelligence or optimism. Youth with hope set goals, recover from setbacks more quickly, and persevere with greater energy. But hope is not a personality trait—it is a skill. And skills can be taught, nurtured, strengthened.

Young people learn hope through the questions we ask: "What helped you get through that hard moment? Where did you show bravery today? What's one thing that feels possible, even if it's small?" These questions shift their attention from despair to capability—from "I can't" to "I did." Supporting hope does not erase hardship. It simply illuminates a path through it.

And woven into hope is possibility—the gentle widening of the mind that says, There is more than one way for my life to unfold. Possibility is not certainty. It is spaciousness. It blooms through creativity, curiosity, and the freedom to imagine beyond what is immediately in view. Adults can cultivate possibility by offering young people moments of wonder: "Look at that sky." "Listen to the rain—doesn't it sound alive?" "Have you ever noticed how many colors are in one leaf?" "I wonder what amazing thing your future self will be doing."

Possibility opens journeys untaken. We naturally see more possibilities when we slow down enough to embrace moments of awe. Awe doesn't require mountains or masterpieces. It happens when a toddler sees Santa and reindeer or their first snowfall. When a teenager pauses to watch a sunset and sees all the colors embedded into the sky. When a child notices the kindness of a stranger holding open a door. Awe reorganizes us. It reminds us that we belong to a world that contains beauty, mystery, and hope. A world that has possibility after possibility.

And alongside awe sits gratitude—one of the most accessible, protective practices in the entire field of positive psychology. Gratitude gently redirects attention from what is missing to what is present. It reinforces the truth that even in moments of struggle, there is goodness woven into the fabric of our days.

Gratitude is not about dismissing pain or forcing positivity. It is about anchoring ourselves in what is life giving and beautiful. Adults teach gratitude when they model it aloud: "I'm grateful for the way you helped your brother today." Or, "I'm grateful for this warm cup of tea." Or, "I'm grateful we get to talk about hard things together." When youth hear gratitude spoken as part of daily life, they begin internalizing it as part of their own inner voice—a voice that steadies them, reminds them of their strengths, and expands their sense of meaning.

RISE INVITATION

Gratitude rewires the mind when spoken, not just thought. Say one sentence aloud.

...something I am grateful for...
...something that supported me today...
...something that I often take for granted...
...someone who is a consistent, loving person...

Choose something simple and real—warmth, connection, the way a young person laughed today, the sunrise, a moment of peace.

Let it land in your body.

Hope, awe, possibility, and gratitude work together like threads woven through the tapestry of meaning. They lift the eyes. They soften the heart.

They expand the imagination. They see all the colors, feel the wind— transform the soul, spiritually.

Meaning and purpose are not abstract ideals; they are lifelines. They anchor youth to the belief that their story is still unfolding—that they are needed and deeply significant.

When a young person feels their life has meaning, hope rises naturally.
When they know they can contribute, possibility widens.
When they feel significant, awe becomes more visible.
When they are rooted in purpose, gratitude finds them even in the small moments.

RISE INVITATION

Take a moment—just a few quiet breaths—and soften into this reflection.

Hope, awe, possibility, and gratitude are not abstract ideas; they are practices we can choose, notice, and nurture in daily life. Putting it into practice with youth. Choose an element each day—awe, hope, possibility, or gratitude—and weave it naturally into conversations with the youth you support.

Awe: "Come look at this with me—isn't it beautiful?"
Hope: "What helped you get through that hard moment today?"
Possibility: "What feels even a little bit possible right now?"
Gratitude: "I'm grateful for sunshine today."

CHAPTER ELEVEN

Efficacy

As we arrive at the final Indicator of Wellbeing in the RISE framework, we turn toward something both deeply practical and profoundly personal: efficacy. It is easy to mistake efficacy for achievement or performance. So many of us were raised to believe that capability must be proven—through grades, trophies, relentless effort, and visible success. However, through the RISE lens, efficacy means something far more tender and transformative.

Efficacy is the felt belief that we are capable—capable of meeting expectations, navigating challenges, making healthy choices, and shaping our own path forward. It is the quiet conviction inside a young person that whispers not only: "I can do it," but "I can choose how and why I do it." It is the belief that our doing can be aligned with our being—with what matters to us, what energizes us, and what reflects who we are becoming.

For much of my life, I lived inside a tangle where doing had completely eclipsed being. I stayed busy without any real connection to why I was so busy. I still find myself slipping back into those patterns when I am not being intentional. I thought efficacy meant being the best. Achieving. Outperforming. I believed capability was proven by how exhausted I was, how many responsibilities I carried, how many unrealistic expectations I could meet without breaking. I pushed myself past my limits, convinced that effort equaled worth. I worked harder, faster, longer—obsessed with deadlines, perfection, and impossible standards I set for myself. I said yes to everything, not because it aligned with my values or passions, but because it made me feel needed.

In the rare moments someone noticed, I drank in that praise like oxygen. I chased it. I waited for it. I organized my life around earning it. I was chasing a certificate that read, "You are enough," even though no one else would ever be allowed to hand it to me—and even if they had, my inner critic would have crumpled it up and whispered, "That's not real. Try harder. Do more." The truth is, none of that was efficacy. It was survival. It was perfectionism masquerading as purpose.

It was armor disguised as ambition. It was people pleasing dressed up as productivity. It was the quiet, relentless belief that if I just did enough—long enough, well enough, perfectly enough—I might finally feel worthy. Sacrificing our wellbeing to earn worth is not efficacy. And yet, this is the message so many youth are absorbing and so many adults are living. As a society, we nudge children toward constant achievement: get straight A's, stand out, be impressive, stay busy, don't fall behind, don't be lazy, be involved in everything, collect the accolades that signal you matter.

We fear that if we do not push hard enough, the world will swallow them whole—leaving them unprepared, unmotivated, or stuck. But in our fear, we risk teaching something far more dangerous: that they are their accomplishments. That worth is conditional. That perfection equals love. That success equals safety. As anxiety, depression, burnout, and disconnection increase among young people, we have to ask a painful but necessary question: "What if the very pressure we believe will make youth strong is what is making them brittle?"

Because true efficacy is not built on output alone. It is not rooted in perfection or constant production. True efficacy grows when action is aligned with intention—when effort is connected to meaning, passion, and self-understanding. It is the inner knowing: "I am capable because I can keep learning." "I can grow because I understand myself." "I can rise through challenges because I've done it before." "I can trust myself to choose when to say yes—and when to say no."

Efficacy Matters

Efficacy is not simply a motivational idea—it is one of the most powerful psychological protectors a young person can carry into adolescence and adulthood. When youth believe they can influence their own outcomes, the entire landscape of their inner world begins to shift. Efficacy plants the seed of possibility and teaches a transformative truth: "I can." And when a young person begins to sense that—even faintly—the world around them starts to expand.

Albert Bandura (1997), whose research altered the field of human development, found that efficacy shapes nearly every aspect of functioning—from academic performance to emotional regulation, from problem solving to long-term wellbeing. Yet long before science named it, families, communities, and cultures understood it intuitively: when we believe we are capable, we behave in ways that help us become capable.

Research consistently shows that youth who carry a strong sense of efficacy experience steadier emotional health across development. They show lower rates of anxiety and depression, greater emotional regulation, more adaptive coping strategies, increased life satisfaction, and a stronger, more durable sense of hope. This is not because life becomes easier, but because their relationship to difficulty changes.

Youth with a growing sense of efficacy interpret hard things differently. Difficulty does not immediately signal danger or inadequacy—it signals challenge. Instead of shutting down, they pause. Instead of spiraling into self-doubt, they grow curious. They recover from conflict more quickly, trust their ability to navigate big emotions, and seek help without collapsing into shame. A child struggling with a math problem under low efficacy might say, "I can't do this. I'm just bad at math." A child with developing efficacy might take a breath and say, "Okay... what else could I try instead?"

That small shift—from finality to possibility—is resilience taking shape. Within it lives the belief, "I am capable of figuring things out." Because they have lived experience—internal evidence—that effort can create movement, and with that, youth are less likely to collapse into helplessness or overwhelm. As they try, falter, persist, and eventually succeed—even in small ways—they begin forming an identity rooted in capability rather than comparison or competition.

This is where flexible thinking emerges. It is where growth mindset becomes embodied rather than conceptual. It is where problem solving begins, curiosity deepens, and creativity finds room to breathe. Over time, these micro-moments accumulate, strengthening a young person's inner story about who they are and what they can do. Slowly, their language shifts from "I must be perfect" to "I am learning," from "I am failing" to "I am growing," from "I can't" to "I can try," and eventually, "I can." This identity becomes a stabilizing force they carry into classrooms, friendships, teams, and communities—especially during adolescence, when identity often feels fragile and uncertain. Efficacy helps young people internalize not only what they can do, but also who they are becoming.

At its core, efficacy teaches a young person: "my choices matter. I am not powerless. I can influence what comes next." And this belief does not grow from instruction alone—it grows from lived experience. From trying. From stumbling. From recovering. From being supported rather than rescued or shamed. It grows in moments when adults say: "I see how hard you're working," "Try again—I'm right here," "You don't have to be perfect. Just keep going."

Only then does efficacy truly bloom—because only then do young people feel safe enough to try, to reach, and to imagine themselves as capable. As this belief takes root, youth begin setting goals that feel meaningful—not because an adult told them to, but because something inside them feels worth pursuing. They begin asking future-oriented questions that widen possibility: "Who do I want to be? What truly matters to me? How do I want to contribute? What step could I take next?"

This shift—from doing what others expect to doing what feels aligned—is one of the clearest markers of healthy development. Agency allows youth to become participants in their lives rather than passengers. Children do not persist because they enjoy struggle; they persist because the effort is connected to something that matters to them.

Efficacy transforms difficulty from a stop sign into a stepping-stone. It turns "Why bother?" into "Let me try one more time." It turns "This is too hard" into "This is hard… and I can do hard things." This is why the relational environment matters so deeply. When adults stay with young people through the messy middle—modeling courage, encouraging effort, and helping them notice moments of pride—youth begin to internalize one of the most protective beliefs of all: "I am capable."

This belief does not arrive all at once. It is built through repeated experiences of beginning, struggling, being supported, and discovering that growth is possible. In the next section, we will explore how efficacy takes shape through this lived rhythm—through courage, perseverance, encouragement, mastery, and agency.

RISE INVITATION

Take a quiet moment—and let yourself return to a memory from your own childhood or adolescence. Think of a time when you believed your worth depended on how well you performed. Maybe it was a grade you chased. A team you wanted to make. A role you felt you had to fulfill. A moment you were desperate for someone to notice, affirm, or approve.

With as much gentleness as possible, ask yourself, "what did I learn, in that moment, about what made me "enough"? Let whatever rises come without judgment. You are not trying to fix the memory—you are simply meeting it.

Now shift your attention to a young person in your life—a child you care for, a student you teach, a teen you mentor. Picture the messages they receive today about capability and worth. Invite curiosity. Where might they be carrying the same feelings you possibly carried? Where might they believe their value is something to earn instead of something they already have? Hold that awareness softly. Choose one moment to reflect back to that young person that their worth is not something they must achieve.

It might sound like, "I love watching you try new things—your courage is inspiring." "You're allowed to be human here. Mistakes are welcome." "You matter because you're you—not because of what you do."

Now, gently bring the reflection back to yourself. Invite curiosity. Where in your own life do you still confuse performance with worth? What might it feel like to offer yourself the same compassion you offer children?

How Efficacy Grows: Courage, Perseverance, Encouragement, Mastery and Agency

Efficacy does not grow from lectures or pep talks. It grows from lived experience—slowly, relationally, and often in the smallest moments. It begins with courage, is strengthened through perseverance, and gradually settles into the body as a quiet knowing: "I can." These experiences are not separate skills so much as one unfolding process that teaches a young person how to stay with themselves as they grow.

Courage: Daring to Begin

Courage is where efficacy begins. Before a child can learn, succeed, or persist, they have to dare to start. Courage is not the absence of fear; it is the willingness to take a shaky step toward something new, uncertain, or challenging. And most often, courage grows first in the presence of a steady adult. Think of a child standing at the edge of a pool, toes curled over the tile, wanting to jump but unsure. What usually makes them leap is not some mysterious inner grit—it is the eyes of someone they trust on the other side, saying, "I'm right here. Try when you're ready."

So many courageous moments in childhood share this same shape: something feels risky, and an adult helps make it feel safe enough to try. We cultivate courage not by pushing, but by communicating—through words, tone, and presence—"Mistakes are welcome here. You do not have to be perfect to begin. Trying itself is brave." When adults respond this way, a child's nervous system softens. Fear does not disappear, but it becomes bearable. The risk of trying no longer feels like a threat to their worth. They begin to explore parts of themselves they didn't know existed—raising a hand in class, joining a new team, talking to someone new, attempting something they might not get right the first time. Courage opens the door.

Perseverance: Learning the Rhythm of Rising

Once a young person dares to begin, perseverance becomes the next teacher. Perseverance is not a single act of "pushing through." It is a rhythm—a long, human process of returning, pausing, trying again, adjusting, resting, and re-engaging. It is what allows effort to stay aligned with what matters, rather than collapsing under pressure or rigid expectations. Albert Bandura (1997) observed that people with high self-assurance "approach difficult tasks as challenges to be mastered rather than as threats to be avoided" (p. 39). That mindset does not appear overnight. It is formed through safe relationships, meaningful opportunities, and repeated experiences of moving through something hard and discovering, "I'm still okay."

A central—and often avoided—part of perseverance is failure. Not catastrophic failure. Not moral failure. Just the everyday falling that happens when humans stretch. For many young people, fear of failure becomes the greatest barrier to growth. That fear may come from perfectionism, from pressure after past success, or from environments that celebrate outcomes more than effort. Whatever its source, fear shrinks a child's willingness to try.

However, failure is not the opposite of success. It is often the soil success grows in. Failure teaches flexibility, creativity, and resilience. It invites new strategies, new questions, and renewed courage. The way adults respond matters deeply. When we model vulnerability—"Oops, I messed up," or "I need to try that again"—we normalize falling as part of being human. The children's book Beautiful Oops! captures this truth perfectly: what first looks like a mistake can become the beginning of something imaginative and meaningful (Saltzberg, 2010).

Even our language shapes how perseverance takes root. As Simon Sinek (2018) reminds us, "falling" is something humans naturally do as they grow; "failure" often sounds final (0:45). When we say "You fell forward" or "You're learning," we send a very different message than "You failed." Falling becomes information, not indictment.

Perseverance is not only something we ask of youth—it is something we model ourselves. As caregivers, parents, educa-tors, and helpers, we will misread situations, lose patience, or respond in ways we later wish we had not. In those moments, we get to shake it off and try again. In our house, we call this a reset—we push the reset button and redo the moment in a way that feels more aligned with how we want to be. Each misstep becomes an opportunity to model what perseverance looks like inside a relationship. When we say, "I was too sharp earlier. I am sorry. I'm going to try again," we show that mistakes do not end connection—they invite repair.

I often tell my own kids that I want them to "fail" every day—not to discourage them, but to demystify the myth of failure. We should be falling every day if we are learning, stretching, and staying open to new ways of thinking and being. When failure is held with care, it becomes a teacher and even a friend. When shame is removed, bodies soften. Curiosity returns. Courage grows.

Winston Churchill's familiar words echo this truth: "Success is not final, failure is not fatal; it is the courage to continue that counts." Perseverance is that courage in motion. And perseverance is not rigid. It is not about pushing through at all costs. Sometimes it looks like taking a break. Sometimes it looks like stepping back to breathe. Sometimes it looks like trying again tomorrow or choosing a different path altogether. What matters is that a young person stays engaged with their life, rather than shutting down or giving up.

The heartbeat of perseverance sounds like this: "I can fall, learn, and re-center." And when that rhythm becomes familiar—when falling isn't feared, effort is honored, and returning is supported—efficacy begins to take root in a deep and lasting way.

RISE INVITATION

Choose one young person in your life and think of something they are hesitant to begin—something new, unfamiliar, or a

little scary. It might be academic, social, creative, or emotional.

Start with courage. In your next interaction, offer a simple message that makes beginning feel safe—remind them they don't have to be perfect, that trying is brave, and that you are there with them. Notice how permission softens pressure.

Then, support perseverance. When they reach the messy middle, respond with calm reassurance. Let them know it's okay that it feels hard—that this is part of learning—and that they can take a breath or a break and then keep going, step by step. Let your presence be the anchor.

Finally, offer yourself the same compassion. Where in your own life do you need to remember that struggling is a normative part of growth?

Encouragement and Sitting "With": Fuel for the Journey

Courage opens the door. Perseverance carries a young person through it. But encouragement is the steady fuel that allows them to keep going long enough for growth to take root. It is not a cheer from the sidelines or a quick "good job" tossed over the shoulder. Real encouragement is relational. It is attuned. It helps a child feel accompanied rather than evaluated

Encouragement is not the same as praise. Praise spotlights the outcome—the score, the grade, the performance, the correctness. Praise often says, "You impressed me," "Good job," which subtly teaches children to look outward for evidence of their worth. Encouragement does something entirely different. It reflects back what the young person is experiencing—their effort, courage, persistence, creativity, emotions, awareness. Encouragement draws their attention inward, helping them notice their own experience. Slowly, these reflections become an internal voice—a voice that does not disappear when adults are not watching.

Encouragement sounds like: "You are working so hard on that." "I noticed how much focus you brought to this." "You're smiling as you figure that out—learning feels good." "You're frustrated, and you listened to your body and took a break. That shows you know yourself." "You didn't give up. This clearly matters to you." "You tried a new strategy—that took courage." "Look at how much you've grown since last time." "You stayed kind while figuring this out." These statements are specific, grounded, and sincere. They help a child notice what is happening inside them. They develop their own sense of pride rather than relying on external approval to feel worthy.

Encouragement is most powerful in the middle of the journey—the place where excitement has faded, progress feels slow, and frustration gets loud. This is where many youth want to quit. Encouragement here does not remove the challenge; it makes the challenge survivable.

Encouragement also reshapes how young people relate to one another. When encouragement becomes part of a home, classroom, or team culture, children begin echoing that language back to each other. You hear it in hallways before a test, whispered on the sidelines before a game, spoken softly to a nervous friend: "You've got this." "I'll help you." "We can work together." Encouragement becomes a shared language of being together.

This matters because so many youth grow up in environments that quietly communicate that success is a competition—that someone else's achievement diminishes their own. That there is only so much "enoughness" to go around. Encouragement interrupts that narrative. It teaches a different truth: "Your success doesn't diminish mine. We can grow together. We can shine together."

In classrooms, this looks like students clapping just as loudly for the child who finally mastered a skill as for the student who always aces the test. On teams, it sounds like players celebrating the one who rarely scores, not just the star. In families, it shows up when siblings celebrate each other's effort—not just the wins, but the tries. Encouragement changes culture be-cause it changes what is valued: not perfection, but presence. Not winning, but willingness. Not comparison, but collective growth.

Underneath it all is something very simple: encouragement asks us to stay. Sometimes staying means sitting inside the messy—when tears come, when tempers flare, when confusion feels too big for words. Young people don't need adults who fix everything. They do not need perfect responses or quick solutions. Often, hardship isn't something to solve; it's something to sit with—patient, steady, warm.

Some of the most powerful encouragement is quiet. It sounds like: "That is really hard that you didn't make the team." "That feels confusing when you worked so hard." "Your heart is sad you didn't get that part." These small phrases become a kind of emotional shelter. They communicate, I am here with you, your feelings make sense, and you are not alone in this moment.

Sitting with a young person—offering compassion, letting their emotions rise and fall without rushing or shutting them down—creates the very conditions their nervous system needs to integrate what happened. The wave crests, the wave softens, and something inside them releases. That release is not indulgent; it is essential. It is what allows them to carry disappointment without collapsing into shame. It is what makes space for self-love to remain intact even when out-comes hurt. Because we will all face rejection. We will all face moments where we are not chosen, not celebrated, not seen the way we hoped.

However, true efficacy does not crumble under those moments. True efficacy is what helps a young person hold onto their identity—sturdy, rooted, enough—so that rejection becomes a feeling to process, not a truth about who they are.

RISE INVITATION

Take a moment to think of a young person in your life. Picture where they are developmentally, emotionally, and relationally. Invite curiosity. Where are they already showing signs of "I can," even if they do not see it yet?

It may be in small moments—how they approach something new, adjust their thinking, or stay engaged just a little longer.

Look for a simple opportunity to nurture that sense of efficacy. Not a big moment—just a small doorway where they are trying, stretching, or figuring something out. When it appears, gently reflect what you see. Name their effort, their thinking, or their process. Help them notice their own capability beginning to take shape.

Your role is not to evaluate or praise, but to see—and to help them see themselves. "I saw you struggle and then step back and try a new way, you're really capable."

Notice how this shifts the experience—from pressure to possibility, from performance to growth. Invite curiosity. What signs of "I can" are you noticing in your own life? How are you acknowledging your own effort, learning, and growth?

Mastery and Agency: The Quiet "I Can"

Over time, as courage is practiced, perseverance is learned, and encouragement is received, something new begins to take shape: mastery. Mastery is not perfection, and it is not performance. It is the quiet, embodied knowing of, "I can do this now." It is competence that lives in the body, not just the mind—the feeling that comes from repetition, practice, taking risks, and experiences that go well just often enough for a young person to feel genuine pride. Not pride that needs an audience, but pride that settles internally and says, "I trust me. I can figure it out."

Mastery grows when youth are trusted with real responsibility—moments where their effort matters and their choices have impact. A child invited to lead the warm-up at practice. A teenager trusted to organize part of a family gathering. A student asked to teach a peer a skill they have been working hard to develop. These moments communicate something powerful: "Your abilities are influential."

It is here that mastery begins to fuel agency. Agency is the felt sense of, "I can influence what happens." It is the internal shift from reacting to life to participating in it. Agency is not control, and it is not constant striving. It is alignment—the ability to make intentional choices about when to act, when to rest, when to say yes, and when to say no. It is deeply connected to self-actualization: living in a way that reflects who you are, what matters to you, and how you want to contribute.

Agency emerges when a young person can trace a clear line between effort and outcome: "I tried, and something hap-pened." "I stayed with it, and something improved." "I cared about this, and it made a difference." As those experiences accumulate, confidence blossoms. Fear loosens its grip. The world feels more navigable. Young people begin to see themselves not as passive recipients of life, but as active participants in living. This is where efficacy fully comes online.

Courage opens the door.

Perseverance carries them forward.

Encouragement sustains them through the middle,

Mastery anchors their confidence.

Agency naturally follows.

Together, these experiences create a deep, quiet sense of efficacy—a belief that does not depend on perfection or performance, but on lived experience. A belief grounded in knowing, "I can align what I do with who I am." And when a young person truly feels that—when doing and being begin to work together—a new chapter of their life opens. One grounded not in earning worth, but in living from the steady truth that they are already enough, exactly as they are.

This brings us to the deeper essence of the RISE framework. The four Indicators of Wellbeing—Safety, Connection and Belonging, Meaning and Purpose, and Efficacy—are not separate ideas or isolated goals. They are an ecosystem. A living, breathing climate we create around young people every day. Each one strengthens the others. Each one fills a space the others cannot reach alone. Together, they form the foundation of wellbeing—and the architecture of resilience.

INTERLUDE

Stories from the Long Distance Call (11-14)

By this point, I had evolved—not healed, but adapted. A child scientist, testing hypotheses with patterns, tactics, offerings, as if affection could be engineered, if I just found the right sequence. Somewhere along the way, boxes began to form. Containers. Cubbies. Systems meant to hold the chaos still so nothing could fall out and shatter in front of anyone.

Yet still, I kept searching for the yellow brick road—as if it were hidden in the mazes of my life, as if it could lead me, save me, without first asking me to understand how pain can be both monstrous and formative—how something so deprived can grow in the dark.

Middle school is where everyone seems to struggle with identity. However, I came with no foundation—no walls that did not shake, no roof that didn't spin. Just the internal storm. The instinct to scan.

I didn't belong when I started. A small town ten miles away. Sixth grade. A new social universe. I didn't have nice things. My parents didn't have a recognizable last name. My older siblings hadn't paved a hallway for me to walk down. So when the popular girl turned her face toward mine, it felt like a door cracking open, and my whole body leaned toward the opportunity.

This is how the story repeats itself, isn't it?

Different setting. Same hunger.

This new era was simply giving the chaos a new cast of characters.

Middle school girls can be a different kind of weather—cruelty with lip gloss, betrayal in matching outfits, manipulation disguised as best friends.

Oh how closeness had taken on so many definitions by the age of fourteen. Still, I was excited. I wanted to be chosen. And being chosen felt like a small miracle, one that lifted me briefly out of my hell hole. They lived in a world that was foreign to me—dance outfits, makeup, their own bedrooms, two parents home at night.

Not a fantasy of wealth. A fantasy of structure. A fantasy of family. A fantasy of the things I thought were only on TV.

In sixth grade, near the end of the year, I had my first boyfriend. The coolest girl brought me into the group like a ceremony. They all had boyfriends. They knew how to move among boys—a language I did not speak, because my version of boyhood had been dirty footballs, chasing bugs, and trying to be tough. Being with her made me feel like I was one of them. Being one of them made me feel something foreign. It made me feel special.

Then summer came. In addition, summer always came with distance. Ten miles. No ride into town. No way to stay visible. So I did what my nervous system had already been trained to do.

Pursue. Monitor. Reach.

Long-distance calls like lifelines, like proof of existence. What are you doing? Where are you? Do you still remember me? I did not know the meaning of trust. I did not know regulation. I knew the feeling of being left behind.

I called and called until the phone bill arrived, and my dad demanded I work it off—as if belonging were something, you could purchase in minutes and then be punished for needing.

One day they told me they were at the bowling alley. They said one of their parents was coming to pick me up. I waited. Checked in. Waited again. They were not there. Then the punchline: we were just messing with you. We cannot come. And over that same long-distance line—that same wire carrying my hope like a live current—I learned my boyfriend was breaking up with me. My friends set him up with another girl.

The loneliness dropped into my body like something old returning home. Hypervigilance, as familiar as the backyard lookout. The storm did not need to arrive. I could feel the wind before it touched the trees.

As summers kept coming, I kept trying.

My best friend suggested we journal every day and exchange notebooks at the end of summer—a promise we could hold in our hands. Notebooks would hold proof—that I had mattered, that the effort was mutual, that love left a paper trail. That summer was heavy with big feelings and friendship dynamics that felt like rope burns: triangulation, comparison, competition.

You're my best friend.

No—she's my best friend.

Prove it.

She called saying she was going to hurt herself, that she was locking herself in her room. And old patterns reached out through that long distant call.

Fix. Caretake. Protect.

Loyalty felt like vigilance. Love felt like anxiety.

When we exchanged notebooks, at the end of summer, I opened hers like a gift. But page by page, I read how annoying I was. How obsessed. How she wondered if I was a lesbian because I always wanted to be around her. Then—pages later—how I was the best friend she'd ever had. How no one had ever cared for her the way I did.

There it was again: the terror of not knowing how to be.

I couldn't tell which parts of me were wrong and which parts were lovable. So I did what I always did. Retreat. Then pursue again. Walls up. Walls down. The maze had no clear path out.

I didn't have language for it then, but something inside me was organizing for another type of survival. Parts took on roles. Exiles formed memory by memory, determined never to feel like a failure, never to be unworthy, never to need too much. The internal architecture, molding again and again.

I didn't feel like I could master anything—not friendships, not home—and then I realized those worlds were colliding. My mom drove the bus for the school. Morning and afternoon routes. Sports trips. Ski trips.

My friends still tell the story of the eighth-grade ski trip—my mom found at the bar, and the question they asked out loud was the one I'd been asking silently for years: so how do we get home?

Skeletons needed bigger locks.

My birthday—a coed party, music and laughter, a glimpse of what normal might feel like. I went inside for food, walked into the garage with the music blaring, and saw my mom grinding on two of my male classmates. In that moment, something occurred to me, it would never be just about me. This maze wasn't built with an exit.

Church came next.

Church offered clean lines. Clear boundaries. A script. And still—control lived there too. Shame and purpose intertwined. Judgment and hypocrisy. I had already learned that dichotomy well. Yet Jesus loved me, this I know. For the bible tells me so. They said I could count on that love. I had never counted on love.

My first mission trip lit something in me. Altruism. Perspective. Gratitude. I learned how to find silver linings, how to be thankful for what I had. I didn't feel so alone.

Confirmation class made me feel proud, accomplished—part of something. Even as my curious brain wrestled with contradictions: hell and love, forgiveness and cruelty, devotion and behavior that never aligned. In all my curiosity, in all my questions, my pastor remained patient, remained kind. My confirmation party was held in our garage. Community members, family, alcohol, the hum of uncertainty. My confirmation picture stood beside a homemade cake while extracurricular activities and my mom's affairs shared the same space. My cousin said she was in the bathroom making out with his girlfriend. It felt fitting, in a devastating way, that the night devoted to purity would expose what had tried to hide the longest.

That night the winds shifted past repair.

After confirmation night, my dad took us camping and told us they were getting a divorce. I felt relief and fear intertwined. What would the next chapter require of me? Who would I need to be?

A week later at church camp, I sought rebirth. I confessed sins publicly—beer, cigarettes, stealing— sins from the backyard. I wanted to be washed clean of anything that made me like them. I shared about the divorce. I cried. I didn't know it was being recorded.

The tape became a joke. Played back over and over. Laughed at. A friend's mom told everyone I was lying for attention. After that, the parts of me that felt hope, stopped reaching for rescue. I learned what happens when you hand people the truth.

The next week my dad moved out, and whatever childhood I had left quietly changed jobs.

The thing is, I had always protected Sky. Four years younger, but somehow decades behind me in what the world had already asked. I watched him the way you watch a candle in a room full of drafts—cupping my hands around his innocence, trying to keep the flame steady when everything around us kept leaning in.

At fourteen, I got my school permit and tasted freedom for the first time—not joy, not rebellion, but access. Movement. The ability to steer us toward safety instead of waiting to be carried there.

One morning my mother didn't come home. Morning has a sound when it's wrong—that I had come to know. She was in jail. Sky needed to get to basketball practice.

So I drove.

Hands barely old enough for the wheel, law already bending under necessity, learning early what no one teaches you outright: laws are a luxury when no one is holding the world in place.

I told him she was out doing fun things. I told him he was to stay at our aunt's for a few days. My aunt, the constant shelter for him. I folded the truth small enough to fit inside his clean pocket.

The puppeteering had started long before, but now my hands were steadier—arranging reality like stage props, keeping the boat afloat, even as water kept finding new ways in.

And it wasn't just Sky. Sara, too. Two years older, but the world met her differently—her mind moving on its own rhythm, her heart too sensitive for how cruel the world can be. A sister should be a best friend, but sometimes love looks like protection—shielding from kids at school, strangers, laughter that landed wrong.

Sometimes I wonder who has it harder: the one who sees everything or the one spared just enough to still believe. When there are no expectations, does the love you get feel like enough?

My parents moved from one shared tornado into separate hurricanes, and we stayed in the wind—learning how to lean without falling apart.

Because my age demanded fairness and equity, with no map telling us where to go, my brother and I rotated between houses. Nowhere was home. My dad slept on the couch. We slept on a twin mattress in the living room, knees knocking, elbows overlapping, learning the geography of each other's breathing.

We tried to learn who this man was, without instructions. I became a mother there—cooking, cleaning, remembering what needed remembering, and holding the shape of a household with hands that were still so small.

This was the era where control started to feel like safety.

My dad grieved loudly and quietly at once. Funny. Playful. Drunk. Silent. Somber. Gone.

Thursday bowling nights meant scanning his eyes, counting, assessing, and deciding how we'd get home before the question had to be asked. Sometimes we played tricks on him, when he passed out—drawing on his face, convincing him he was filling ice trays with air and still somehow had ice in his glass. Laughter became a pressure valve. A brief escape hatch.

Here was the contradiction— the same thing that felt dangerous with my mother made my father softer, more present, more ours. The nervous system hates contradictions, but my childhood was built on them.

I became the go-between. The journal keeper. The translator of tone and threat. The holder of secrets whispered and swallowed.

At fourteen, I was controlling outcomes before they existed— holding tokens never meant for my hands, playing chess with lives that were not mine to move. It felt like power. It felt like oxygen. A false sense of control, eroding something sacred in me.

Underneath it all, I was still that little girl. I painted my bedroom walls a rainbow and splattered paint across them. Two parts of me in coexistence—innocence still searching for the yel-low brick road, and the shell of me who learned to float away at four. The part that knew how to numb an emotion before it arrived—tight chest, shaky hands, a throat closing like a door.

Sitting at a football game, wrapped in a blanket, I watched teens run and play. Parents cheering. Couples holding hands. I started to cry. I wondered why I had been dealt these cards. I wondered what the point of living was.

That moment freed me and shackled me. I decided I would never cry again.

And for three years, I didn't.

But the long-distance call taught me something important. It taught me how to disappear—long before anyone could see me fall.

RISE INVITATION

As you sit with these stories, notice what lingers. Not just what you remember—but what your body remembers.

Were there moments when you learned to disappear in order to survive? Times when control felt safer than connection? Where crying felt too dangerous and numbness became protection?

Notice if any part of you recognizes the child who learned to float away. The one who stayed quiet. The one who got loud and tried to control.

Place one hand on your chest, or somewhere that feels steady. Take a slow breath—not to change anything, just to arrive. If it feels right, imagine a version of you who needs you now. Offer that part a message it never received in time: "You are resourceful." "You are smart." "You made it. You are older now."

This is the work of RISE—not erasing the past, but honoring the wisdom of survival while gently making room for something new.

PART IV:

SOCIAL AND EMOTIONAL DEVELOPMENT

The "S" part of the RISE framework centers on Social and Emotional Development (SED)—the everyday capacities that help young people relate to themselves, others, and the world around them with steadiness, awareness, and care.

This section is deeply meaningful to me because these skills were not always modeled or taught in my early life. Growing up, I often found myself in relationships where I could sense that I was frustrating people or coming across as defensive, angry, or "too much," yet I did not understand why. I was simply using the relational templates I had learned—so why weren't they working in other environments?

People did not argue the way I expected. They did not engage in chaos in familiar patterns. Sometimes my caretaking felt overbearing to others. My intensity felt abrasive. My choices did not land the way I intended. It was not until college, when I was introduced to the concept of emotional intelligence, that these patterns finally made sense. For the first time, I understood that what I had been missing were not character traits—but skills.

From that point on, I began an intentional journey of cultivating my own emotional intelligence. As I learned new ways of relating, practiced regulating my affect, and gained insight into relational rhythms, something shifted. I felt calmer. Healthier. More grounded. The more I grew these capacities, the more connected, purposeful, and effective I felt in my life.

For a long time, Western culture has emphasized cognitive intelligence—IQ—above all else. But research and lived experience now consistently affirm what many of us have felt intuitively: emotional intelligence (EQ) plays a far greater role in long-term wellbeing, relationships, and success. It doesn't matter how strong someone's academic skills are if they struggle to communicate, regulate emotions, show respect, or navigate social dynamics—skills essential in classrooms, workplaces, families, and communities alike.

Social and emotional development is about teaching and modeling these foundational life skills. It means helping young people understand their internal states, regulate emotions, engage in relationships with awareness and intention, and make thoughtful choices. Just as we explicitly teach academic skills, we must also intentionally teach emotional intelligence—through daily interactions, modeling, reflection, and repair.

Social and Emotional Development in RISE was added because wellness and resilience require more than safety, belonging, meaning, and efficacy alone. Young people also need tools. Tools to understand themselves. Tools to manage emotions. Tools to navigate relationships. Tools to make values-aligned decisions under pressure.

These capacities do not develop overnight. They grow through experience, consistency, and the presence of trusted adults who model steadiness, openness, and curiosity—especially in moments of stress or uncertainty. Not all young people naturally develop emotionally intelligent ways of engaging with the world. They need adults willing to teach, practice, and nurture these skills alongside them.

This section explores four interwoven areas that shape social and emotional development through the RISE lens:

- **Awareness:** Developing insight into thoughts, feelings, and internal cues
- **Affect Management:** Understanding emotions and practicing regulation
- **Relational Rhythms:** Building and sustaining healthy, adaptive relationships
- **Healthy Choices:** Integrating thoughts and emotions to guide

wise decisions

When adults cultivate these capacities, young people gain more than awareness and regulation—they develop relational confidence and a stronger sense of self in the world.

CHAPTER TWELVE

Awareness

Awareness is the gentle act of noticing—what is happening within us and what is unfolding around us—and allowing that understanding to guide how we respond. Before a young person can regulate emotions, navigate relationships, or make thoughtful choices, they must first learn to notice themselves. Awareness bridges the inner world and the outer one, helping youth connect thoughts, emotions, body sensations, and needs to how they show up with others.

Awareness does not arrive fully formed. It grows slowly, through experience, reflection, and relationship. It is shaped in everyday moments—when a feeling is named, when a pause is supported, when someone stays close long enough to help a young person make sense of what just happened.

Consider Aaron.

Aaron is usually cheerful, the kind of child who moves easily through his day. But lately, something has shifted. School has felt harder. Friendships feel uncertain. He hasn't quite been able to name what's wrong—only that his body feels tight and his patience thinner than usual. One afternoon, when his younger sister accidentally breaks something important to him, Aaron snaps. The reaction surprises even him. Almost immediately, guilt follows.

With his mom's steady presence, Aaron begins to untangle what happened. He realizes his frustration didn't start with his sister—it started days earlier, in the quiet loneliness of recess and the effort of trying to fit in. This moment—connecting his inner experience to his outward reaction—is awareness taking shape. Not perfectly. Not all at once. But enough to pause, reflect, and begin again.

Self-awareness is not simply about naming emotions. It is about living consciously. It involves noticing thoughts, feelings, and physical sensations—the clenched jaw, the racing heart, the heaviness behind the eyes—and learning to slow the leap from sensation to reaction. Many young people move quickly from discomfort to action without realizing what is happening inside them. With guidance and support, they can begin to stretch that space. And in that space, choice becomes possible.

As Aaron grows in awareness, something else begins to happen: his attention turns outward. One day, he notices a classmate sitting alone, shoulders slumped, eyes downcast. Instead of walking past, he pauses. He checks in. The interaction is small, but meaningful. Later, his teacher reflects this moment back to him—not as praise, but as noticing. Aaron begins to understand that awareness is not just about knowing himself; it is also about noticing others.

This is one of the quiet gifts of awareness. As young people learn to recognize their own inner states, they become better able to recognize and respond to the emotional experiences of those around them. Awareness deepens empathy. It strengthens connection. It allows youth to move through the world with more attunement and care.

Over time, awareness also supports values-driven choices. Aaron begins setting small personal goals—improving at soccer, practicing patience with his sister, choosing honesty when things feel hard. These choices are not about perfection; they are about alignment. Awareness helps him notice what matters to him and act in ways that reflect that truth, even when it feels uncomfortable.

Awareness is not self-criticism. It is not rumination or over-analysis. It is the practice of building an honest, compassionate relationship with oneself. When youth are supported in developing awareness, they gain a clearer, more balanced view of who they are—their strengths, their challenges, and their growing edges. A young person who is aware and well can say, "This is something I'm good at," without arrogance, and "This is something I'm still learning," without shame. They can acknowledge mistakes without collapsing into defensiveness. They can take responsibility without losing their sense of worth. When challenges arise, awareness and feeling a sense of wellbeing, allows them to respond with curiosity instead of avoidance, and accountability instead of blame.

As awareness grows, resilience follows. Setbacks become information rather than identity. Mistakes become moments of learning rather than proof of failure. A young person who understands their internal experience is better able to repair relationships, adapt to challenges, and move forward with healthy choices and confidence—because awareness strengthens affect management. A child who can say, "I feel frustrated," is far more equipped than a child who can only act out that frustration.

Awareness is not a fixed trait. It develops through multiple, interconnected layers as youth grow—awareness of internal states, self-perception, social expectations, the emotions of others, and the broader cultural contexts they move within. These layers build upon one another, weaving together into a deeper understanding of self and world. This chapter explores those layers of awareness within the RISE framework—not as a checklist to master, but as an unfolding process that supports emotional intelligence and intentionality.

Level 1: Understanding Self-States

Young people learn to notice themselves in the presence of adults who slow down with them, name what they see with tenderness, and help them connect inner experiences to outward choices. When we guide youth to tune into sensations, feelings, thoughts, and behavior—without shame or urgency—we help them build the first layer of emotional intelligence: recognizing what is happening inside them. The most foundational form of awareness begins in the body.

Sensations State

This state is about noticing physical cues—racing hearts, tight shoulders, clenched hands, and lightness in the chest, heaviness in the stomach, and fatigue behind the eyes. Youth experience these sensations constantly: hunger, restlessness, calm, tension, butterflies, and sleepiness. Often, these are the earliest signals that something deeper is happening.

When adults help youth check in with their bodies, they are giving them access to information. The body is often the first place a need shows up. Adults can model this naturally: "My shoulders feel tight, so I'm going to stretch," or "I'm noticing my breathing is shallow—I think I need a slow breath." Gentle prompts like, "How does your body feel right now?" or "What do you notice in your body when you're excited?" invite awareness. Sometimes offering language helps: "I notice you're wiggling—does your body feel restless?" Even brief grounding practices—feet on the floor, a few breaths, stretching—teach youth that the body is something to listen to, not ignore.

Feelings State

Once youth begin noticing the body, emotions become easier to name. Feelings come and go, and the broader a young person's emotional vocabulary, the more clearly they can understand what is happening inside. Joy, sadness, anger, embarrassment, shame, pride, jealousy, disappointment—these feelings can be intense, but they are also meaningful. They carry information about what we value, what we need, what matters to us, what feels unfair, what feels scary, what feels hopeful.

Too often, children receive messages—spoken or unspoken—that certain emotions are "bad," especially anger. That can teach youth to suppress emotions, judge themselves for feeling them, or become afraid of their own inner world. In reality, no emotion is inherently wrong. Emotions may be uncomfortable, but they are still valid—and they can be expressed safely.

Adults support this state by naming and validating emotions with steadiness: "That felt frustrating," "This is really exciting," "You smiled; I am guessing you are happy." You can expand the feeling by connecting it to context, "It seems like you're feeling disappointed that didn't work out the way you hoped," or "You look really worried—I wonder if you are feeling something bad might happen?"

We build vocabulary through daily life—books, movies, story moments, family conversations, role-play. We normalize emotions by sharing our own experiences appropriately: "I felt nervous before my presentation today, and my heart was beating fast." And we invite reflection in a way that builds coping: "When you feel this way, what helps even a little?" Over time, youth learn that feelings are not something to hide—they are part of being human.

Thought State

As youth become more aware of sensations and emotions, they can begin to notice thoughts—the inner narration that shapes how they interpret the world. Many young people experience automatic, loud thoughts, especially when they are stressed: "I'm dumb. Nobody likes me. I always mess things up. This is going to be terrible." The important lesson here is gentle but powerful: thoughts are not who we are. They are not facts. They are mental events—sometimes helpful, sometimes distorted, often temporary.

Adults can support this level of awareness by first helping youth feel heard. One of the simplest and most powerful tools is paraphrasing or restating content—simply reflecting back what a young person has said without judgment or correction. Statements like, "You said you don't want to go to school today," or "I hear you saying you think the rule feels dumb," let youth know their thoughts have landed. Often, that acknowledgment alone is enough to help them settle and move forward.

At times, adults can gently extend restating content by pairing it with curiosity, giving space for other thoughts to generate. For example, "That sounds like a really loud thought—what else is your brain saying?" This process invites flexibility without dismissing the original experience. The goal is not to argue with a thought, but to soften its grip by validating it was heard.

Adults can also model this process by sharing their own inner dialogue aloud in age-appropriate ways. Saying things like, "Part of me is thinking I might mess this up, but I'm going to try anyway," or, "I feel overwhelmed right now, so I'm reminding myself that I can take this one step at a time," helps youth see that thoughts come and go—and that we don't have to obey every one of them.

Some youth benefit from creating a bit of distance from their thoughts. Writing them down, drawing them, or labeling them—"I'm having the thought that…"—can be especially powerful. This small shift in language helps a child externalize a thought rather than become it, creating space between what they think and who they are. When a thought is urging immediate action, adults can help youth pause and reflect: "If you acted on that thought right now, what might happen?" Or, "That thought is telling you to get revenge—what if we sat with it for a little while and checked back in later to see if it still feels like the choice you want to make?"

These moments strengthen discernment and self-trust. It is important to remember that reflecting or restating a young person's thoughts does not mean agreeing with them. At times, adults may worry that validating a statement like, "I hate school," or, "They're all against me," reinforces the belief. In reality, the intention is not to confirm or deny the thought, but to communicate, "I hear you."

When youth hear their words reflected back, they are given the opportunity to listen to themselves in a new way. Thoughts that once felt automatic or unquestioned can become visible, creating space for awareness and choice. Often, it is in hearing their own thinking—spoken aloud by someone else—that young people begin to recognize patterns, reconsider meaning, and discover that their thoughts are something they can notice, not something they have to become. The goal is never to police or eliminate thinking. It is to help young people learn that thoughts are information, not instructions—and that they always have more than one possible response.

Behavior State

This state connects the dots. Behaviors do not appear out of nowhere—they grow out of sensations, emotions, and thoughts. Often, behavior is simply the outward expression of an inner world that has not yet been named or understood. When youth learn to pause and ask themselves, "What am I feeling right now? What am I thinking? What does my body need?" they begin to realize that behavior does not have to be automatic. It can become a choice. That realization alone is powerful. It shifts young people from reacting to reflecting, from being driven by impulses to being guided by awareness.

Adults reinforce this learning when they notice and name intentional behaviors. Saying things like, "I noticed you took a breath before answering—that helped you stay calm," or "You felt frustrated and chose to walk away to take space," communicates that behavior is linked to other states of being. Highlighting these moments helps youth recognize their own strengths and reinforces the behaviors we want to see more of.

Adults also support this state by gently making connections visible—without shaming or blaming. Reflections such as, "You yelled because you were angry, and that hurt your friend's feelings," or, "You slammed your book; it seems like you might have felt embarrassed," help youth link inner experiences to outward actions.

When youth are regulated, these moments can naturally move into reflection and repair: "What could you do differently next time?" or "How can you make this right?" It is important to remember, however, that learning and repair—teaching more skillful or adaptive behaviors—can only happen when a young person's nervous system is calm enough to engage. If a youth is dysregulated or operating from their "downstairs brain," the first step is co-regulation: offering presence, safety, and support before moving into teaching, problem solving, or accountability.

This is where awareness becomes actionable—not as a tool for compliance or control, but as a pathway toward affect management, adaptive relational rhythms and healthy choices.

Integrating It All: A Way of Being with Youth

Supporting awareness is not a script—it's a way of being present. Before we invite a young person to regulate, reflect, or slow down, we check in with ourselves. What is my tone? My energy? My pace? My body language? A regulated adult creates a safer nervous system around them. That steadiness becomes a model long before any words do. From there, we lead with curiosity rather than judgment. We use relational skills that feel natural in conversation—simple, human tools that help youth make meaning of their internal world.

Sometimes we track what we observe: "I notice you're tapping your foot," or "You're smiling right now." Sometimes we reflect feelings: "It seems like you feel proud," or "You look worried." Sometimes we restate content so they feel understood: "You worked really hard, and you're disappointed it didn't turn out how you hoped." And sometimes we offer clarifying prompts that invite depth without pressure: "How so?" "Tell me more," "Help me understand."

When these approaches are woven together, they create conversations that gently connect the dots: "What do you notice in your body right now?" "What feeling is showing up?" "What's going through your mind when that happens?" "What do you want to do with it all?" In those moments, our job is not to diagnose or label. It's to create space for a young person to become curious about themselves—without fear, without shame, without being rushed.

And when youth experience that kind of steady companionship, awareness begins to grow naturally. They start to understand their inner world and how it connects with outward navigation.

RISE INVITATION

Image a twelve-year-old storming into the room after school, drops their backpack on the floor, and says sharply, "School is so stupid. I'm not doing my homework."

As adults, it's easy to feel pulled toward fixing, correcting, or setting limits immediately. But this moment also offers a powerful opportunity to cultivate awareness.

Before reading further, pause for a moment. If you were with that youth, what might you say first—if your goal was to build awareness rather than compliance? Take a breath. There is no "perfect" response. Now, here is one way this moment could sound when awareness skills are woven together.

Tracking: "I notice you dropped your bag pretty hard and your voice sounds tight."

Reflecting feeling: "It seems like you're really frustrated."

Restating content: "It sounds like today felt overwhelming, and homework feels like too much right now."

Clarifying prompt: "Do you want to tell me what made today so hard?" or "What's the part that feels the heaviest?"

Notice what this approach does—and what it does not do. It does not agree or disagree. It does not remove expectations. It does not rush toward a solution. Instead, it creates space.

As you think about youth in your life. Invite curiosity. What might you track without judgment? What feeling could you gently reflect? What content could you restate so they feel heard? What simple prompt could invite more awareness?

Awareness grows when we slow down, stay present, and remain curious. Over time, these shared moments become something more—an inner voice that helps them understand themselves wherever they go.

Level 2: Self-Perception—Seeing Ourselves More Clearly

If self-awareness is about noticing what is happening inside us, self-perception is about how we make sense of it. It is the lens through which we view ourselves—the story we tell about who we are, why we act the way we do, and what our experiences mean. That lens is never neutral. It is shaped by beliefs, values, emotional triggers, preferences, past experiences, and unmet needs. It shifts constantly, influenced by daily interactions and the feedback—spoken and unspoken—we receive from the world around us. Two young people can experience the same event and walk away with entirely different conclusions about themselves.

At this level of awareness, youth begin moving beyond what they do and start exploring why they do it. They begin noticing patterns in their reactions, choices, and relationships. This is where deeper insight becomes possible—and where intentional growth begins to take shape.

One of the most powerful tools adults can use here is metacommunication—gently noticing and naming what is happening within the interaction itself. These moments are not interrogations or corrections. They are reflective invitations that help youth see themselves with more clarity. An adult might say, "I wonder if you're feeling disappointed that your project didn't work out because success really matters to you," or "When I picked up my phone, I noticed you looked over—you seem concerned about what I'm doing." Or, "When I said I was going to call your mom and you said 'no,' I'm wondering if you're worried about what I might say."

These observations slow the moment down. They help youth connect internal experiences to outward behavior without feeling blamed or judged. Over time, the goal is for youth to begin to recognize their own patterns: "I shut down when I feel embarrassed. I get loud when I feel unheard. I say yes even when I don't want to, because I don't want to disappoint people." This is an important part of self-perception—developing congruence between how we experience ourselves and how others experience us. When that alignment grows, youth gain a stronger sense of authenticity—who they believe they are begins to align with how they engage with the world.

Because self-perception is shaped by interpretation, adults must remain aware of their own internal lenses. Our assumptions, biases, and personal histories can quietly influence how we interpret a young person's behavior. This is why adult self-reflection matters so deeply at this level. Debriefing intense moments with a trusted colleague, supervisor, or counselor helps ensure we are responding to the youth in front of us—not to our own unexamined narratives.

Youth learn to question assumptions, recognize how values and needs influence behavior, and see themselves through more than one lens when adults consistently use practices such as: tracking observations, reflecting feelings, paraphrasing, clarifying, metacommunicating. Seeing themselves more clearly gives them, greater freedom to make decisions aligned with who they are—and who they are becoming.

RISE INVITATION

Think of a recent moment with a young person—something small where they reacted, withdrew, or pushed back. Invite curiosity. First, consider their inner world. What might they have been feeling, needing, or thinking in that moment?

Now, gently shift outward. How might they have been experienced by others? Hold both—without choosing one over the other.

If you were to return to that moment, you might simply invite awareness by asking: "What was going on inside of you right then?" "How do you think that came across to others?"

Stay curious. Keep it simple. This is the practice—helping young people see themselves more clearly, both from the inside and in relationship with others.

Level 3: Awareness of Social Norms—Understanding the Shared World

As self-awareness and self-perception deepen, awareness naturally expands outward. Youth begin learning that they are not navigating life alone—they are moving within systems, communities, and relationships shaped by shared expectations. This is where awareness of social norms comes into focus.

Social norms are the often-unspoken agreements that guide how people interact within a group. They shape what behaviors are expected, welcomed, or discouraged. Youth encounter social norms everywhere—at home, at school, on teams, online, within peer groups, and through media. These norms influence how they speak, listen, show respect, manage conflict, and take responsibility. Some norms are relatively universal. Others are contextual. What is expected at home may differ from what is expected at school. What works in one peer group may not translate in another. Learning to navigate these shifts is a critical part of social and emotional development.

Adults play a central role in making social norms visible and understandable. We are not born knowing how to wait our turn in conversation, read tone, or recognize when humor crosses into harm. These skills are learned through modeling, explanation, and practice. When adults consistently demonstrate behaviors like greeting others respectfully, listening without interrupting, speaking clearly, or pausing before responding, youth absorb those rhythms. When adults name them—"I waited my turn so everyone could be heard," or "I noticed you lowered your voice so others could concentrate"—youth begin connecting actions to impact.

This level of awareness is not about rigid conformity. It is about helping youth understand how their behavior affects others and how shared expectations help communities function. With guidance, youth begin to see themselves as contributors, not just participants. They learn that their presence and choices shape the spaces they move through.

As youth develop awareness of social norms, they gain confidence in navigating classrooms, friendships, teams, workplaces, and communities. They learn how to adapt without losing themselves—how to belong without abandoning authenticity. When social norms are taught with clarity and compassion rather than shame or control, youth are far more likely to internalize them as values rather than rules.

Level 4: Awareness of Others—Learning to See Beyond Ourselves

From the very beginning of life, our brains are wired for connection. Mirror neurons—specialized brain cells that fire both when we act and when we observe others acting—allow us to feel alongside one another. They help infants attune to caregivers, support cooperation, and form the neurological foundation of empathy. However, while this capacity starts forming early, the ability to integrate empathy, perspective-taking, and emotional regulation develops gradually.

Awareness of others is the growing ability to recognize, understand, and respond to the emotions, perspectives, and experiences of people around us. It begins simply—recognizing that someone is upset or happy—and expands into sensing why they might feel that way and allowing that understanding to guide our response. For young children, awareness of others might sound like, "She's crying. She's sad." As youth mature, this skill becomes more complex. It requires reading emotional cues, interpreting body language and tone, and imagining what someone else might be thinking or feeling—all while still learning to manage their own internal world.

One common challenge in developing awareness of others is what psychologists call the transparency illusion—the belief that our intentions, emotions, or thoughts are obvious to others (Gilovich, Savitsky, & Medvec, 1998). In reality, there is often a wide gap between what we intend and how we are perceived. A child concentrating deeply may appear angry. A teenager feeling overwhelmed may come across as dismissive. Youth often lack the experience to recognize that behavior usually carries a story beneath the surface.

Adults play a vital role in bridging this gap. One of the most effective tools is curiosity. Rather than correcting or assuming, adults can invite perspective taking through gentle wondering: "I wonder what it might feel like to be in their place," or "What do you think they might be experiencing right now?" This process—sometimes called mutual puzzling, exploring, or circular questioning—positions adult and youth as co-learners. Instead of delivering answers, we explore together. We model that empathy is not about certainty, but about openness.

Play can also be a powerful teacher. Games involving mirroring, imitation, or guessing emotions help youth practice reading nonverbal cues in ways that feel safe and engaging.

Everyday modeling matters just as much. When adults name their own empathic observations—"It looks like she might be disappointed after what happened earlier"—youth learn that understanding others is something we practice, not something we simply know.

Developmentally, this matters. As Dan Siegel and other researchers note, empathy is not fully formed in early childhood. Some youth struggle to take another's perspective not because they do not care, but because their brains are still learning how to hold more than one emotional reality at a time. When adults understand this, they can respond with patience instead of judgment—and approach empathy as a skill to be taught, modeled and practiced, not a trait to be expected or forced.

Sometimes, the deepest growth in awareness of others comes from asking directly. A kind of "presence audit" with trusted people—questions like, "What's your experience of me?" or "What could I do that would help you feel more connected to me?"—requires courage and humility. When adults model this openness, listening without defensiveness and noticing patterns rather than isolated comments, youth learn that awareness of others and being curious as to our impact on others, are lifelong practices.

I often try this with my own children, asking, "What's one thing you've enjoyed about me lately, and one thing you wish I did differently?" These conversations are not always easy, but they open doors to honesty, repair, and deeper connection. In those moments, staying curious—rather than defensive—matters deeply. Phrases like, "Tell me more," or "I wonder what you would have preferred instead," help me develop awareness of their experiences and my potential role in that. Then, when appropriate, sharing our own experience afterwards models a desire for shared awareness of each other and how to continue to grow relationally.

Awareness of others is complex. It asks youth to integrate empathy, perspective-taking, and emotional literacy while still discovering who they are. Nevertheless, when adults create environments that value curiosity over certainty and openness over blame, youth develop the capacity to connect with others in ways that are thoughtful, compassionate, and real.

Level 5: Cultivating Cultural Awareness—Expanding the Circle

As awareness continues to expand, youth begin locating themselves within a broader context. Cultural awareness is the ability to recognize that our lives are shaped not only by personal experiences and relationships, but also by family systems, communities, histories, and global realities. It is the understanding that we belong to something larger than ourselves. This level of awareness invites youth to consider questions of identity, impact, and responsibility: "Who am I in relation to others? How do my experiences differ from those around me? How do my voice and choices matter in the world?"

One of the most meaningful ways adults can nurture cultural awareness is by staying connected to a young person's interests and passions. When we understand what matters to them, we can help them see how those interests connect to the larger world. Encouraging youth to engage with causes they care about—locally or globally—helps them experience themselves as contributors rather than passive observers.

At the same time, cultural awareness must be cultivated with care. Flooding youth with distressing news or complex global issues without support can overwhelm their nervous systems and lead to hopelessness. Instead, adults can help youth engage with the world in ways that feel grounding and empowering—balancing honest conversations about injustice with stories of resilience, collective action, and possibility.

Whether youth are learning about environmental issues, social justice, cultural traditions, or global health, these conversations widen perspective. They help youth see that difference does not equal danger, and that curiosity can replace fear. With guidance, youth learn to approach diversity with openness and humility. Cultural awareness ultimately reinforces a sense of belonging to humanity itself. It invites youth to hold pride in who they are while remaining open to who others are. When adults support this level of awareness thoughtfully, youth develop not only compassion and perspective, but also a deeper sense of purpose—one rooted in connection, contribution, and care for the wider world.

Awareness is the first step, but it is not the final one. Noticing what is happening inside a young person creates possibility, but regulation is what helps them stay with that awareness when stress increases. Once youth can recognize sensations, feelings, thoughts, and social cues, the next task is learning how to manage those experiences without becoming overwhelmed.

This is where affect management comes in—helping young people integrate awareness into regulated states of self.

RISE INVITATION

Take a moment to pause and think about a young person in your life. Invite them into conversations. You might ask: "What was one part of your day that stood out to you?" "How do you think someone else might have experienced that moment?" "Did you notice anything about someone who is different from you today—what did you learn?"

Listen with curiosity. Let their words be enough. This is the practice—creating small pauses where young people can begin to notice their experiences, understand others, and make meaning of their world.

Over time, these moments of reflection become an inner habit: the ability to pause, notice, and respond with awareness of both self, others and the larger world around them.

CHAPTER THIRTEEN

Affect Management

As we deepen our understanding of self-awareness, the next step is learning how to manage what we sense, feel, and think. This is where affect management begins. Affect management is not about controlling emotions, numbing sensations, or making thoughts disappear. It is about learning how to notice our internal experiences and stay connected to ourselves as they move through us in a regulated way. It allows us to respond rather than react—to remain in relationship with what is happening inside without becoming overwhelmed by it.

At its core, affect management helps young people recognize what is happening within them, so they do not lose themselves to the storms that inevitably come and go. With support and practice, youth begin to understand that their internal experiences are information—not commands. They learn that even when something feels intense, there is often a small but meaningful pause between what they experience internally and what they do next.

This matters because thoughts, feelings, and sensations are not occasional visitors. They are constant companions, shaping how youth experience relationships, learning, and their sense of self. When young people lack support in understanding their internal world, those experiences can feel confusing, frightening, or out of control. When they are supported, those same experiences become something they can notice, name, and work with rather than be swept away by.

In this chapter, we explore how the RISE framework supports the development of affect management by honoring children's internal experiences rather than dismissing or punishing them. In many settings, the focus is placed almost exclusively on outward behavior. We want calm bodies, compliant actions, and "good choices." Without meaning to, we can send the message that big inner experiences are the problem—especially when they result in big behavior.

RISE offers a different path. While we absolutely want youth to learn how to make healthy choices, we recognize that the ability to do so depends on their capacity to understand and regulate what is happening inside them. Affect management is not about excusing behavior; it is about building the internal capacity that makes healthy behavior possible.

I know this personally. As a child, I had big feelings and strong body sensations that often felt like a storm inside me. The message I absorbed—often unintentionally—was that I was "too much." Over time, I learned to disconnect from uncomfortable feelings in order to be accepted. However, when we learn to cut off from sadness, embarrassment, or fear, we also lose access to joy, excitement, and connection. We build protection, but at a cost.

Children are born knowing how to feel. A toddler's emotions are big, raw, and deeply connected to their body—hunger, fatigue, curiosity, frustration. They show us, in their most authentic form, the mind–body connection. I often think of a moment when one of my children was a toddler and spotted dog poop on the sidewalk. Curious, they moved toward it. I scooped them up and said, "Icky poop, no thank you," and immediately they began to cry and yell, "I want!"

It is a silly moment, but a powerful metaphor. My child wasn't misbehaving—they were experiencing disappointment, frustration, and a loss of control. In that moment, my role wasn't to eliminate the feeling, but to stay present with it. I reflected: "That's hard. You really wanted that." Over time, these moments teach children that their internal states can be felt, managed, and integrated. This is where affect management begins—not with stopping those experiences, but with creating safety around them.

How Internal Experiences Build: The Escalation Cycle

Internal experiences rarely appear out of nowhere. More often, they build gradually, following a pattern that can be understood and anticipated. Most emotional experiences begin in a regulated state, when youth feel safe, open, and connected. Then something happens—a trigger that introduces stress or discomfort. Early signs may be subtle: restlessness, a shift in tone, difficulty concentrating. As internal experiences intensify, the body becomes more activated, thoughts narrow, and emotions grow stronger. Without support, this internal experience can continue to build until it peaks, overwhelming the youth's capacity to cope.

Remember the Neuroscience Chapter in the Foundations Section. These are the moments often described as "flipping your lid," a term coined by Dr. Daniel Siegel. When this happens, the brain's ability to reason, reflect, and make intentional choices temporarily goes offline. This occurs when youth are pushed outside their window of tolerance—the range in which they feel safe, balanced, and able to manage stress. Inside this window, emotions still rise and fall, but youth remain grounded enough to think clearly, stay connected, and recover from challenges. Outside of it, the nervous system shifts into survival.

Some youth move into high arousal, where emotions feel explosive and the body is flooded with energy. Others move into low arousal, where they feel shut down, numb, or disconnected. Both responses are protective. They are the body's attempt to restore safety when something feels like too much.

What matters is not preventing these states altogether, but learning to recognize them and find pathways back to balance. When youth begin to notice what it feels like to drift out of their window of tolerance, they gain something essential: agency. They learn that their body is communicating, not betraying them.

Over time, even the strongest emotional surge settles. The body calms, energy decreases, and safety returns. In this recovery phase, youth are once again able to reflect, connect, and learn from the experience. Every child's cycle looks different. What matters most is noticing the early signals—when support is most effective and least intrusive. When youth understand that these internal experiences come but also go, they gain hope. They learn that feelings are temporary and that support is available long before things reach a breaking point.

Affect management is not about preventing emotions or demanding perfection. It is about building confidence in the ability to move through internal experiences and return to balance.

RISE INVITATION

When we learn to notice the early signals, we gain more choices. This practice invites you to explore the escalation cycle with curiosity and compassion.

Think of a recent moment when a youth moved from calm to distress. Bring your attention to the early stage of the escalation cycle. Did you notice subtle body cues? Changes in tone, energy, or engagement? Did you notice shifts in focus or connection?

Now gently trace what happened next. How did the body respond? How did emotions intensify? How did thoughts or behavior begin to narrow or escalate?

Consider where the youth may have been in their window of tolerance. What might have pushed them closer to the edge? Were there moments when support could have helped bring them back toward balance?

Now imagine responding earlier in the cycle. What support might have helped at the first signs of agitation? Would connection, movement, a pause, or environmental adjustment have made a difference? Invite curiosity. Which early signals are easiest for you to notice? Which ones do you tend to miss? How does your own nervous system influence what you see?

Co-Regulation: Borrowed Calm before Self-Control

Before youth can regulate themselves, they must first experience regulation in relationships. Emotional regulation does not develop in isolation.

Children learn how to calm their bodies and minds by being with adults who can remain grounded when emotions rise. Co-regulation is the process through which youth borrow the calm of another nervous system until their own capacity grows.

When a young person is overwhelmed—by fear, anger, or frustration—they need more than directions or consequences. They need an anchor. Someone who can stay present, steady, and connected even as emo-tions surge. Our role in these moments is not to control behavior or rush toward solutions, but to meet youth where they are and model what regulation looks like in real time.

This is especially important for youth who have experienced trauma or chronic stress. Many of these children did not have consistent caregivers who soothed them, named their feelings, or helped them return to safety. Without those early experiences, self-regulation did not have the opportunity to develop. Co-regulation becomes the bridge—offering repeated, embodied experiences of calm that the nervous system can begin to recognize and internalize.

Consider Alex, a child whose early life was marked by chaos. In the classroom, frustration often spilled out as yelling, throwing objects, or leaving the room. One teacher responded differently. She stayed close, lowered her voice, and offered steady reassurance: "I'm here. You are safe. Let's breathe together." At first, Alex resisted. Over time, something shifted. He began seeking her presence before reaching his breaking point. One day, after calming himself successfully, he smiled and said, "I did it like you do." In that moment, regulation had begun to move from borrowed to owned.

This is how regulation grows—not through instruction alone, but through lived experience. The body learns patterns of safety by being in relationship with calm, attuned adults. Neural pathways strengthen through repetition. Sometimes that learning happens quickly. Other times it takes hundreds—or thousands—of moments of steady presence. We rarely know when a particular interaction will take root. Our work is not to measure or rush the process, but to keep offering the conditions for growth and trusting that those moments matter, even if they do not take root until after our time with them.

Co-regulation is not about being perfect. It is about being present. When we attend to our own emotional state first, we offer youth a model of what regulation looks like in practice. When we name emotions without judgment and remain connected through discomfort, we teach that feelings can be felt and survived.

Through patience, empathy, and consistency, we help youth build the internal resources they need to manage their emotions. We lend them our regulation until they are able to create their own. The goal is not to eliminate stress or emotional intensity, but to create relationships and environments that help youth stay within—or return to—their window of tolerance, where learning, connection, and growth are possible.

When youth experience adults who help them return to balance, they begin to trust their internal world. Still, regulation cannot rely only on what happens in moments of distress. The most effective affect management is shaped long before emotions boil over—through the daily rhythms, interactions, and environments that support regulation from the start.

In the next section, we turn our attention to how affect management can be supported proactively, woven into everyday life in ways that strengthen regulation before escalation occurs.

Proactive Affect Management

Proactive affect management is most powerful when it becomes part of the everyday rhythm of a child's life. Rather than something we reach for only when emotions are already overflowing, it is built quietly—through relationships, routines, environments, and experiences that support regulation long before distress appears.

When youth know what to expect, feel seen and supported, and trust the adults around them, emotional regulation becomes more accessible. Consistency and predictability create a sense of safety, and safety is the foundation for regulation. One way to think about this is to imagine stress as water slowly filling a bucket. Each demand, transition, or disappointment adds another drop. What keeps the bucket from overflowing are the release valves—movement, connection, reflection, laughter, music, downtime, reminders, and play. When these are woven into daily life, stress does not have to build silently until it spills over. It can be noticed, shared, and released along the way.

This process begins with the adults. Youth take cues from the nervous systems around them. When adults are grounded, predictable, and aware of their own energy, they create an external sense of regulation that children can lean into. Simple things—consistent routines, clear transitions, gentle reminders, and calm tone—send powerful signals of safety. When adults slow down, narrate what is coming next, and stay emotionally available, they reduce the amount of stress that ever enters the bucket in the first place.

From there, proactive affect management moves into the body. One of the simplest ways to support regulation is by offering regular pauses throughout the day. Short moments to reset give youth the chance to release built-up tension and return to balance. These pauses might look like stretching between activities, taking a few slow breaths, shaking out the body, or engaging in brief, playful movement. While small, these moments communicate something essential: it is okay to stop, notice what's happening inside, and take care of your body.

This is especially important in environments that place heavy demands on the nervous system. I see this clearly with my youngest child when we spend long stretches in basketball gyms for her older siblings. After an hour or two, her behavior often begins to shift. She may become restless, loud, or less cooperative. It would be easy to view this as misbehavior, but when we pause and look beneath the surface, her body is communicating something else entirely. The gym is loud—whistles, bouncing balls, cheering parents. The lights are bright. The energy is high and constant. Her nervous system is overstimulated. What she needs in that moment is not correction; it is relief. A break outside, quiet connection, movement, or rest helps her body reset. When we meet the need, the behavior resolves.

The environment matters. Calm, thoughtfully designed spaces can significantly support proactive regulation. Quiet areas with softer lighting, comfortable seating, or sensory tools give youth a place to regroup before stress escalates. Many classrooms and programs create calm corners, cozy nooks, or coping tents—spaces that communicate, "You're allowed to take care of your mind and body here." For some youth, having access to these spaces independently becomes an early form of self-regulation: noticing their internal cues and responding with care. As the body feels safer and more supported, we can begin to gently build awareness of the internal world.

Mind–body practices help youth tune into the present moment and make sense of what they are experiencing. Mindfulness activities such as guided breathing or noticing sensations build awareness without judgment. Movement-based practices like yoga or stretching combine physical release with emotional grounding. Creative outlets—art, music, journaling, or storytelling—offer additional pathways for expression, especially for youth who struggle to find words for their feelings. These practices give emotions somewhere to go, reducing the likelihood that they will spill out in ways that feel overwhelming or disruptive.

Regulation is also deeply connected to basic physical needs. Regular movement, nourishing food, hydration, and adequate rest all support a regulated nervous system. Play and laughter are equally essential. Unstructured play allows youth to release stress, explore social roles, and experience joy, while shared humor strengthens connection and resilience.

Choice and autonomy further strengthen this process. When youth are invited to help choose coping strategies, activities, or ways to reset, they begin to take ownership of their emotional experience. This sense of agency builds confidence and reinforces the belief that they are capable of caring for themselves with support. Regulation becomes something done with them, not to them.

Many proactive strategies are most effective when they are practiced during calm moments. Regular emotional check-ins—using feeling words, visuals, or brief reflection—build emotional literacy. Teaching coping skills when youth are already regulated makes those tools easier to access when stress increases.

Just as importantly, adults model regulation in real time. When we name our own feelings and demonstrate healthy coping—pausing to breathe, asking for help, or taking a break—we show youth what affect management looks like in action.

When these supports are woven into the fabric of everyday life, they form a strong foundation. Youth are more likely to remain within their window of tolerance and to recognize early signs of stress before emotions escalate. And still, even with the most thoughtful proactive supports in place, there will be moments when emotions rise faster than skills can keep up. In those moments, how we respond—especially under pressure—matters deeply.

RISE INVITATION

Co-regulation begins not with what we say or do, but with how we arrive. The regulation we offer others begins within us. Before focusing on a child, notice your own nervous system. What sensations are present in your body right now—tension, ease, fatigue, restlessness? Without judgment, name your current state.

Now, bring to mind a recent time when a child or youth was overwhelmed. It does not need to be a crisis. As you reflect, notice what was happening in their body or behavior—and what was happening inside you at the same time.

Notice the nervous system conversations. Co-regulation is an exchange between nervous systems. Did you feel rushed, tight, or activated? Or grounded, steady, and present? How might your internal state have influenced theirs? There is no right answer, only information.

Now imagine yourself responding from a place of steadiness. What would it look like to slow your movements, soften your voice, and stay present without fixing? Perhaps it means saying very little, sitting nearby, breathing, or offering quiet reassurance. Notice how this version of you feels in your body.

What helps you stay regulated when others are not? What pulls you out of regulation most quickly? What support do you need to offer calm more consistently?

Each time you tend to your own nervous system, you strengthen your capacity to support others. Each time you stay connected through discomfort, you teach that big feelings can be felt, held, and survived.

When youth borrow our calm, they are not becoming dependent—they are learning. Over time, that borrowed calm becomes their own.

When Proactive Is Not Enough: Responding in the Moment

There will still be times when a young person becomes overwhelmed. When emotions escalate more quickly than they can manage, regulation becomes difficult to access. These are the moments that test us most—not because we don't know what to do, but because they stir something in us, too. When rules are broken or behavior feels disrespectful, it is easy to react from frustration or urgency. Yet these moments, when handled with intention, can become some of the most powerful opportunities for learning, connection, and trust. Not because we eliminate limits, but because we lead with relationship.

I often share this story in trainings. Let us pretend that one day, I came home to find my child sitting on the couch eating, even though the rule in our house is "no eating on the furniture." Without thinking, I blurted out, "Hey, what are you doing eating on the couch? Get to the kitchen!" My child shot back, "That's so dumb! I can eat here if I want!" The older version of me would have felt angry and disrespected. However, through RISE, I have learned to remember that kids have greatness within them, and that all behavior is communication.

Therefore, instead of reacting, I paused. I took a breath. I chose a different path. I sat down next to them and said calmly, "You're saying the rule feels stupid—you feel like you should be able to eat wherever you want."

"Yeah," they said. "It's a dumb rule, and I'm not making a mess, so it's no big deal."

"This doesn't feel like a big deal to you," I reflected.

"Yeah. Leave me alone. I've had a hard day."

"Today has felt really heavy," I said softly. I stayed there, breathing, rubbing their back, letting the mo-ment settle.

Eventually, they said quietly, "None of my friends talked to me today, and I don't know what I did wrong."

"That's really hard," I said, pulling them into a hug. "Let's go to the kitchen and talk about it." *(Because you're not going to eat in my living room.)*

This moment captures what it means to talk to the "downstairs brain" in order to reach the "upstairs brain" (Siegel, 2020). When a child is upset, their thinking, logical brain is not fully available. If we lead with rules, lectures, or consequences, we are speaking a language they cannot hear yet. Connection must come first. This is where time-in becomes so powerful. Instead of sending a child away to calm down alone, we stay present—offering attunement safety, and support until they are ready to re-engage.

In the story, we moved from the living room to the kitchen, where we talked about what the day had felt like for them. We then talked about how it felt for me to come home and see the norms and boundaries dishonored. I was able to share my feelings and we were able to explore ways they could make it right and what was needed for the rest of the night and tomorrow, in case similar experiences happened at school again.

From this place of connection, regulation and growth become possible. What follows is not a rigid script, but a relational flow. These six stages help guide us through moments of dysregulation with intention, compassion, and clarity.

Stage 1: Awareness—Beginning with Yourself

Before we can support a dysregulated child, we must first check in with ourselves. This is the pause. The moment where we notice our own body, thoughts, and emotions. Are our shoulders tense? Is our voice tight? Are we reacting to the behavior in front of us—or to something it touches inside us? Awareness invites curiosity rather than judgment.

We ask ourselves what this moment is bringing up and gently adjust our expectations. Sometimes success does not mean immediate compliance.

Sometimes success means maintaining safety, connection, and dignity long enough for regulation to return. In the story, my instinct was to enforce the rule. Awareness gave me just enough space to breathe, shift my perspective, and remember that the behavior was communication—not defiance.

Stage 2: Attuned Responding—Leading with Presence

Once we are grounded, we turn our attention fully to the child. Attuned responding is the practice of connecting before correcting (Siegel and Bryson, 2018). Children sense our emotional state long before they process our words. When we slow our movements, soften our tone, and stay physically present, we offer our calm as an anchor for their nervous system. This might mean sitting beside them instead of standing over them. It might mean matching their emotional energy without matching intensity—acknowledging frustration, sadness, or anger while remaining steady ourselves.

This is where time-in truly begins. We communicate, often without words, "I'm here. You're not alone." And for many children, that presence alone is enough to begin settling the body and bringing regulation back online.

Stage 3: Talking to the Downstairs Brain—Validation and Connection

With presence established, we begin to put words to the experience. We reflect what we see and hear. "You feel like the rule is unfair." "This doesn't feel like a big deal to you." "Today has felt really heavy." These reflections are not agreements or permissions—they are bridges. Validation tells the child, "I see you. I hear you. Your feelings make sense."

When children feel understood, their nervous system softens. From that place, they are far more able to re-engage their thinking brain. Only after regulation returns can we meaningfully revisit expectations, boundaries, and repair. Connection first creates the conditions for learning later.

Stage 4: Physiological Coping—Supporting the Body

Sometimes words are not enough. Emotions live in the body, and regulation often requires physical support. This stage is about offering tools that help calm the nervous system. Gentle breathing can slow the heart rate and bring oxygen back to the brain. Movement—stretching, walking, squeezing a fidget—can release built-up energy. Sometimes the most effective intervention is meeting a basic need: water, a snack, or rest. And sometimes space is needed first, honoring if a child requests some time alone. Sometimes a fresh face is needed. Sometimes a pause.

In the story, quiet presence was enough. In other moments, a blanket, a stuffed animal, or movement might be what helps. Regulation is rarely one-size-fits-all. It is often a process of trial and discovery—learning along-side the child what helps their unique body and brain feel safe again. Over time, these shared experiences build awareness and confidence. This is where time-in becomes true co-regulation, even if we have to take a little space, the access to our "presence" is still available. We lend our calm while the child's nervous system finds its way back to balance.

Stage 5: Assessing and Adjusting the Environment—Reestablishing Safety

Finally, we consider the environment itself. Sometimes stress is being amplified by noise, lighting, temperature, or sensory overload. Small adjustments—moving to a quieter space, dimming lights, offering a soft object, or simply changing rooms—can dramatically shift a child's ability to re-engage. In the story, moving to the kitchen provided a natural reset. The environment changed, safety returned, and conversation became possible.

Stage 6: Restoring Regulation—Making Things Right

Children do not act out because they want to misbehave. They act out because they are struggling. When we respond with connection and co-regulation, we offer exactly what helps them grow: time together instead of isolation, understanding instead of rejection, and learning instead of punishment. We show them that even in hard moments; they will not be abandoned with their experiences.

Once regulation is restored, we can talk through expectations, explore repair and problem-solve together. These conversations build self-awareness, empathy, and accountability—without shame. They teach children that mistakes are opportunities for growth, and that relationships can hold both boundaries and care. This approach preserves dignity. It strengthens connection. And most importantly, it works. These moments may still involve natural consequences or consequence, depending on the harm done—but they are intentional, collaborative, and centered on growth rather than control.

In our fictitious example, once we were in the kitchen and had debriefed, we talked together about how to make things right. The child apologized for not following norms and they were able to name how their choices had affected me. They then identified and practiced a coping strategy they could use in the future when similar feelings arise, rather than responding in ways that break shared expectations.

Over time, these repeated experiences shape how children relate to themselves and others. They learn that sensations and emotions can be felt and managed, that support is available, and that they are capable of navigating challenges. Regulation becomes not something imposed, but something practiced—together, over time. Affect management is not about getting it right every time. It is about returning—again and again—to connection, balance, and the belief that growth happens in relationship.

RISE INVITATION

The six stages of regulation are not something to perform perfectly. They are a way of orienting yourself when emotions are high and thinking feels hard. This practice invites you to slow down and move through them with curiosity and compassion.

Think of a recent interaction with a child or youth where emotions rose. It does not need to be intense—just a moment that felt activating.

Awareness—Pause and Turn Inward

Notice what is happening inside you. What sensations, emotions, or urges are present? Take a slow breath and remind yourself, behavior is communication.

Attuned Responding—Offer Presence

Notice how you arrive. What shifts when you soften your tone, slow your movements, or stay physically present? Your steadiness creates safety before words are spoken.

Talking to the Downstairs Brain—Name and Validate

Gently put words to their experience. "It seems like this feels overwhelming for you right now." Stay curious—no fixing or correcting.

Physiological Coping—Support the Body

Consider what their body needs—movement, stillness, breath, water, or quiet. Regulation is often physical before it is cognitive.

Assess and Adjust—Reestablish Safety

Look at the environment. What might be adding stress? What small shift could help—less noise, a new space, added comfort?

Restoring Regulation—Making Things Right

Once calm returns, consider what is needed for repair and growth. Is there something to teach, restore, or support moving forward?

Afterward, take a moment and invite curiosity. What felt natural? What felt harder? What did you notice about your own regulation? There is no "right" way to move through these stages. Some moments may only allow for one or two. What matters most is not perfection, but presence.

Building a Brighter Tomorrow: A Collective Responsibility

As we talk about affect management, it is important to acknowledge a difficult reality. There are moments—particularly in systems serving youth with significant trauma, mental health needs, or developmental challenges—when immediate safety must take priority. In extreme circumstances, adults may need to intervene to prevent a young person from harming themselves or others.

In residential treatment programs, hospitals, schools, and juvenile justice settings, this can sometimes include practices such as physical restraint, seclusion, or medically induced containment. RISE does not deny that these practices exist, nor does it suggest that safety should ever be compromised. When there is imminent danger, adults have a responsibility to act. At the same time, we must be clear about what these interventions are—and what they are not. They are safety measures, not experiences that teach regulation.

Affect management develops through repeated experiences of safety, connection, and co-regulation. Force, isolation, and loss of control—no matter how clinically framed—do not build these skills. For many youth, especially those with histories of trauma or adversity, these experiences can deepen dysregulation, reinforce fear, and erode trust. They may stop behavior in the moment, but they rarely support long-term healing or growth.

This is why RISE holds a firm stance: while safety interventions may sometimes be necessary in extreme situations, our responsibility as adults and systems is to reduce the need for them as much as possible. That work begins long before a crisis. It requires understanding how nervous systems respond to stress and recognizing how environments, interactions, and expectations can unintentionally push youth outside their window of tolerance. It asks us to consider not only, "How do we respond when things go wrong?" but also, "How are we creating conditions that make regulation more likely in the first place?"

In practice, this means designing spaces that support regulation rather than overwhelm it—sensory rooms instead of seclusion rooms, calm corners instead of isolation, and therapeutic outlets for physical release rather than punishment for big energy. It means limiting access to objects that can cause harm, offering safe ways for bodies to discharge stress, and ensuring adults are trained to recognize early signs of escala-tion.

It also means taking a hard look at our systems. Housing large groups of youth with trauma histories together without adequate support, predictability, or relational consistency often creates nervous systems in constant collision. When dysregulation becomes contagious, restraint and seclusion are more likely—not because children are "too much," but because the system is under-resourced and overwhelmed.

RISE calls us to advocate for something better.

A society that waits until a child is sixteen and then invests heavily in residential care—or later funds incarceration for those carrying the deepest childhood wounds—has intervened far too late. If we truly want to reduce harm, we must invest earlier: in families, caregivers, early childhood systems, schools, and communities that support healthy nervous system development from the very beginning.

We currently live in a world where corporate systems generate immense profit while educators struggle to meet basic needs, and where human services and nonprofit organizations operate under chronic burnout, compassion fatigue, and self-sacrifice in an effort to support communities. These conditions are not separate from the struggles we see in children—they are part of the same system. Children enter classrooms and programs every day carrying stress, trauma, and unmet needs. We can choose to respond with understanding rather than punishment, prevention rather than reaction, and dignity rather than control.

This is not about pretending we live in a utopia. It is a commitment to doing better. It is a belief that our systems can be built around care rather than crisis, and around connection rather than control. A society that supports pregnant mothers, invests in families, and creates a village of safety and belonging for developing youth is one that reduces harm before it ever takes root. When we build communities that offer regulation, connection, warmth, and safety early in life, we reduce the likelihood that force will ever be needed later. Affect management is not just an individual skill. It is a collective responsibility.

But this kind of commitment asks more of us. It asks us to examine the systems we have inherited—systems that have not been built with equity or healing at their center. Too often, they have reinforced patterns of power and control rather than connection and care. To move forward, we must be willing to deconstruct and intentionally build something different—something rooted in dignity, compassion, and shared humanity. This is how we begin to create not just regulated individuals, but healthier communities for generations to come.

CHAPTER FOURTEEN

Relational Rhythms

Relationships are like a dance—sometimes slow and steady, sometimes full of energy and movement, and sometimes requiring a pause to find the rhythm again. Throughout our lives, we move through these relational rhythms as we form connections, navigate challenges, and learn how to stay in step with those around us. For youth especially, relationships play a powerful role in shaping identity and long-term wellbeing. Through interactions, young people begin to understand who they are in relation to others and how relationships can support their growth.

Like any dance, relationships have steps that can be learned, practiced, and refined over time. In this chapter, we explore the essential movements of relational rhythms: building, evaluating, maintaining, repairing, and reintegrating relationships.

Building relationships is where the dance begins—with curiosity, openness, and the courage to reach out. As relationships grow, youth begin to evaluate them, learning to notice which connections feel safe, supportive, and aligned with their values. And just as in any dance, missteps happen. Repairing relationships involves recognizing when something has gone wrong and learning how to make it right—taking responsibility, extending grace, and growing through conflict. Sometimes, after time apart or moments of rupture, relationships find their way back together. Reintegration is the hopeful return to rhythm, where trust is rebuilt and connection is given space to flourish again.

When youth understand and practice these relational rhythms, they gain the skills to communicate openly, set healthy boundaries, navigate conflict with courage, and nurture relationships that bring joy and belonging. Like a meaningful dance, relationships become most powerful when we learn the steps, listen to the music of shared humanity, and move together with intention and heart.

Building Relationships: The Four C's of Connection

Building relationships is one of the most meaningful skills youth can develop as they grow into their sense of self and community. Social and emotional development is not an abstract concept—it is the daily, lived practice of learning how to connect with self and others in ways that feel safe, respectful, and authentic. At its core, building relationships requires courage, curiosity, communication, and care. These four capacities reflect key indicators of wellbeing and show how social and emotional development comes to life in real relationships.

Relationships do not begin with perfection. They begin with a willingness to step forward—to say hello, to engage, to risk being seen. From there, connection deepens through curiosity, is sustained through communication, and the building of relationships is strengthened through care. Adults play a critical role in cultivating each of these capacities—not by forcing connection, but by creating environments where connection can grow.

Courage: The Willingness to Begin

Courage is the foundation of relationship building. It is the emotional risk required to initiate connection without knowing how the other person will respond. For many youth, this step feels daunting. Fear of rejection, uncertainty about what to say, or past experiences of hurt can make reaching out feel unsafe. Yet it is through these moments of bravery that relationships begin to take root.

Courage is not confidence—it is trying despite discomfort. A youth who approaches a peer, joins a group, or speaks up has already practiced a vital relational skill, regardless of the outcome. Reflection afterward—"What felt good? What was hard? What might I try next time?"—helps transform effort into learning and resilience.

Adults cultivate courage by:

- Normalizing nervousness, "It makes sense this feels hard."
- Encouraging effort rather than outcome, "I noticed you tried."
- Creating low-stakes opportunities for interaction—partner work, small groups, shared tasks, joining a club or team.
- Modeling initiation themselves—greeting others, introducing themselves, repairing missteps.
- Teaching emotional regulation skills that help youth tolerate the discomfort of social risk.

When youth learn that discomfort is part of connection—not a signal to stop—they become more willing to try again.

Curiosity: The Desire to Know and Be Known

Curiosity allows relationships to move beyond surface-level interaction. It is the openness to learn about another person—to ask questions, listen closely, and notice shared interests and differences without judgment. Curiosity communicates openness. A smile, a kind word, or remembering something important about someone. Curiosity is also deeply connected to awareness. Youth are learning not only who others are, but also how relationships work. This includes understanding that people have different ways of connecting.

Attachment patterns—shaped by early experiences—influence how youth seek closeness, respond to stress, and navigate emotional needs. Some youth crave reassurance and proximity, while others feel safer with independence and space. These differences are not flaws; they are adaptive strategies. By teaching youth about attachment styles, we help them recognize relational patterns and gain greater flexibility in how they relate to others. A peer's need for space no longer has to mean rejection, and a desire for closeness does not have to feel overwhelming.

Adults support curiosity by:

- Modeling genuine interest, "Tell me more about that."
- Teaching open-ended questions instead of yes/no questions.
- Helping youth notice differences without judgment, "People connect differently."
- Naming attachment needs in age-appropriate ways, "Some people like closeness, some need space."
- Naming how different people have a variety of preferences and interests. Introversion vs. extroversion. Down time vs. lively activities.
- Encouraging perspective taking, "How do you think that felt for them?"

Curiosity builds empathy, and empathy creates room for connection to grow.

Communication: The Bridge between Intention and Connection

Communication is how courage and curiosity turn into building a relationship. Even when youth want to connect, they may struggle to find the right words, read social cues, or express themselves clearly. Each person has a unique communication style—some are expressive, others quiet; some process out loud, others internally. When styles align, connection feels easy. When they do not, misunderstandings can arise.Teaching youth that communication differences are normal—and not a personal rejection—reduces shame and builds adaptability. Skills such as starting conversations, listening actively, and expressing thoughts and feelings respectfully are learned through practice.

Nonviolent Communication (NVC), developed by Marshall Rosenberg (2003), offers one helpful framework, guiding youth to observe without judgment, name feelings, identify needs, and make clear requests. Through this lens, communication becomes a tool for understanding rather than defense.

Adults cultivate communication by:

- Modeling regulated speech, especially during stress.
- Demonstrating active listening—reflecting, summarizing, validating.
- Teaching feeling and need language explicitly.
- Practicing conversation starters.
- Slowing interactions down so youth can think and respond.
- Showing what it looks like to ask questions that help others feel heard and seen.
- Teaching how to make requests in a way that keeps the other person open vs. defensive.
- Role modeling how to communicate accountability for mistakes.

When youth experience communication that lands—where they feel understood—they learn how to offer that same gift to others.

Care: Kindness and Cooperation

Care is what sustains us when we are building relationships. It shows up through kindness, consistency, cooperation, and respect for both our own boundaries and those of others. Care is not a feeling; it is a practice. Care grows through shared experience. Working together, solving problems, playing, and contributing. This builds trust and belonging. These moments teach youth that relationships are built through both being and doing.

Adults cultivate care by:

- Creating cooperative experiences rather than competitive ones.

- Teaching boundary-setting and consent explicitly.
- Reinforcing accountability, repair, and responsibility.
- Modeling kindness and follow-through.
- Helping youth notice reciprocity, "Does this feel balanced?"
- Protecting emotional and physical safety within relationships.

Care teaches youth that healthy relationships are sustained through mutual respect, not self-sacrifice. The four C's—courage, curiosity, communication, and care—are not checkboxes. They are capacities that grow through experience, modeling, and practice. Adults are the architects of the environments where these capacities either flourish or shut down. When youth are given opportunities to practice these skills—and are supported when it is hard—they begin to trust their ability to build relationships. These small, everyday moments form the foundation for the friendships, partnerships, and communities that will carry them through life.

The next section will explore how youth learn to evaluate relationships—deciding which connections feel safe, mutual, and worth sustaining.

RISE INVITATION

Take a moment to reflect on a recent interaction where a relationship was forming or deepening. Gently walk through the Four C's of Connection.

Where did courage show up?
How was curiosity expressed?
What supported or blocked communication?
Where did care, respect, or cooperation appear?

Invite curiosity. Which of these capacities feels strongest for the youth you support? Which one may need more modeling or practice right now? What is one small opportunity you could create this week to help grow it?

Relationships are built one moment at a time. Each act of courage, curiosity, communication, and care helps youth grow their confidence in connection—with themselves and with others.

Evaluating Relationships: Learning Discernment and Choice

Evaluating relationships is just as important as building them. As youth begin forming connections, they need guidance in understanding that not every relationship will be a good fit—and that this is not a failure. Relationships, like a dance, require shared rhythm, responsiveness, and care. Some connections move easily, with both people staying in step. Others require constant adjustment, and some never quite find a rhythm that feels safe or sustaining, no matter how much effort is invested.

Teaching youth to evaluate relationships is like helping them notice which relational rhythms feel grounded and supportive—where they feel respected, seen, and able to move freely—and which ones feel strained, unsafe, or out of sync. This process builds discernment, a core element of healthy relational development. Rather than asking youth to judge people, we can teach them to notice patterns—how they feel, how they are treated, and how the relationship impacts their sense of self.

Lens One: Safety—How Does This Relationship Feel

The first and most essential lens for evaluating a relationship is safety. This includes emotional, relational, and sometimes physical safety. Youth benefit from learning to tune into their internal signals—their bodies, emotions, and instincts. We can guide them to gently reflect on questions like: "Do I feel safe being myself with this person? Can I share my thoughts or feelings without fear of being mocked or dismissed? Do I feel calmer or more tense after spending time together?"

These questions draw directly from self-awareness skills developed earlier. When youth learn to notice whether a relationship feels grounding or draining, they gain important information. A relationship that consistently creates anxiety, shame, or fear may be signaling the need for boundaries or reevaluation.

Adults can support safety awareness by:

- Validating youth's internal signals, "Your feelings are giving you information."
- Helping them name emotions and body sensations after interactions.
- Normalizing that discomfort can be a signal, not something to ignore.

Reinforcing that safety is a requirement—not a luxury—in healthy relationships.

Lens Two: Mutuality—Is there Balance and Respect

A second lens is mutuality—the presence of balance and respect. Healthy relationships involve reciprocity. Both people contribute, care, and feel valued. A helpful metaphor is the idea of a "friendship bank." In nourishing relationships, both people make deposits through kindness, honesty, inclusion, and compassion, creating balance over time.

Youth can be supported in noticing patterns such as who initiates contact, who compromises, who apologizes, and who feels heard. When one person is consistently giving while the other is withdrawing, youth may begin to feel unseen or taken for granted. This doesn't mean the other person is "bad," but it does signal that the relationship may not be mutual.

Adults help teach mutuality by:

- Asking reflective questions like, "Does this feel equitable to you?"
- Helping youth notice patterns over time rather than focusing on one moment.
- Teaching that mutuality does not mean keeping score, but

noticing balance.

- Reinforcing that effort and care should flow both ways.

Understanding mutuality helps youth move away from relationships built on people-pleasing or self-sacrifice and toward relationships rooted in shared care.

Lens Three: Alignment—Does This Relationship Support Who I Am

The third lens is alignment. Relationships shape identity, and youth benefit from reflecting on whether a relationship supports who they are and who they are becoming. Questions such as: "Do I like who I am when I'm with this person? Am I encouraged to be myself—or pressured to change? Does this relationship pull me toward or away from my values and goals?" help youth assess whether a relationship aligns with their sense of self.

A relationship may feel comfortable or familiar, yet still pull a youth away from growth. Learning to notice alignment supports choices rooted in self-respect rather than fear of loss.

Adults support alignment by:

- Helping youth identify their values and personal "bottom lines."
- Reinforcing that boundaries are acts of self-care, not rejection.
- Role-playing language for stepping back respectfully.
- Normalizing that relationships can change as people grow.

Adults bring relationship evaluation to life through intentional practice. Stories and books that portray both healthy and unhealthy friendships offer powerful teaching moments. After reading or observing interactions, adults can ask reflective questions such as: "What did you notice about how they treated each other? Where did it feel respectful—or not? What choices did the character have?" These conversations help youth translate abstract ideas into lived understanding.

Creative activities also support integration. A "healthy friendship recipe"—listing ingredients like trust, honesty, fun, respect, and safety—gives youth a concrete reference point. Supporting youth in identifying their own bottom line clarifies what they will and will not accept in relationships. Practicing boundary setting through role-play builds confidence in saying "no" with clarity and kindness. Youth learn that stepping back from a relationship does not require blame or cruelty—only honesty.

Evaluating relationships gives youth the power to be intentional about who they let into their inner circle after the building phase of relational rhythms. By teaching them to assess safety, mutuality, and alignment, we equip them to choose relationships that feel respectful, supportive, and life giving. Like a dancer who learns when to lean in, slow down, adjust their steps, or step away altogether, youth can learn to care for relationships that help them grow—while gracefully releasing those that no longer allow them to move with safety or authenticity.

The next sections explore what happens after evaluation: how relationships are maintained, repaired when harm occurs, and reintegrated with intention and care.

RISE INVITATION

Think of a relationship in a young person's life. How do you think this relationship feels for them—do they seem more open and at ease, or more guarded and withdrawn? Is there a sense of shared effort, or does it feel one-sided? Does this relationship support who they are becoming, or ask them to shrink or change?

Now reflect. How can you support their own awareness? You might simply offer a question or be curious about an observation.

Maintaining Relationships

Maintaining relationships is where connection deepens and becomes real. While building and evaluating relationships create the foundation, maintaining them requires ongoing attention, flexibility, and commitment.

Staying connected over time means learning to notice subtle relational rhythms—changes in tone, mood, or energy—and responding with intention. It is a continual process of giving and receiving, like a dance that only works when both partners stay aware of one another's movements and adjust as the music shifts.

Consider a middle school friendship that has lasted a few months. At first, everything feels easy. Then one day, a joke lands wrong. Someone pulls away. There's a silence that wasn't there before. Nothing big happened—but something changed. This is where relationships are either quietly lost or intentionally maintained, if it feels right. Maintaining relationships centers itself around attunement—to ourselves, to others, and to the relationship as a whole. Youth benefit from learning that connection is shaped by a rhythm between people—body language, emotional presence, and responsiveness.

A pause before responding, a change in posture, or a sigh can communicate just as much as spoken language. When youth learn to notice these cues, they become more skilled at staying connected rather than reacting impulsively. This requires self-awareness and affect management. When young people can recognize their own sensations, emotions, and internal reactions, they gain the ability to choose responses that align with their values rather than being driven by the moment.

From an Internal Family Systems perspective, strong emotional reactions often come from protective parts of ourselves that are trying to keep us safe. A youth might snap defensively, shut down, or cling tightly—not because they want conflict, but because a part of them fears rejection or shame. When these reactions are met with curiosity rather than judgment, youth learn something powerful: "I am not my reaction." That realization creates space to pause, regulate, and respond with more intention and compassion.

Adults can cultivate attunement and parts curiosity by:

- Naming reactions without labeling, "Something in you really wanted to feel safe just now."
- Wondering aloud rather than correcting, "I wonder what part of you showed up there."

- Teaching youth to check in with themselves before responding, "What's happening inside right now?", "What story are you telling yourself?"
- Modeling curiosity toward their own reactions instead of self-criticism.
- Slowing moments down so regulation can happen before problem solving.

As relationships continue, growth becomes unavoidable. Needs change. Misunderstandings happen. Differences surface. Maintaining relationships does not mean preventing these moments—it means learning how to stay present when they arise.

Conflict is an inevitable part of relationships. When youth are taught to see conflict not as a threat, but as a signal, that something needs attention, it becomes an opportunity for understanding rather than rupture. People approach conflict differently. Some avoid it, hoping it will pass. Others escalate quickly, driven by strong emotion. Others move toward problem solving right away. Helping youth recognize these tendencies—both in themselves and in others—builds empathy and flexibility.

We can explicitly teach this by having youth explore their own conflict patterns through reflection, discussion, or simple assessments that highlight how past experiences shape present reactions. One practical way to support engaging in conflict is by offering a simple structure that prioritizes regulation and respect: pausing before reacting, naming what is happening, thinking through options, choosing a path forward together, honoring each perspective, and normalizing conflict as part of relationships. When youth learn to speak truth in love, they discover that honesty and compassion can coexist.

This matters deeply in a world where many youth experience conflict primarily through social media—where public shaming, avoidance, or cutting people off replaces accountability and understanding. These responses may feel powerful in the moment, but they rarely lead to trust or resolution. Healthy conflict, when handled with care, allows relationships to resynchronize—to find rhythm again with greater understanding.

Maintaining connection also means learning how to receive feedback without collapsing into shame or becoming defensive. Feedback is inevitable in close relationships, yet many youth experience it as a judgment of their worth rather than as information about a rhythm. Many youth have never been taught how to give feedback appropriately or how to sit and receive feedback openly.

Adults can help reframe feedback as an opportunity for deeper connection by modeling curiosity instead of defensiveness. When youth learn to ask, "What can I grow from here?" rather than "What's wrong with me?" they build resilience and self-respect.

Adults can cultivate healthy feedback practices by:

- Separating behavior from identity, "This is about what happened, not who you are."
- Pairing care with honesty rather than delivering feedback cold or harshly.
- Modeling how to pause before responding to feedback.
- Modeling open, honest dialogue.
- Saying aloud what they are doing internally, "I feel defensive, but I want to stay open. I know that is just a part of me."
- Practicing feedback in low-stakes moments.

Adult modeling is especially powerful here. When youth see adults receive feedback with humility, reflect openly, and make adjustments without shame, they learn that growth is safe and relational. These moments quietly teach that maintaining relationships is not about being right—it is about staying connected and honoring differences.

Youth also need support in recognizing when conflict is escalating and moving away from constructive connection. These are the moments when people shift out of their grounded selves and into reactive protector responses—raising voices, shutting down, becoming sarcastic, or withdrawing entirely. Helping youth identify early warning signs—tightness in the body, racing thoughts, clenched fists, and a rising voice—gives them the chance to pause before harm occurs.

Simple tools such as taking a break, breathing deeply, or naming what they are feeling can help youth return to a more regulated state. Frameworks like the Gottman Institute's "Four Horsemen"—criticism, contempt, defensiveness, and stonewalling (Gottman & Silver, 1999)—offer helpful language for noticing when conversations are drifting toward disconnection. Youth do not need to memorize these concepts; they benefit from learning to recognize when communication has shifted from understanding to protection.

Finally, maintaining relationships also includes learning how to stay grounded in difficulty that cannot be easily resolved. One of the hardest lessons youth face is realizing that some relationships—or people—will remain challenging, even when they do everything "right."

Sometimes the difficult relationship is with someone they cannot avoid: a teacher, coach, peer, or family member. In these moments, the work shifts from establishing harmony in the relationship to maintaining the self within it. Youth cannot control others' behavior, but they can choose how they respond. This realization restores agency. Instead of trying to change someone else, youth can focus on staying aligned with their own values.

Separating others' behavior from personal worth becomes essential. Harsh words or dismissive actions reflect the other person's capacity, not the youth's value. Naming unkind behavior while maintaining internal dignity helps prevent shame from taking root. Self-awareness again plays a central role—helping youth notice what is activated and choose grounding strategies that keep them centered is a key element of managing difficult relationships.

Adults can cultivate strength in difficult relationships by:

- Helping youth identify what is and is not within their control.
- Teaching boundary-setting language that is clear and respectful.
- Supporting planning for challenging interactions.

- Reinforcing that seeking support is a sign of wisdom, not weakness.

By teaching these skills, we empower youth to maintain relationships without losing themselves in the process. They learn that connection does not require self-abandonment, and that boundaries and integrity are part of healthy closeness. While they cannot always choose who is in their lives, they can choose how they respond—with clarity, regulation, and self-love.

RISE INVITATION

Think of a relationship a young person is actively trying to maintain. This could be a friendship, peer connection, or relationship with an adult. Bring to mind a recent moment where there was tension, misunderstanding, or a shift in the interaction.

First, notice patterns in communication. How does this youth tend to express themselves—directly or indirectly, quietly or expressively? How do they respond to tone, feedback, or change? How does your own communication style interact with theirs—where does it align, and where might it create tension?

If helpful, you might explore a Behavioral, Social, and Communication Style Questionnaire to better understand differences in how people interact and process communication:

https://www.bradfordvts.co.uk/wp-content/onlineresources/communication-skills/behaviour-analysis/behavioural%20social%20and%20communication%20style%20questionnaire.pdf

These styles are not right or wrong—they simply help make patterns more visible.

Next, consider how conflict shows up. When tension arises, does this youth move toward it, avoid it, or become overwhelmed? What do you notice in their body or behavior—and in your own? What seems to support connection, even in small ways? You may also find it helpful to reflect using a Conflict Styles Assessment to identify typical responses to tension:

https://blake-group.com/sites/default/files/assessments/Conflict_Management_Styles_Assessment.pdf

Now, choose one small practice to try this week. Name a relational cue you notice. Normalize that conflict is part of relationships. Or highlight your communication patterns.

This is the practice—slowing down enough to notice patterns, understand differences, and respond with intention. Over time, these moments help youth build the skills to stay connected, navigate conflict, and maintain relationships with greater awareness and care.

Repairing Relationships

Repairing relationships is one of the most powerful lessons we can teach youth. Every relationship will experience moments of rupture—words said that could not be taken back, actions that cause harm, misunderstandings that create distance. These moments can feel heavy and uncomfortable, but they also hold possibility. When we guide youth through repair, we teach them that strong relationships are not strong because they are perfect—they are strong because they can bend, break, and be rebuilt with care.

Imagine a moment in a classroom or home when voices rise. A comment meant as a joke lands as an insult. Someone storms away. Later, the room feels different—quiet, tense, unsettled. Nothing has been resolved, but everyone feels it. This is the space where repair becomes possible.

Not immediately. Not perfectly. But intentionally.

Repair begins with two essential goals: acknowledging and healing the harm, and restoring a sense of relational safety. Youth need to know that when harm happens, there can still be a way back toward connection. Not a shortcut. Not a pretend "we're fine," but a real path forward—one that honors truth, accountability, and dignity.

Adults play a vital role in this process by becoming anchors of safety. In moments of rupture, our nervous systems set the tone. When adults slow down, stay regulated, and remain present, they signal that honesty and vulnerability are welcome. Repair cannot grow in an environment of humiliation or fear. Youth are far more willing to take responsibility when they believe mistakes will be met with guidance rather than shame.

One of the simplest ways to invite repair is through reflective questions—questions that open space rather than assign blame. Asking, "What do you think happened?" or "What do you think the other person experienced?" helps youth shift from defensiveness to awareness. Asking, "What can we do to make it right?" centers accountability without punishment. Affective language deepens this process by bringing emotions into the open. Questions like, "How did that make you feel?" or "What do you wish had happened instead?" allow both the person who caused harm and the person who was hurt to name their experience. When feelings are acknowledged without judgment, we invite humanity back into the space.

Restorative questions, rooted in Restorative Justice Practices developed by Ted Wachtel (2013) and the International Institute for Restorative Practices (IIRP), offer additional structure, especially when emotions are high. For the person who caused harm, reflecting on what happened, what they were feeling, who was impacted, and what responsibility looks like helps transform guilt into accountability. For the person who was hurt, being asked how they were affected, what felt hardest, and what they need to feel safe again affirms that their experience matters. These conversations teach youth a critical truth: repair is not about punishment—it is about restoring trust through honesty, care, and responsibility.

In certain situations and settings, restorative circles can be especially powerful. They create intentional space for all voices to be heard and for shared understanding to emerge. Youth learn that communities and relationships can rupture—and still come back together with care. Repair becomes more than a private moment; it becomes a shared value.

Adults can cultivate meaningful repair by:

- Sowing the moment down rather than rushing to resolution.
- Modeling accountability before expecting it from youth.
- Using curiosity-based questions instead of accusations.
- Making space for both harm and impact to be named.
- Protecting dignity while still holding responsibility.

Repair also requires action. A sincere apology matters, but repair often asks for more than words. Writing a note, replacing something that was taken, helping with a task, or changing behavior over time teaches youth that trust is rebuilt through consistency. These acts show that accountability is something we do, not just something we say.

Understanding apology languages can make this process more meaningful. People experience apologies differently—some need to hear regret, while others need responsibility, restitution, commitment to change, or an invitation to forgive (Chapman & Thomas, 2006). When adults model apologies that include more than a quick sorry, youth learn what real repair looks like in practice. For example, an adult might say: "I'm sorry I raised my voice earlier. I was wrong to speak to you that way. You deserve kindness, even when I'm frustrated. Next time, I am going to take a breath before I respond. Will you forgive me?"

This kind of apology weaves together regret, responsibility, and commitment. It shows youth that repair is not performative—it is relational. When repair is avoided, ruptures remain open. Over time, they harden into distance, resentment, and disconnection. However, when we lean into repair, we teach youth one of life's most powerful truths: relationships can survive mistakes. More than that, they can grow stronger because of them.

A recent experience with my own children reminded me how delicate—and important—repair can be.

My two oldest were with me at work one day as we prepared materials for our therapeutic childcare program. We were with a few colleagues, organizing items intended to support regulation for young children. As we worked, I found myself pointing out certain tools and sharing how my own children had used similar items when they were younger. My intention was to normalize these supports—to help others see that using them is not "coddling," but a meaningful way to care for children's bodies and brains. I also wanted to model that I believed in these tools enough to use them in my own home.

But I didn't slow down to consider how it might feel for my children to hear their personal experiences shared in that setting. At one point, my oldest looked at me, and I knew I had crossed a boundary. Later, in the hallway, he said, "You do that when you're around work people—you embarrass us." I asked him to tell me more. He shared that it felt like I was talking about their needs in a way that felt embarrassing.

In that moment, I realized that while I believed I was advocating for wellness, I was also meeting my own needs—wanting to be seen as a "good mom," wanting others to understand my values. In doing so, I had overlooked his sense of autonomy, dignity and confidentiality.

I apologized. I acknowledged that I had crossed a boundary, and I told him I would do better to slow down, to be more aware, and to stay attuned to what felt okay to share. We talked about his preferences and what respect would look like moving forward. Repair in relationships often asks us to look inward. It calls us to examine our motives, our insecurities, and the ways our own needs can show up in our interactions with others.

This is where repair connects deeply with the You Intervention—knowing yourself well enough to recognize what is driving your behavior in the moment. The more we integrate the earlier elements of RISE, the more equipped we are to show up with awareness, take accountability, and repair when harm occurs.

By teaching youth the language and practices of repair—through affective questions, restorative approaches, meaningful apologies, and real opportunities to make amends—we give them a lifelong gift: the knowledge that making things right is always worth the effort, and that relationships are resilient when we care for them with intention. And when we do, we not only restore connection—we strengthen it.

RISE INVITATION

Repair is not just about saying, "I'm sorry." It is about helping the other person feel understood, respected, and safe again.

Think of a recent moment where harm occurred—something small or significant—between a young person and someone else. What kind of apology was offered, if any? Did it seem to land—or did something still feel unfinished?

Now, consider how repair is experienced. People give and receive apologies in different ways. If helpful, you might explore an Apology Language Assessment to better understand these differences:

https://5lovelanguages.com/quizzes/apology-language

Invite curiosity. Which type of apology feels most meaningful to you? What might feel most meaningful to this youth? Where might an apology fall short—not from lack of care, but from mismatch?

Now return to the moment. What might repair look like if it matched the other person's needs more closely? What words could name the impact? What action could help rebuild trust? What follow-through might show change?

You might model something like, "I'm sorry for what I did. I understand how it affected you. Here's what I'll do differently next time." This is the practice—helping youth see that repair is not a performance, but a pathway back to connection.

Reintegration, Restoration, Release

Reintegration is the step that comes after repair: deciding what it means to move forward. It is the process of finding a healthy path ahead—either bringing the relationship back into connection or creating closure that allows both people to move on with peace. Reintegration matters because without it, youth can be stuck in extremes: cutting people off impulsively, avoiding repair or staying entangled in resentment without resolution. Reintegration offers a healthier alternative—one that honors both safety and dignity.

Imagine two students who had a conflict on the playground. The apology has been made. The tears have dried. And now comes the quiet, often unspoken question: "What happens next? Will we play together again? Do we keep our distance? Do we pretend nothing happened?" Reintegration is where those questions are answered with intention.

Sometimes, after repair, both people are ready to step back into connection with renewed understanding. The relationship may return to something familiar—or it may evolve into something more thoughtful. Reintegration often includes clearer expectations, more intentional communication, and a deeper commitment to attunement and awareness. It is like returning to the dance, this time with a steadier rhythm and more care in the steps. This teaches youth something hopeful: conflict does not have to be the end of connection. When both people are willing to learn and grow, relationships can become stronger—not weaker—through rupture and repair.

Other times, the healthiest choice is not to return to the same level of closeness. Reintegration can also mean choosing closure. This is not avoidance or rejection, but an intentional closing of a chapter—acknowledging what happened, naming what is needed, and stepping back without cruelty or blame. This might sound like: "I care about you, but I need to take a step back from this friendship. I want to be respectful, and I need more space to feel okay." Teaching youth this kind of language shows them that relationships can change without becoming bitter. It helps them understand that boundaries are not punishment—they are an honoring. And that peace can be a sign of maturity, not failure.

Adults play an essential role in supporting reintegration. By modeling these conversations, facilitating restorative circles when appropriate, and guiding youth through realistic next steps, we help them move forward with clarity rather than impulse. Questions such as, "Do you feel ready to reconnect?" or "What do you need to feel safe moving forward?" invite reflection and agency. Sometimes reintegration is as simple as returning to play after an apology. Other times it involves clear agreements about boundaries, expectations, or what will happen if harm repeats.

Adults can cultivate healthy reintegration by:

- Normalizing that there is more than one "right" way to move forward.
- Helping youth think through options instead of rushing decisions.
- Supporting clear, respectful language for reconnection or closure.
- Reinforcing that safety and dignity matter more than keeping peace.
- Modeling how to leave relationships with honesty rather than hostility.

Reintegration reminds us that relationships are not all-or-nothing. They can bend, shift, and transform in ways that honor both people's needs. Whether a relationship is rekindled or released, the goal is the same: to move forward with honesty, safety, and respect. Teaching youth this practice gives them tools for navigating relationships with maturity and compassion—showing them that even after hurt, there can still be a way forward.

Relationships are not a single moment or milestone—they are a living process that unfolds over time. The RISE framework reminds us that connection is built through small, intentional steps: the courage to reach out, the wisdom to reflect on what we need and value, the care to maintain connection over time, the humility to repair when harm is done, and the grace to reintegrate in ways that honor safety and growth.

When we guide youth through these relational rhythms, we give them tools that last a lifetime. We teach them that relationships require effort and vulnerability—but that they are also the source of joy, resilience, and well-being. By modeling attunement, awareness, accountability, and compassion, we show youth that healthy relationships are built through everyday acts: listening closely, encouraging often, apologizing sincerely, making amends, and trying again when things get hard.

In Relational Rhythms, the core idea is simple: relationships are not static. They grow, rupture, repair, and evolve. And through each cycle, youth can become more grounded, more connected, and more confident in who they are with others.

RISE INVITATION

Think of a relationship where harm, conflict, or misunderstanding has occurred—recently or in the past.

What harm was done, and how was it acknowledged? Do you think it feels emotionally safe for the youth to move forward—or is there hesitation? What options feel available to the youth right now—reconnection, space, or closure?

Now, consider your role in supporting them through this. What curious questions might help them express what they need? Choose one small way to support this process.

Relationships are not resilient because they avoid harm, but because they know how to respond to it.

CHAPTER FIFTEEN

Healthy Choices

As we reach the final chapter in this section on Social and Emotional Development, we arrive at something quietly powerful: the ability to make healthy choices. As young people learn how to make thoughtful decisions, it helps to have something larger guiding them. They need a sense of direction—a feeling that their life is going somewhere, even if the destination is still unclear. They need motivation, the energy that keeps them moving forward. They need hope, the belief that their actions matter. And they need agency, the understanding that I have the power to influence what happens next. When these elements come together, choices begin to feel different.

A young person who feels hopeless may think, "What's the point? Nothing will change." But a young person with hope and direction can think, "This is hard—but it matters." In this way, healthy choices are deeply connected to meaning, purpose, and a sense of efficacy. They do not emerge in isolation or through willpower alone. Without these foundations in place, asking youth to make better choices is often asking too much, too soon.

Healthy choices are not a separate skill we tack on at the end. They emerge when everything we have been building—indicators of wellbeing, awareness, affect management and relationships—come together in real life. They show up in the pause before reacting, in the decision to try again, and in the everyday moments that guide behavior. At its simplest, healthy decision-making is the ability to choose with intention, clarity, and foresight. It is not about always picking the right option or avoiding mistakes. It is about learning to engage the whole brain—to balance emotion with reasoning, impulse with reflection, and the needs of the moment with the hopes we carry for the future.

Earlier in RISE, we explored whole-brain integration: the partnership between the downstairs brain, which governs emotions, impulses, and survival instincts, and the upstairs brain, which allows for reasoning, problem solving, and perspective. When these systems work together, young people can pause, think, and choose with greater care. However, when stress, trauma, or underdeveloped skills interfere, that integration can break down—leaving youth more reactive, overwhelmed, or stuck. This chapter builds on that foundation by bringing these ideas into everyday moments of choice.

Making sound decisions requires more than logic alone. Choices are shaped by awareness, affect management, and the ability to think ahead. They are most challenged in moments when emotions are loud and time feels short—when reacting would be easier than slowing down. Healthy choices are how young people move from moment to moment with intention.

While youth learn from what we say, they learn just as much—if not more—from what we do. Every time we pause before responding, admit a mistake, change course, or talk through a decision aloud, we offer a living blueprint for how choices can be made. In truth, we are learning alongside them, shaped by the same moments, practicing the same skills in real time.

Every young person is writing the story of who they will become, often without realizing it. Each choice—big or small—becomes a sentence in that unfolding narrative. Some choices are ordinary and routine, like deciding what to eat for breakfast or whether to finish a task. Others feel heavier: whether to stand up to a friend, try something unfamiliar, tell the truth, or resist the pull to fit in.

As adults—parents, caregivers, mentors, teachers—we do not get to hold the crayon for them. But we do get to stand beside them. We can offer guidance, encouragement, and opportunities to practice choosing wisely. Healthy decision-making is not about perfect answers; it is about learning to make choices that align with one's values, needs, and long-term wellbeing.

We often assume that decision-making improves with age, but it is not that simple. Decision-making is a muscle—and like any muscle, it grows through use. For youth who have experienced trauma, chronic stress, or inconsistency, this muscle may be underdeveloped. They may act on impulse, avoid responsibility, or freeze when faced with decisions. These responses are not signs of defiance or immaturity; they are signals that support and practice are needed.

Helping youth develop strong decision-making skills is one of the most meaningful ways we can support their growth into emotionally intelligent, resilient individuals. While it may appear to be something that develops on its own, effective decision-making must be intentionally modeled, taught, and practiced—especially for young people navigating complex emotional and relational experiences.

At its core, decision-making is the process of choosing between options and acting with purpose. But when emotions are overwhelming or the future feels uncertain, the brain often prioritizes short-term relief over long-term outcomes. In those moments, young people may react quickly, shut down, or avoid choices altogether. Healthy decision-making, then, is not just about the choice itself—it is about building the internal capacity to pause, reflect, and choose in ways that align with values, goals, and relationships.

When we actively guide youth through this process, they begin to see that choices have consequences—and just as importantly, that they have agency. In the sections that follow, we will explore the internal and external skills that support healthy choices. Together, these skills support wellbeing and resilience. These capacities do not appear all at once—they are built gradually, from the inside out.

RISE INVITATION

Think of a young person and one recurring "choice moment" where they get stuck, reactive, or impulsive.

Now, consider what may be shaping their ability to choose. Do they have a sense of direction? Enough motivation to try? Hope that change is possible? A belief that their choices matter? Which of these feels most limited right now? If something is missing, the moment may be asking more of them than they can yet hold.

Now choose one way to support them: plan, simplify choices, offer a pause, name effort, allow a redo, or model your own decision-making. Offer one steady sentence that builds agency without pressure. For example, "Let's slow down together. Pause first, then decide."

After the moment, take a brief pause. What showed even a small step forward? What helped the moment feel safer or clearer? What is one small step to try again?

The Inner Work of Choosing Well

Every young person knows the feeling of wanting something right now. The last cookie on the counter. The urge to snap back when someone says something hurtful. The thrill of breaking a rule just to see what happens. In those moments, impulsive choices often win—not because youth do not care, but because the feeling in the moment is louder than the voice of reflection.

Healthy choices do not begin with willpower. They begin with internal capacity. And that capacity is built step by step, often with adults holding the structure until young people are ready to hold it themselves. Before youth can consistently pause, wait, and reflect, they need foundations that make those skills possible. This is the inner ladder to healthy choices—and it is largely cultivated in relationships.

Capacity One: Felt Safety

Waiting is only possible when the brain feels safe. For many youth—especially those who have experienced inconsistency, stress, or trauma—waiting feels like a risk. "What if it never comes? What if I forget? What if I lose my chance?" Predictability quiets those questions. Clear timelines, consistent routines, and advance planning reduce uncertainty and lower the cognitive load on a developing brain. When youth know what to expect and when to expect it, they do not have to make as many decisions in moments of stress. In this way, adult structure becomes the decision-making system for the child until their own system is more developed.

Adults can cultivate predictability by:

- Creating clear timeframes—"after dinner," "on Friday," "after recess" rather than "later."
- Maintaining predictable routines and rituals.
- Following through consistently so waiting feels safe.
- Narrating planning aloud—"We're waiting because…"

Predictability does not limit freedom—it creates the conditions for greater future choice.

Capacity Two: Growing the Pause

Once safety is present, the next step is learning how to pause so that healthy choices can follow. The pause is the moment when the "downstairs brain" and "upstairs brain" reconnect—when choice becomes possible. This pause often begins in the body. Tight fists. A racing heart. Heat in the face. Helping youth notice these signals builds awareness, a skill introduced earlier in RISE. Simple tools—taking a breath, stepping away, counting slowly to ten—may seem small, but they create just enough space for reflection to return.

Let's consider a young person who struggles to find that pause. If his sister teased him, he yelled. If a video game frustrated him, the controller went flying. There was no space between feeling and action. One evening, his father shared something that had helped him slow down as a kid. The next day, when his sister grabbed the remote, the familiar surge of anger rose: tight chest, clenched fists, heat in his face. He started counting without really meaning to.

One… two… three…

He did not calm down completely. But he didn't explode either. Instead of yelling, he said, "I was watching that." It was a small moment, but a meaningful one. Over time, those borrowed pauses began to turn into his own.

Adults can cultivate the pause by:

- Helping youth notice body cues that signal rising emotion.
- Teaching simple pause tools—breathing, counting, stepping away.
- Modeling pauses themselves in moments of stress.
- Prompting youth to practice pause skills during calm moments as a proactive skill.

Capacity Three: Delaying Gratification

Impulse control and delayed gratification are not traits youth either have or lack. They are capacities that develop gradually, through repeated experiences of being supported, guided, and given just enough structure to succeed. Early on, many young people rely on adults to help them slow down, think ahead, and hold limits—especially when emotions are high or rewards feel immediate.

Scaffolding means recognizing when a young person's brain is still learning how to manage impulse, wait for something meaningful, or consider future consequences. In those moments, adults temporarily hold that capacity with them. One of the clearest places this scaffolding shows up is in delayed gratification: the ability to wait for something meaningful rather than reaching for immediate reward. Waiting is hard, especially in a world designed around instant access and quick dopamine hits.

For many youth, the discomfort of waiting can feel overwhelming or unsafe. Yet the ability to delay gratification is one of the strongest predictors of long-term success—not because youth are naturally good at it, but because it can be learned through supported practice.

One of my children struggles with wanting to spend money the moment it lands in his hands. Rather than framing this as a problem to correct, we treated it as a skill to practice. Together, we tried a simple experiment. Whenever he received money, we agreed he would wait two weeks before spending it. If he still wanted the item after that time, he could buy it, with a small-added incentive for practicing the wait. What surprised us both was how often the urge passed. Most of the time, it was not really about the item—it was about the rush of buying something in the moment. This is developmentally typical, especially for youth whose brains are wired for novelty, reward, and immediate feedback.

For some young people, including those with neurodivergence, the pull of dopamine can make delayed gratification even more challenging. But practices like this do something deeper than delay a purchase. They teach young people how to sit with discomfort, how to notice the difference between immediate wants and longer-term needs, and how to work toward something intentionally. When he finally made a purchase after saving, the joy felt different—deeper and steadier. He had not just bought something; he had practiced patience, self-control, and follow-through.

In moments like these, the adult is holding the timeline, the structure, and the future in mind—so the child doesn't have to do it alone. Over time, with enough supported experiences, that external structure becomes internal skill.

Adults can cultivate capacity by:

- Reducing decision load during high-stress moments.
- Holding timelines and expectations when waiting feels hard.
- Starting with small, manageable challenges and gradually increasing responsibility.
- Making decision boundaries explicit—"I decide bedtime; you decide dessert."
- Naming the process, not just the outcome—"You waited—even when it was uncomfortable."
- Gradually increasing autonomy as skills strengthen.

Scaffolding is not about lowering expectations or controlling choices. It is about matching support to development. As youth grow, the scaffolding naturally fades—and what remains is a young person who knows how to pause, wait, and choose with intention.

Capacity Four: Do-Overs and Choosing Again

Healthy choices are not built through perfection. They are built through making choices repeatedly. When youth react impulsively, the most powerful learning often happens after the moment has passed. Offering do-overs—"That decision didn't go the way you wanted. Want to try again?"—teaches that mistakes are part of growth, not evidence of failure.

Adults can cultivate repair by:

- Allowing do-overs without shame.
- Using "pause and choose again" language.
- Separating behavior from identity and choices from personhood.
- Reflecting internal effort, not just outcomes.

As these capacities strengthen, youth become increasingly able to reflect not just on what they do—but on how they think.

From Capacity to Cognition

As youth learn to pause, wait, and repair, they become more capable of noticing how their thoughts influence their choices. This is where cognitive skills—thought stopping, challenging, and changing—begin to take root. Today's youth are growing up in environments shaped by scarcity, speed, and constant stimulation. Short-form videos, online gaming, and endless comparison often reinforce impulsive happiness over long-term reward. These messages matter. They shape how young people interpret discomfort, effort, and waiting.

Sometimes the first step in working with thoughts is simply learning how to interrupt them. When a young person becomes stuck in anxious, all-or-nothing, or self-critical thinking, a mental pause—imagining a stop sign, taking a breath, or quietly saying, "Not helpful right now"—can interrupt the spiral long enough to regain balance. For example, a youth who thinks, "I already messed up, so what's the point?" may be able to pause that thought before it turns into shutdown or acting out.

From there, youth can learn to gently challenge their thoughts by asking questions such as: "Is this thought based on facts? Am I assuming the worst? What would I say to a friend in this situation?" A young person who thinks, "No one likes me," may begin to notice exceptions—one friend who texted, one teacher who checked in. This kind of flexible thinking helps youth see that thoughts and impulsive feelings are not always truths.

The final step is learning to replace unhelpful thoughts with ones that are more supportive and realistic. This is not about pretending everything is fine. It is about acknowledging difficulty while choosing thoughts that encourage effort and growth. Shifting from "I can't do this" to "This is hard, but I can keep trying" builds resilience over time. Another example might be a youth replacing "I always mess things up" with "I didn't handle this well, but I can learn from it."

When youth practice pausing, waiting, and reshaping their thinking, these skills begin to work together. With repetition and adult support, they become more natural—showing up in moments of stress, conflict, and decision-making. These internal processes form the foundation of healthy choices, giving young people the capacity to respond thoughtfully rather than react automatically.

RISE INVITATION

Healthy choices depend on capacity. This practice helps you notice what may be missing—and what to build before expecting a different choice. Think of a young person and a moment where choices often go sideways—impulse, shutdown, avoidance, or conflict. Which capacity seems most fragile in that moment?

Felt safety (waiting feels risky).
The pause (no space between feeling and doing).

Delayed gratification (immediate wins override future goals).
Do-overs (shame or stuckness after mistakes).

Which one needs the most support? Match your response to the need. You might create more predictability, teach and practice a pause, simplify waiting with clear structure, or offer a chance to try again without shame. Offer one steady sentence that keeps the pathway open.

"Pause first, then decide."
"You're safe—we can take this step by step."
"Want a do-over? I'll stay with you."

Healthy choices grow when capacity grows. Your steadiness is the bridge until theirs is ready.

Turning Thought into Action

Internal skills—pausing, waiting, and working with thoughts—prepare young people to make healthier choices on the inside. However, healthy choices do not stop there. They eventually move outward, into action. Decision-making becomes visible when youth begin to solve problems, weigh options, follow through, and reflect on the outcomes of their choices.

Healthy choices are not about finding the perfect answer. It is about learning how to move through decisions with curiosity, flexibility, and intention. For many young people—especially those who have experienced stress, instability, or repeated failure—even small decisions can feel overwhelming. Breaking challenges into clear, manageable steps restores a sense of agency and possibility.

Action Skill One: Naming Clearly

Every effective decision begins with understanding what is actually happening. When youth are supported in slowing down and naming the situation or decision clearly, they are more likely to move forward productively. This means identifying all the elements at hand. Often, youth jump straight to solutions without fully understanding the moving parts—or they react to the feeling without naming the situation. Adults can help by modeling curiosity rather than correction.

Adults can cultivate clarity by:

- Helping youth name the situation—"What's the hardest part right now?"
- Separating feelings from the situation itself.
- Inviting multiple perspectives without assigning blame.
- Slowing the process and exploring the situation more objectively.

Action Skill Two: Generating and Weighing Options

Once naming and externalization has occurred, creativity can emerge. Generating options teaches youth that there is rarely only one way forward. Brainstorming together sends a powerful message: "You don't have to solve this alone." This stage is not about choosing yet—it is about expanding thinking. Adults play an important role in keeping this space judgment-free so youth feel safe sharing ideas, even imperfect ones. After options are generated, youth can begin to evaluate them thoughtfully. This includes considering short-term and long-term impact, personal values, and how choices affect others.

Adults can cultivate discernment by:

- Encouraging multiple options before choosing.
- Asking guiding questions—"What might happen next?"
- "How does this align with what matters to you?"
- Helping youth consider both benefits and consequences.

- Avoiding rescuing or deciding for them too quickly.

This teaches youth that decisions are not just reactions—they are reflections of values and priorities.

Action Skill Three: Acting and Reflecting

Taking action requires courage. Once a decision is made, youth practice following through—testing their thinking in real life. But action alone is not the end of the process. Reflection is what turns experience into learning.

A middle school teacher noticed a student repeatedly shutting down during group projects. Instead of addressing the behavior in the moment, she invited the student to talk after class. Together, they named the problem: group work felt overwhelming and unsafe. They brainstormed options, including choosing a partner, having a clear role, or working independently with check-ins.

The student chose to try working with one peer he trusted. After the project, the teacher checked in again: "What worked? What was still hard? What would you do differently next time?" The choice was not perfect—but it was informative. Over time, the student learned that decisions could be adjusted, not judged.

Adults can cultivate reflective learning by:

- Normalizing that not every choice will work.
- Asking reflective questions after action—"What did you learn?"
- Separating outcomes from self-worth.
- Treating reflection as part of the decision, not a consequence.

Reflection teaches youth that choices are data—not verdicts.

Action Skill Four: Goal Setting, Staying the Course, and Pivoting

As youth become more comfortable making decisions, they begin to think more intentionally about the future. Goals provide direction, helping young people connect today's actions to tomorrow's possibilities. Healthy goal setting includes learning when to stay the course, when to adjust, and when to stop. Small goals build momentum. Larger goals build patience and persistence. Both matter.

Adults model this process constantly—when they set plans, adjust expectations, or name progress aloud.

Adults can cultivate future-oriented thinking by:

- Helping youth set small, achievable goals before larger ones.
- Naming progress, not just completion.
- Modeling flexibility, "This isn't working—let's adjust."
- Asking future-focused questions, "What do you want your future self to thank you for?"

In this way, problem solving and goal-setting work together. One helps youth navigate the challenges of today; the other helps them move forward with intention. Together, they transform healthy choices from isolated decisions into a way of living—one thoughtful step at a time.

RISE INVITATION

A quick, repeatable way to turn everyday decisions into learning moments—without rescuing. Choose a real, low-stakes decision a young person is facing or recently faced.

Guide them through four simple steps:

Name the decision and what they are feeling.
Generate a few options (including doing nothing).
Weigh what helps now and what matters later.
Choose one small next step.

Afterward, invite curiosity. What worked? What didn't—yet? What did you learn for next time? You might offer a steady reminder:

"We're not looking for perfect—we're learning."
"Choices are information, not judgment."
"Let's try it and adjust."

This is the practice—helping young people learn to name, choose, try, and grow.

Opportunities Are the Real Classroom

The strongest skills are not built through lectures, rules, or perfect explanations. They are shaped through real life—through moments of trying, stumbling, reflecting, and trying again. Youth learn best when they are given opportunities to practice making choices, and when those opportunities are met with guidance rather than judgment. Over time, each experience becomes a teacher, quietly shaping their understanding of responsibility, consequences, and personal agency.

Of course, this kind of learning must happen within a safe and supportive container. Youth need space to make decisions without facing harm that is too great or consequences that are irreversible. When adults intentionally create environments where mistakes lead to learning rather than shame, young people begin to trust the process. They discover what works, what doesn't, and—most importantly—why their choices matter.

One of the most important truths to hold is that there is no universal right choice. What is healthy for one young person may not be healthy for another. Context matters. Capacity matters. Values matter. Healthy choices are those that align with a young person's needs, goals, beliefs, and current capacity, while also considering the impact on the people around them. This understanding invites curiosity instead of control and reflection instead of rigid rules.

Adults can support this growth by asking questions that invite thinking rather than demand answers. Questions like, "What does your future self-need right now?" or "How might this choice affect the people you care about?" gently guide youth toward insight without taking ownership of the decision away from them. Every pause before reacting, every "let's think this through," every goal set and promise kept plants a seed. Some sprout quickly—like the first time a young person stops themselves before acting on impulse. Others grow slowly, taking root over years. Sometimes their impact is only revealed later, when a young adult stands at a crossroads and quietly remembers, I have done this before. I can choose with intention.

Healthy choices are not built in a single moment. They are formed through everyday decisions, repeated practice, and the growing belief that our actions shape our future. As youth learn to pause, think ahead, solve problems, and act with intention, they strengthen not only their decision-making skills, but also their sense of self. In this way, healthy choices plant lasting seeds of hope, direction, and agency.

Yet, decision-making does not exist in isolation. Our ability to choose well is deeply connected to the health of our minds, bodies, and spirits. When young people feel emotionally balanced, physically well, and spiritually grounded, they are better equipped to make choices that reflect their values and goals. Noticing this connection helps support resilience, growth, and the development of fully integrated, well individuals.

INTERLUDE

Stories from the Locker Room (15-18)

Stories from the locker room began shaping me as much as the stories and lessons that had already marked me. These are the stories of building armor—and learning that even the strongest shield leaves something exposed.

High school offered distance from middle school pain. New hallways. New hierarchies. New rules of survival. My parents were separating. The ground at home was unstable, so I walked into school determined to construct something solid.

Yet I had no true confidence. No steady sense of self. No identity that felt rooted. By now, I learned to compartmentalize. Nevertheless, I learned quickly that even the safest containers were fragile—transparent enough to allow protector parts to examine, breakable enough for exiles to fragment if exposed too much.

I worked hard to act like nothing personal mattered—while secretly tracking everything—trying to assemble the puzzle of my life, one edge piece at a time, while the insides were losing their place. I wanted to be mature. Controlled. Advanced beyond ordinary teenage vulnerability.

By then, I had mastered my parents' patterns. I could read their states like weather systems. I knew the hiding places. The tells. The shifts before impact.

My mom had stepped into a new world—relationships outside marriage. Letters to men afar. Journal entries naming people I knew. Consuming like a bucket with a slow leak—never empty, never full, never really contained.

My dad's construction company—the one he had given our lives to—began to collapse. What had been built on loyalty and family, dissolved into distrust. Recreational drug use became a daily ritual at job sites. Steady deterioration.

Little by little, the pride and identity he built eroded.

After a while, nothing surprised me.

Perhaps less like resilience and more like rehearsal. And I knew how to play the part. Here's what happens when you grow up studying your parents' secrets: perception sharpens, trust vanishes. Respect drains, and love loses.

Expectations felt like calculus—always solving for X, except X kept shifting.

When the divorce finally became official, after years of threats and weary negotiations, it altered the paperwork but not the pattern. They remained entangled—two addresses, one orbit.

I'd get calls when my mom was intoxicated, threatening to end her life. I knew they were still sleeping together, as if familiarity was the only language their bodies still trusted. They could despise each other and still reach across the dark.

I couldn't understand how your enemy could become your refuge, or why I was expected to manage the wreckage of their days while they collided again at night. Maybe it wasn't comfort that drew them back. Maybe it was momentum. Maybe it was the pull of something unfinished.

The divorce didn't heal anything. It didn't set anyone free. It only shifted the coordinates of the war.

Then came the disclosure about my dad's lab—another crisis slipped quietly onto my to-do list. My job to strategize. To minimize damage. To contain the fallout.

Without a consultant.

Loyalty wasn't optional. It was inherited. It was assumed.

Drugs. Accusations. Shifting alliances.

And somehow, in the middle of it all, I was still expected to play teenager.

As the fractures kept widening, my mom went to substance use counseling after her OWI. Part of the process was a family "input statement." She asked each of us to write how her addiction had shaped us.

I wrote pages. The kind of truth that makes your hand cramp, as if your body is trying to outrun the memories.

Her counselor chose me to join her. Me—an angry teenager, drafted into repair.

And yet, somewhere inside that anger lived an ache. Maybe there was room for amends. For something that might resemble a beginning.

I remember the feeling of the office. The windows at my back. The still air. The too-soft chair. The way the counselor's voice stayed calm, as if calm could make facts disappear. She told me how proud she was of my mom—the goals she was meeting, the progress she was making, the "monumental sobriety" she was achieving. And something in me raged. Because it felt like watching someone applaud a magic trick when I already knew where the rabbit was hidden.

So I told the truth.

Liquor bottles behind the washer. More tucked beneath the sink. Real beer poured into nonalcoholic cans. Afternoons passed out in a lawn chair, still chasing a tan. I said it matter-of-factly. Being empty of emotion was the only way I knew how to survive it.

My mom stood abruptly. Stormed out.

And I followed, stepping onto the sidewalk like stepping out of one life into another—suddenly a child again, back on a different sidewalk, in a different panic: the little girl left on the side of a highway. The same question rising up through my stomach and chest. Landing in my throat.

How am I getting home?

One night, after my mom slapped me during an argument, a friend asked why I stayed. "Because she's my mom," I said.

The next week her mother offered me a room in their home. I moved into the attic. Maybe the yellow brick road finally led me to Oz?

The house was quiet. Dinner at the table. Cookies baking. Family movies. And instead of comfort, I felt disoriented. My nervous system didn't know how to exist without scanning. Calm felt unnatural. Silence felt loud. My body searched for something to manage. Hyper-awareness had nowhere to go.

So I went back home. In that moment, I understood something clearly: Oz was only an illusion.

But at least home had Skyler. And with him, love was simple.

Trampoline nights while he finished homework. Couch cuddles. Doritos with melted cheese. Skipping school for brownie batter until our stomachs hurt. Sky was warmth when everything else ran cold. A little brother who let me practice being the mom. Protecting him gave me purpose. It gave me direction when everything else felt untethered.

His warmth held.

However, it was not intended to steady everything.

So, I found another kind. Other warmth—like heat from an electric blanket—came from structure and achievement, especially when so many of my other efforts felt exposed and weak.

It didn't love me back. But it kept me from freezing.

Volleyball. Basketball. Tennis. School. Work. Volunteering. Church. These were not just activities—they were anchors. Places where effort equaled outcome. Points tallied. Grades calculated. Paychecks earned.

Clear systems. Clear results.

They became my map—places I could go when the internal terrain felt impossible to navigate.

As high school dynamics settled into place, so did my inner critic. I built rules like fences around a house still under construction.

No sex until marriage.

No drinking.

No drugs.

If the lines were clear, maybe I could be.

Even when friends made different choices, I held my ground. I drove them home. I held their hair back. Sometimes I hosted—because in my house, boundaries were already blurred.

Adults and kids in the same rooms. Supervision and participation interchangeable. Our house was the "cool" house.

And through it all, I polished my halo—stern, certain, composed—without fully understanding what I was protecting. If I had a gift, it was vigilance. Staying alert while everyone else exhaled. Christianity hovered above me like a low ceiling. I judged choices I secretly envied.

I called rigidity strength, when it was often just fear in a pressed shirt. Fear kept me clothed. Layers of watchfulness. Constant scanning. Listening for the click of a secret about to surface.

I believed if I could see everything coming, nothing could take me down.

But achievement didn't teach me how to be loved.

It didn't teach me how to love.

For all my rules and vigilance, relationships still pulled me off center. I understood loyalty and abandonment. Enmeshment and cutoff. But I did not understand gentleness toward myself. I did not understand worth that wasn't earned.

And beneath all of it was still a girl who wanted what other girls seemed to receive without trying—to be chosen.

Desired. Seen. Loved.

But I didn't get to be soft.

Twiggy. Pepperoni face. Missing teeth. Frizzy hair.

Stern. Strong. Intense. Intimidating.

An underdeveloped girl standing tall in armor made of paper, hoping no one would notice all the creases. I was a sensitive, hopeless romantic raised on evidence that love destabilizes.So I told myself I didn't want it. Forced myself to believe it.

One Lent, I gave up mirrors. Forty days without reflection. I called it devotion. It was avoidance dressed as discipline. If I refused my own reflection, maybe I could outrun shame.

Junior year brought my first real experience of being desired. I had always been "one of the guys." Sleepovers with male friends weren't unusual in a home without guardrails. I wasn't read as feminine—I was safe. Neutral. So when a boy saw me differently, it felt new.

My first relationship was easy. Manageable. I played the role I had studied. Kissing. Labels. School dances. But I kept it shallow. Depth required risk. And risk felt like stepping off a ledge without checking the ground. When he developed feelings for someone else, I felt something close to relief. The ending made sense. The pattern held.

Rejection. Not enough. Alone.

But it didn't hurt. I had mastered this terrain. Protectors could repeat the pattern and keep the exiles tucked safely away.

I felt strong. My armor thicker.

Then the winds shifted.

The second relationship was a maze I had not memorized. Attraction felt real. Magnetic. Like standing too close to something electric.

I did not have language for the pull—only the panic humming beneath it. Wanting unsettled me. My rules strained.

Sex. Alcohol. Marijuana—lines I refused to cross.

But electricity doesn't care about lines. It only knows contact. I could not hold the contradiction. I wanted him. I wanted control. I wanted my compartments sealed. I needed to translate the chaos into something measurable.

So I wrote the story the only way I knew how: If I were enough, he would choose me. Change for me.

It was an old story. Older than him. Older than high school. A story that had been writing me for years.

Rejection. Not enough. Alone.

But this time it hurt. If I was being honest, the real fracture did not start with him. It began before memory.

It began when I was not held long enough to learn how to hold myself. When I was not mirrored clearly enough to recognize my own reflection. When you are made of so many voices, which one becomes your own? When each one swears, it is keeping you safe, which one do you follow home?

I pushed and pulled. Judged and yearned. Externalized blame. Internalized shame. My self-critic sparred without rest. There was one thing that would remain certain; no one was coming to save me.

Who was I? A fighter. A fawn. Water. Fire. Earth or Air.

Senior year forced the questions.

What do I value?

Who do I carry?

What stays? What goes?

I told myself it was temporary. We were all leaving. Nothing here was permanent.

That spring, I wrote about my childhood for the first time—handing it in as one of my final high school assignments. There was a part of me searching for agency. Searching for orientation as I said goodbye.

Two close friends told me I was selfish. That I was turning the lights on in a room everyone preferred to keep dark. That I would leave, but my mom would remain.

How ironic—to be asked to protect someone, who it felt like, never protected me. To long to be seen, and then feel the cost of visibility.

So I made a decision.

No reconciliation. No waiting for repair. No rewriting seventeen years in disappearing ink.

That summer, I experimented with alcohol. And I did it the only way I knew how: with structure. Limits. Conditions. Emotional rules. I would only drink when I felt steady. Never too much. Never too far.

I wanted youth. Freedom. Adventure.

But I feared inheritance—that addiction waited in my blood.

That summer, my friends and I drove to Georgia. Seven days of motion. State lines blurring. Windows down. Independence humming. We got tattoos. On my foot: Dream. I told myself I was charting a new map.

I had chosen my college. My career path—something I'd declared at nine. I believed I was building a way out. I didn't yet understand that distance is not the same as departure.

And leaving was never simple—not when the person I loved most was still standing in the wreckage.

Skyler. My dearest brother.

I had spent years trying to reroute him—steering him toward my aunt's house, away from the chaos that raised us. Before I left for college, I offered him $500 if he avoided drinking and drugs through high school.

He cried. He begged me not to go. He didn't understand the divorce. He wondered if he had caused it. My heart split open. In trying to protect him from the truth, I had left him alone with confusion. I told him it was not his fault. That he was loved. That he had never been the fracture.

The next day I tried to cancel college. The dorm deposit—$4,000—was non-refundable. So we negotiated: one year. I would come home on weekends. I would bring him to campus. If needed, I would move him up with me.

Before I left, I arranged for him to live with my aunt.

A week and a half into freshman year, my dad called. Hysterical. Fragmented. He said when people asked what to write on his headstone, I could say: RIP my daughter killed me. He said I had abandoned him. Taken his last anchor. He said he would end his life.

Panic flooded my body. I grabbed my keys, calculating distance against time, knowing I could not drive fast enough to out-run despair. I called my aunt. She sent my uncle. He was alive.

The next day, my brother said he was moving back home. He told me he would be fine. I felt like I had failed him. We promised to survive the year.

And we did—imperfectly. He visited sometimes. I returned as often as I could. Gradually, he grew into someone who did not need me the same way. I felt the thread of our shared identity stretch thinner. Quieter. Further.

Closing in on the end of that year, in an Intro to Social Work class, I wrote about my family again. My professor asked me to stay after. My body braced. Not again. But he said something different. He said I could write a resignation letter.

Resign from the roles.

Stop playing every part.

Lay down the script.

Release the shackles.

The idea felt impossible. Who was I without something to manage? Who was I without the responsibility of them? Over the next few weeks, I wrote the letter—never fully believing I could press submit.

How do you grieve what shaped you?

How do you loosen your grip on something that still exists?

How do you stay connected without being consumed?

That life had defined me. And I think I was terrified of what might remain if the roles no longer had to.

In the quiet that followed, I began to see it more clearly.

Beliefs had formed. Parts had performed.

Fragments had torn—into armor worn.

The Pleaser.

The Perfectionist.

The Responsible One.

The Analyzer.

The Strategist.

The Planner.

The Controller.

The Independent.

The Self-Critic.

They lean forward. They clear their throat.

They've kept these rules in a hidden note.
If we bend first, nothing will break.
If we soften our edges, nothing will shake.
Needing is messy. Just walk the line.
Carry ourselves carefully—we'll be just fine.
Check every box. Rise above.
Perfection earns safety. Precision earns love.
Hold every piece so nothing can fall.
Meet every need—and we'll matter to all.
Carry the light. It's ours to hold.
Keep it burning. Don't let them go cold.
Over function quietly. Patch every hole.
Protect them all. That is our role.
Study the tone. The timing. The pause.
Read every pattern. Memorize cause.
Plan how the story is likely to go.
Let them be stunned—"How did you know?"
Know our surroundings. Stay three steps ahead.
Rehearse the stories. Recall what they said.
Plan every outcome. Anticipate the hum.
When others hear silence, we hear what may come.
Calculate impact before we get hit.
Weigh every risk. Measure each bit.
Nothing is promised. Love is not free.
Better to map it, than beg it to be.
Have backup plans. Never lean too far.
Keep one hand on the exit, a key in the car.
If we manage the movement, we won't be undone.
Distance feels safer, than needing someone.
Don't trust people. Not completely.
Not even the ones who love us deeply.
Expect the fracture. Prepare for the end.
Certainty is an illusion—don't dare depend.
When it all fails—and sometimes it will—shame returns to take its fill.

It whispers low, "We're broken still." And names us as the one to kill.
But underneath the practiced pose, beneath the armor no one knows,
a quieter current slowly flows—a forgiving voice that gently grows.
A self not built from only fawn or fight.
A self not formed to brace for night.
A self that flickers faint but bright—not yet steady, but facing light.
She does not roar. She does not win. She does not silence all the din.
She only asks, beneath her skin, "What if love begins within?"
Not fearless in the open air, still scanning what is safe to share,
but wondering—perhaps aware—that strength and softness both live there.
At eighteen, standing at the door, uncertain what there is to explore.
The future folded in her hand, wanting to float with wind and land.
Not finished.
Not fixed.
Not finally known.
Just beginning to wonder, can she make the world her own?

RISE INVITATION

As you sit with these stories, notice what they stir in you. What parts of you learned to perform, bend, or protect in order to belong? Who did you become to stay connected?

Pause. Place a hand somewhere steady. Take a slow breath in—and a longer breath out.

Gently notice the beliefs and patterns you carry. What were they protecting? What were they afraid would happen if you let them go?

You don't need to change anything. Just notice. If it feels right, offer a quiet acknowledgment inward:

"Thank you for protecting me."
"You helped me survive."

"I am learning there may be another way."

Notice what softens. Notice what resists. This is the practice—curiosity, awareness, grace, self-love.

PART V: ENHANCEMENTS

The "E" and final part of the RISE framework is Enhancements—intentional experiences that sustain wellbeing across the lifespan. This element holds a special place for me because it reflects a powerful truth: we are whole people. We do not live in separate compartments of mind, body, and spirit; we live as an interconnected system.

Over time, I have come to understand that what supports one part of us inevitably influences the others. What strengthens the body affects the mind and spirit. What nourishes the mind shapes the body and spirit. What restores the spirit often brings clarity and steadiness to both mind and body. Caring for the whole self is not optional—it is essential.

Enhancements remind us that rising is not only about growth or repair, but about ongoing care. These practices deepen and sustain the impact of everything that comes before in the RISE framework, helping us remain grounded, aligned, and capable of showing up with clarity, presence, and purpose.

In this section, we explore three interwoven areas of care:

- **The Body:** Nurturing the physical vessel
- **The Mind:** Maturing thoughts, feelings, and beliefs
- **The Spirit:** Relating to higher energy

Together, these practices support wholeness and help us continue rising—within ourselves and alongside others—throughout life.

CHAPTER SIXTEEN

Enhancing the Whole Person

Wellbeing is something we nurture every day. These practices help us stay grounded, resourced, and present, even when life feels busy or stressful. Enhancements are not a separate layer added onto the framework; they move through every part of it. They are what allow safety to settle in the body, awareness to deepen in the mind, and meaning to remain alive in the spirit. Through these practices, relationships endure, skills integrate, and purpose continues to unfold. Enhancements are not something extra—they are the fuel that keeps wellbeing alive.

The Body: Nurturing the Physical Vessel

Our bodies are our constant companions. They carry us through the world, store our experiences, and communicate our needs long before our words do. The body houses the nervous system—the foundation of regulation, safety, and capacity. It tells us when we are overwhelmed, exhausted, hungry, overstimulated, or in need of care. Caring for the body is intertwined with emotional and relational health, shaping how we experience each. When the body feels unsafe or depleted, the mind struggles to think clearly and the spirit struggles to stay open.

Supporting the body does not require perfection. It requires consistency. Sleep, nourishment, hydration, movement, rhythm, and predictability help regulate the nervous system and expand our window of tolerance. These practices allow the body to move out of survival mode and into a state where growth and connection are possible.

For adults, tending to the body may look like prioritizing rest, eating nourishing meals, getting regular movement, or noticing early signs of stress before they escalate. These moments of care are acts of self-respect. When the body is supported, we are often more patient, emotionally available, and present with others.

For youth, physical care is often the most immediate pathway to regulation. A skipped meal, poor sleep, sensory overload, busy schedules, intense environments, or lack of movement can make the world feel unbearable. Helping children notice body cues and responding with structure, rhythm, and compassion builds regulation from the ground up. Predictable routines and basic physical care create safety the nervous system can trust.

The body is where regulation begins. When we care for it well, we increase our capacity to engage, reflect, and relate.

The Mind: Maturing Thoughts, Feelings, and Beliefs

The mind is the place where experiences are interpreted, meaning is made, and stories are formed about who we are and how the world works. It includes our thoughts, emotions, beliefs, assumptions, and expectations. Neuroscience reminds us that the brain is not fixed. Through neuroplasticity, it continues forming and reshaping pathways throughout our lives. This means learning, healing, and change are always possible.

Honoring the mind means treating it as something to be nurtured and matured as we develop, not just managed or controlled. It invites awareness of thoughts and feelings, flexibility in thinking, and the ability to pause before responding. The words we offer ourselves matter—quiet mantras, gentle reminders, and compassionate self-talk can soothe the nervous system and anchor the heart. Through reflection and mindfulness, we learn to notice patterns, soften unhelpful beliefs, and respond with intention rather than reaction.

For adults, caring for the mind may involve journaling, therapy, daily affirmation cards, or simply pausing to reflect at the end of the day: "What shaped my reactions today? What story was I telling myself?" These practices support insight, emotional literacy, and growth.

For youth, the mind develops through curiosity, play, questions, and guided reflection. When children ask big questions—"Why did that happen? What does this mean?"—they are practicing meaning making. When adults respond with curiosity instead of correction, children learn that their mind is safe to explore.

A well-supported mind becomes more flexible, reflective, and resilient. It learns not only how to think, but how to think about thinking. This reflective capacity invites a more philosophical way of being, where inherited societal structures, conditioned beliefs, and internalized expectations are gently questioned and explored. In doing so, the mind becomes a place of discernment rather than compliance.

The Spirit: Connecting to Higher Energy

The spirit is the part of us that reaches beyond the individual self. It reflects our relationship to higher energy—something larger than what can be named or contained. Whether understood as God, the universe, Buddha, nature, Brahma, humanity, Allah, love, Ra, or a shared life force, spirit is felt more than explained. It is not something we analyze or define, but something we sense, experience, and embody.

Spirituality is about alignment. It is the felt sense of belonging to something larger, of being part of a wider whole. While the mind asks, "What could this mean?" the spirit asks, "What are the elements I am connected to?" Connection to higher energy often shows up as a sense of peace, purpose, reverence, or inner steadiness. It is what helps us orient toward meaning when life feels uncertain and stay anchored when circumstances are beyond our control. Spiritual connection does not remove pain, but it can help us hold pain without losing ourselves.

For adults, nurturing the spirit may involve prayer, meditation, ritual, time in nature, service, or moments of intentional stillness. These practices quiet the ego and invite connection beyond the immediate moment, reminding us that we are not alone in our experience.

For youth, spiritual connection often emerges naturally—through inquisitiveness about life, questions about existence, a sense of wonder about the natural world, or participation in meaningful traditions. Supporting spiritual development does not require answers; it requires space. When children are allowed to wonder, reflect, and connect, they develop an internal sense of grounding that transcends circumstance.

When we honor the spirit, we nurture the soul with flowing energy. We remember that wellbeing is about alignment and being part of something greater than ourselves.

RISE INVITATION

Resilience grows through intentional moments of alignment—body, mind and spirit. Choose one practice.

Move or care for your body.
Notice or reframe a thought.
Connect to something that brings stillness or meaning.

Invite curiosity. What is your body feeling right now—and what does it need? What thoughts or feelings are present—and are they helping? What helps you feel calm, connected, or most like yourself?

This is the practice—learning to notice and align your whole self, so you can show up with greater presence and support others in doing the same.

The Interconnection of Body, Mind, and Spirit

Although we explore the body, mind, and spirit individually, lived experience does not happen in fragments. It happens as a whole. These systems are not separate; they influence one another constantly. When the body is depleted, the mind grows foggy and the spirit can feel distant. When the mind is overwhelmed, the body carries tension and the spirit may lose its sense of meaning. When the spirit feels disconnected, both body and mind often follow. Yet when we tend to one area with intention, the others often respond with more energy, clarity, and steadiness.

What restores the body can settle the mind and soften the spirit. What nourishes the spirit may calm the nervous system and bring clarity to our thinking. What engages the mind can energize the body and offer meaning to the spirit.

Healing is rarely linear—it is layered, relational, and deeply interconnected. Like the roots, trunk, and branches of a tree, the body, mind, and spirit work together to create strength, balance, and growth. When one part is neglected, the whole system feels it. When we live in ways that support the whole self, resilience becomes less about endurance and more about alignment. Enhancements are meant to be lived. They unfold through the ordinary rhythms of daily life—resting, moving, disconnecting from screens, reflecting, creating, and connecting.

Today's environments are often shaped by constant digital input. While technology offers connection and convenience, too much or unintentional use can quietly impact sleep, mood, attention, and overall wellbeing. Creating space for screen-free moments allows the mind and body to reset and return to a more regulated, grounded state. For youth especially, these moments of disconnection are not about restriction, but about restoring balance in a world that rarely slows down on its own.

A quiet walk outdoors may release tension in the body, settle the mind, and restore a sense of peace. A meaningful conversation can lift mood, shift perspective, and renew a sense of belonging. These are whole-person experiences, and their power lies in intention rather than intensity.

When such moments are normalized and woven into daily routines, they quietly support wellbeing over time. This is especially true for youth. And remember, language matters. Rather than labeling an activity as "exercise," we might say, "Let's do something that helps our body feel strong and our mind feel clear." These subtle shifts reinforce wholeness and choice rather than compliance.

Practices such as rest, mindfulness, movement, nourishing food, sleep, gratitude, journaling, time in nature, creativity, meaningful connection, and acts of compassion may seem simple. Yet practiced consistently, they become the scaffolding that supports resilience—steady, accessible, and sustainable. And these practices are not only for youth. When adults tend to their own body, mind, and spirit, they do more than show up healthier—they model what whole-person wellbeing looks like. In homes, programs, and communities, small, repeated practices slowly build cultures of care.

A subtle but powerful shift occurs when we move from self-care to care of self. Care of self is not a reward or an escape. It is a responsibility to our wholeness. It grounds wellbeing in what is essential and accessible—nutrition, rest, movement, connection, and meaning. It is not something we save for moments of stress; it is something we build into the rhythm of daily life.

When we prioritize care of self, we model alignment. We show youth that their needs matter, that balance is strength, and that tending to oneself is not indulgent—it is essential. Resilience is not built in extraordinary moments. It is grown in ordinary ones, repeated with intention.

RISE INVITATION

Think of a recent moment that felt difficult or draining. What was happening in your body, mind, and spirit? Simply notice—there are no right answers.

When my body felt ______, my mind ______.
When my mind felt ______, my body ______.
When my spirit felt ______, it affected how I ______.

What is one thing that might help right now? It could be a pause, movement, rest, a kind thought, time outside, or connection.

With youth, this might sound like: "What would help your body feel a little better?" or "What helps you feel more whole?"

This is the practice—notice, connect, and respond with care. Over time, small shifts restore alignment. Resilience grows not from pushing harder, but from returning to balance—again and again, in ordinary moments.

INTERLUDE

Stories from Flying Free (19+)

Freshman year of college had felt like the first time the ground held. Not perfectly. Not without cracks. But it held. Stability began to take shape in small, ordinary ways. A roommate who felt like a sister—a journal keeper, a witness to stories whispered in the depths of the night. Friendships that felt wholehearted. Rhythms that grew predictable.

Employment that reflected something back to me—leadership, influence, capability.

I was not perfect. Made mistakes. Learning. Growing. Changing.

Values explored and rearranged themselves. Identity began to soften and mold. For the first time, it felt like I was building something instead of bracing.

The summer after my first year in undergrad, I boarded my first plane. Germany bound. Three months. Coworkers I did not know. Camp Adventure—a chance to travel and work with them funding the dream.

I wanted to discover. To stretch. To find myself.

And yet there is something disorienting about being far from everything familiar while simultaneously building a container for new experiences. You are both untethered and expanding.

One weekend, I visited the army base where my mom and dad had met. An ordinary place with extraordinary consequences. I walked those streets imagining two young people in grown-up shoes. Secrets. Betrayals. Fire disguised as love. I wondered how two people could intertwine so tightly in pain—embers transferring to their children. How different could the course have been? What small turn would have altered everything? I wondered what it would take for burns that old to heal.

Coming home from Germany felt stranger than leaving. The house had changed. The roommates had expanded. The rhythm had moved on without me. I wanted everything to feel like freshman year again—secure, predictable, contained. Instead, I felt disoriented.

So I did what I knew how to do. I dove into school. Picked up more shifts. Mapped out goals. Focused on the horizon. If I could just keep moving, maybe the ground wouldn't shift.

Then that winter, I met him. A big smile. Kindness that felt engaged and present. A calm that didn't ask anything from me. I kissed him for a beer and walked home while others crawled toward the bar. A text came in asking me to come back out. But I didn't. Instead, I fell asleep, wanting to be alone.

The next day, he offered to come help clean up after a party. No edge. No "I owe you." No transaction.

Something foreign. Something new. Dating and friendship—an ease that did not erode. He reminded me of the humor only the Three Amigos knew. Familiar. Genuine. True.

So when early summer arrived and deployment papers landed in his hands, the universe seemed to pause and look at me.

Semper fidelis. I had learned that phrase long ago. The role was not foreign. The fear was not either. Fear of loss. Fear of goodbye. Fear of a future I could not control.

However, there was another option.

Say yes. Grow up fast. Sign on a line you once swore you never would. Security. Belonging. A love that felt steady and safe. A role that felt purposeful. Special. One designed for me. The self-critic reminding me—this might be your one shot, remember, "You are impossible to love."

Yet here he was.

At the altar in college, at twenty years old. I knew my place. A future I could unfold. Predictably in my hands.

The next year was quiet.

Work. Graduate early. Care packages and daily letters.

When Eli returned stateside, life began assembling itself like a checklist: Careers. Friends. A Dog. Our first home. The perfect cake rising in the oven.

And in the middle of all that—my brother was struggling. In ways, I could not fix.

To feel your heart walking outside of your body—that is what it was like. To love someone and not be able to alter the outcome. To watch innocence erode in someone who once ran to you before every choice.

An anxiety settled into my bones. The wicked witch returned in my dreams.

When the criminal charges settled, he moved in with Eli and I. We tried to recreate childhood rhythms. Familiar warmth. Shared laughter. But we were different now. Years had happened between us. Experiences that did not intertwine. Demons that did not speak the same language.

One night, intoxicated, he broke.

Sobbing in my arms. Confessing trauma. Fear. Confusion. Pain.

To look into the eyes of a child you tried to save and realize the oxygen you were offering was laced—poisonous from the start—is a particular kind of devastation.

Nature consumes. My nurture was not enough. I was not them. A little boy inside him needed his parents to be better, do better. He told me he was fine. That time would pass and heal old wounds. But in that moment, I knew. Their storm had darkened the one childhood light that had guided my life.

So I did what I knew how to do best, immerse myself into doing. A tangible that warmed me. Full-time work. Full-time graduate school at night. Eli on third shift. Weekends filled with studying, family and friends. Peanut and Bubba. Being their aunt gave me purpose. Surrounding them with love felt natural—unconsciously trying to rewrite something.

Then we chose to foster.

A pattern retelling. Offering others something, I was still mourning not having myself.

Soon after came pregnancy. Blossoming into the next stage.

Married. House. Master's degree. Stability. Predictability. Control in every corner.

Pregnancy was the greatest feeling I had ever known. To carry someone constantly. To rub and sing and whisper. To hold an embrace I had never received. For forty weeks, I was never alone.

Then Micah arrived.

And no book, no class, no preparation could teach you how to hold your own heart outside your body and call it your son. We came home and pretended we knew what we were doing.

He had his own preferences. His own rhythm. His own will. We were along for the ride.

Three weeks later, Eli went back to work. Days in, I got the call. "He's being transported to the hospital. Come to Des Moines." First trip out of the house. Micah crying in the backseat. Eli in surgery.

No one prepares you for the sound that reaches into preverbal memory. The cry that bypasses logic and lands in your nervous system like a siren. Parked on the side of the road, holding our son, I wondered: How do you move forward and stay still at the same time?

Loneliness quietly started to seep in. Old wounds unsealed.

Eli came home injured. Taking care of a newborn and a recovering husband—I had to have strength for this. But in the minutes alone on the bathroom floor, I cried. Wondering why this felt familiar.

Two months into Micah's life, sitting in the ER for Eli's persisting injuries, my sister called. "Come now. Something bad happened." And thirty minutes stretched into a lifetime.

Cop cars. Neighbors gathering. My sister running toward me. There had been an accident. Highway construction. Brake lights. A woman who did not see. My brother-in-law and Skyler were gone.

The next 48 hours blurred.

I held Micah while shapeshifting into management mode. Drove to the hospital. Notified family. Stood over my brother's body while others watched. As if I could squeeze life back into him. As if we were just lying on the couch again, brownie mix on our fingers.

To bring life into the world while saying goodbye to the first person who gave you your name. Parts of me hardened. Parts of me broke.

My sister and kids moved into our home. Mom was haunted by ghosts. Dad, drowning.

And me—obsessed with being the perfect mother.

If the locker room had given me rigid rules to survive, motherhood handed me commandments to crucify myself with. I could not fail this. I would not fail him.

We moved back to Martelle to be closer to family. To be a sanctuary. Even for those whose sins made me bleed. I told myself it was about proximity. About support. About giving Micah cousins and grandparents and open fields to run in. But if I am honest, it was also about proximity to the wound. Staying close enough to monitor it. To manage it. To make sure nothing else exploded without me knowing.

But I should have known by now, just because you can see the storm doesn't mean you can stop it.

The phone rang. My dad was hysterical.

Third OWI. Sitting in the car. Police behind him. He needed me to fix it.

My body moved before my mind could think. Keys. Purse. Out the door. Planning. Plotting. Strategizing. Heart pounding. Urgency in my fumes.

I was already halfway there when I realized what I was doing. I was performing a role I had carried since childhood —the stabilizer, the rescuer, the one who fixes chaos. The one who fights the storm. But I had a baby at home. A husband. A life I had built.

I pulled the car over. My hands were shaking. For the first time, a different thought surfaced:

I can't save him.

With tears in my eyes, I turned the car around.

I realized trauma was not gone. It was only waiting for the right cues.

Dad went to inpatient rehab to avoid prison. Across state lines, I let myself believe this would be the pivot point. The moment insight would bloom. We talked on the phone. His voice steadier now. Reflective. "I know life was tough," he said. "But you made it out, you've done good kid."

And just like that, I was fifteen again in that counselor's office.

As if my survival had been a choice.

As if resilience meant the past no longer mattered.

As if the life I built had nothing to do with what I endured.

Gratitude instead of grief. Achievement instead of acknowledgment.

As if love had fueled my outcomes.

Not hypervigilance.

Not fear.

Not the constant drive to outrun becoming them. I hung up feeling incred-

ibly invisible.

By March 2020, the world was unraveling.

My grandpa called and asked me to come over. There was something in his voice. I called my sister and said, "Something's wrong." We walked into the house together. And there he was.

My dad on the floor. Incoherent. Years of flirting with death finally demanding attention. Admitted to the ICU. The doctors said what we all already knew.

If he drinks again, he will die.

Break or bend.

It is a strange thing to watch your parent stand at the edge of their own life and still hesitate. Three children alive. Grandchildren growing. Yet the pull toward grief felt stronger than the pull toward life.

I sat in reflection and felt two truths at once: I did not want him to die. And I was exhausted from trying to keep them alive.

Later that year, my sister said she wanted to find her father. She searched records. Made calls. Followed paper trails. Then one day—a letter. Then a phone call.

And suddenly it was real. Flights booked. Suitcases zipped. Hope palpable.

I watched her get ready the first night we were there. Curling her hair. Putting on makeup with hands that trembled just slightly. A little girl inside a grown woman waiting to be claimed.

For days, I watched her be seen, loved, accepted. They laughed. They hugged. Asked about her life. Looked at her as if she was one of theirs.

She fit.

I was so happy for her. And I was jealous in a way that exhausted me. The next day, back at the Airbnb, while they went to explore, I sat with feelings that were complex. I had lost something long ago that she was just beginning to find. I wanted a new beginning too.

Years continued to unfold. Stories remembered. Some never told.

Time moving whether we were ready or not.

Rhythms change. Patterns remain. So much the same. So much yet to name.

After Skyler passed, I tattooed butterflies on my foot.

"Fly Free."

It felt important to mark my body with something that meant release. I imagined him somewhere light. Air surrounding him. Joy without weight. No shame. No demons. No nights drowning in his own mind.

Just freedom.

When I look into the bluest sky, I feel him. In the warmth of the sun on my face. In the way the kids laugh. In the stillness right before sleep.

And at 38, when I wake multiple times in the night—heart racing for no visible reason—I imagine he knows a peace I am still learning to access. In so many ways, RISE was created for him. For kids like him. For kids like me.

He was the first person who saw my light and said, "Go. Shine it bright."

He was also the first to see my darkness. To sit with me in it. To love me despite it.

Healing has not been linear. It is a spiraled, rutted, often muddy dirt road.

On good days, trauma has made me resilient.

Capable. Compassionate. Courageous. Calm. Connected.

On hard days, trauma is panic.

Survival. Doing. Managing. Controlling. Shaming. A quiet wondering if true rest only comes the way it came for him.

However, when I wake in the morning and see the sun break through the horizon—I remember—I can rise.

And when I lay down at night, daring to dream in a body that has carried so much, I rub my feet together—feel the butterflies etched there, and remind myself—I can fly free.

EPILOGUE

When we began this journey through the RISE framework, the invitation was simple—and profound—to see ourselves not only as adults and caregivers, but also as co-learners. As people willing to walk alongside young people as they make sense of their experiences, cultivate wellness, build emotional intelligence, and discover their own capacity for growth.

That vision is rooted in my own unfolding—the highs and heartbreaks of my own healing and years of showing up with children and youth through both the ordinary and the unbearable. Through honoring my own story and witnessing so many others, one truth has surfaced again and again: what matters most is not perfection, but presence.

RISE was born in those moments.

It is not a checklist.

It is not a rigid model.

It is a way of being—of noticing, reflecting, and connecting—that honors what children truly need from the adults around them.

More than tools or strategies, my hope is that this work offers you permission.

Permission to pause.

Permission to reflect.

Permission to reconnect with your own values and humanity as you care for others.

Because when we model wellness and resilience, we are doing more than supporting youth—we are showing them what is possible. And in that process, we allow ourselves to lean into what sustains us, too.

Throughout the RISE framework, each part unfolds with care—because resilience is not built in a single moment or mastered through one skill. It grows through layers of experience, shaped slowly and relationally, over time.

Relationships are where resilience first takes root. Through everyday moments with caring adults—through shared experiences, reflective practices like the You Intervention, and the steady presence of intentional characteristics—young people learn what it feels like to be truly seen. Relationships calm the nervous system, offer mirrors for identity, and create a safe place from which growth feels possible.

From that foundation, RISE turns toward Indicators of Wellbeing, gently naming the conditions that help young people flourish. When the body feels safe, when connection is present, when identity holds meaning, and when action builds a sense of efficacy, youth are supported not just to endure—but to thrive. These conditions quietly answer an essential question: What needs to be true around a young person so growth can begin?

As those conditions settle in, the work naturally moves inward, into Social and Emotional Development. This is not a new idea layered on top, but the living expression of everything that came before. Here, young people learn how to live well inside supportive conditions—how to regulate their inner world, understand themselves and others, make thoughtful choices, and move through relationships with greater compassion and care.

And finally, RISE invites us into Enhancements, where resilience becomes integrated and lasting. Enhancements tend to the whole person—body, mind, and spirit—offering practices that help restore balance, deepen wholeness, and support integration.

Together, these elements form a living continuum. Not a formula to follow, but a rhythm to return to. Growth does not happen in isolation, or all at once.

Research tells us that happiness and life satisfaction often rise following periods of challenge. This does not mean we seek suffering. But it does remind us that healing rarely happens by going around hard things. Growth happens through them.

We do not need to shield young people from every struggle. What they need most is support to make meaning of their experiences, to walk through difficulty with connection, and to discover strength they did not yet know they had.

If there is one truth I hope you carry with you, it is this: You matter deeply in the lives of young people—not because you have all the answers, but because you show up.

You notice.

You reflect.

You repair.

You stay connected, even when it is hard.

You will not always get it right. None of us do.

But you do not need to be perfect.

You need to be present.

You need to be real.

And you need to stay anchored in the very things we know help youth feel seen.

I invite you to return to this framework—not as a rulebook, but as a reminder. A reminder of what nourishes you. A guide for how to support those who matter most.

Resilience begins in relationships.

It deepens through reflection.

Start there. Return often.

And trust that each day offers a new opportunity to rise—together, and within yourself.

I often return to a story from the movie Moana (Clements & Musker, 2016). I had seen it countless times. I had two toddlers then, and on a cold winter day, we were curled up watching it again. But that day, something shifted. For the first time, I truly saw the story. It moved me to tears—the kind that arrive without warning and refuse to be contained.

In the film, Moana realizes that Te Kā—the terrifying lava monster destroying everything in her path—is actually Te Fiti, the Mother Island. Te Kā is not evil. She is enraged, in pain, and protecting what remains after her heart has been stolen.

There is a moment when Moana, holding the stolen heart, turns to the ocean and says, "Let her come to me."

The water parts. Moana walks forward—calm, steady, grounded—and sings words that still give me chills:

They have stolen the heart from inside you.

But this does not define you.

This is not who you are.

You know who you are.

Who you truly are.

Moana does not fight. She does not flee. She stays open. She stays present.

And when Te Kā reaches her, full of wrath, she notices that Moana sees her, truly sees her. With her eyes closed, Moana and Te Kā connect, and Moana gently restores the heart. The rage dissolves. The lava cools. And what remains is Te Fiti—whole, beautiful, and radiant. She was never gone. She was simply alone and lost.

Watching that scene, I realized how often life steals pieces of us. Adversity can take our sense of safety, our identity, our hope. It can make us guarded, reactive, or withdrawn.

But then—there are the Moana's of the world.

The people who come alongside us. Who see us when we cannot see ourselves. Who reflect our worth back to us, moment by moment, until we remember who we truly are.

That is the opportunity we are given every single day with the children in our lives.

To come alongside them.

To walk toward, not away.

To shine light back on them.

To remind them of the goodness and wholeness already within.

That is sacred work.

It is beautiful. It is powerful. And you make it possible.

Thank you for taking this journey with me.

Go Forth. Be a Moana.

AFTERWORD

I want to take a moment—at the end of these pages—to acknowledge the stories held here. In trying to help the reader understand how adversity shapes a child, many of these chapters lean toward the hard. Toward the moments that bruised and bent me. Those memories are mine. They live in my body the way I remember them.

But memory is a living thing. It is shaped by the eyes that saw it, the nervous system that carried it, the meaning a child had to make in order to survive it.

I know my parents and my siblings hold their own versions of these years. Their memories may be different. Softer in places. Sharper in others. I want to honor that. This book tells my story—not the whole story.

And even within my own remembering, there was more than pain.

There was joy.

There was a long drive to California to see Grandpa—the hum of tires on pavement, log cabins, pools, desert air stretching wide around us. Adventure woven with belonging.

There were days outside—tubing on the water, dirt on our legs, sun on our shoulders. Martelle summers. T-ball games. Church projects. Grandma Alta's annual clean-up day where everyone had a job. Holidays at Grandma Barb's, thick with tradition and familiar smells.

Dad—I remember driving home from camping with you. AC/DC blasting through the speakers. You let me stick my head out the window, wind tangling my hair. For a moment, nothing was complicated. I felt wild. Alive. Free.

Mom—you kept the house so clean and organized. A special Sunday night pot roast. The sound of dishes settling after dinner. You brushing my hair. Cleaning my ears. Riding in the car while you sang country music, your voice filling the space like something sacred. I was in awe of you. You felt magical to me. Like someone, I wanted to become when I was big.

Dad, you would give the shirt off your back to a stranger. You talked to everyone. Your laughter filled rooms. Your energy draws people in like warmth on a cold day. You have a work ethic that helped push my own passions to deep purpose.

Mom, you give and give and give—cleaning homes, caring for the elderly, feeding students, tending to whoever needed you. Your nurturing heart shaped mine more than you may ever know.

You both have supported me in countless ways. Sports. Taking me to friends. Moving me. Laundry. Construction. Repairs.

I have said it before, and I will say it again and again—I know, deep in my bones, that you both did the very best you could with what you knew and what you had.

That is the complicated inheritance of generational trauma.

When I look at you now, I do not just see my parents. I see two children once longing for love and steadiness themselves. I see young adults trying to build something without ever having been shown how to shape it safely. I see patterns that were handed down long before they ever reached our front door.

I know you carried your own bruises.

I know some of what shaped you was never your choice.

And I have watched you grow. I have watched stability take root. I have watched settling unfold in quiet, courageous ways over these last several years. I am endlessly grateful for the partners beside you now—for the love and connection, you both deserve. I see you working hard to be loving grandparents.

As you move into the seasons of your lives, I hope you look back and see your story met with grace. Not denial. Not shame. Grace. I hope you see your resilience. Your survival. Your humanity.

It has never gone unnoticed.

And I know I was not always easy to raise. I felt a lot. I could be a lot. I carried sharp edges, anger, and judgment like armor. I said things that were fueled by hurt and know that I caused pain in return. For the ways I added weight to what was already heavy—I am sorry.

Thank you for being my parents.

I love you, for being you.

I always will.

Xoxo,

Tawny/Butterfly

POSTSCRIPT: POETRY FROM THE JOURNEY

Every journey leaves behind both wounds and teachings. These poems are pieces gathered along the way—from places of struggle, moments of reckoning, and quiet glimpses of hope. They carry the echoes of what it means to be human: the longing for safety when life feels uncertain, the ache for connection and belonging, the search for meaning and purpose, and the courage it takes to reclaim one's own sense of agency.

Each poem is both deeply personal and quietly universal. They are an invitation to pause, to feel, and to remember that healing is not linear—it is layered, lived, and unfolding. Just as RISE reminds us that resilience is cultivated through relationships and intentional care, these poems offer another truth: that expression, too, can hold us, guide us, and become a companion along the healing journey. As you move through these pages, consider your own forms of expression.

Where do your thoughts go when they need somewhere to land? What helps you release what feels too heavy to carry alone? In what ways do you give shape to what lives inside your heart? When you put words or images to your experience, what begins to shift? There is no right way to express what is within you—only the invitation to begin.

A Tortured Soul

Made in this world, but not of this world
The mysteries of me
What you cannot see

Born out of chaos and pain
Centuries in the making, unresolved disdain
You witness strength and fire
But below the shields is a craving to rewire

Always making the decisions and in control
Desiring to fly free, not shackled and responsible to everyone else's coal
Drunk on my loyalty and care
Can't you see your hold is stripping me bare

You long for my energy, passion and force
But only until you can dominate and conquer my course
Fleeting affection, not loving all my parts
Never to the extent of nurturing my heart

Not wanting to set fire to give me life
While covering yourself in my ashes, hydrating from my blood on your knife
Don't exploit my vulnerabilities
Don't love the wisdom but reject the instabilities

Suffering in the darkness
Pushing down, executing numbness
Compassionate, kind, strategic in the light
Hidden in the shadows, the devil in flight

It is why I can never be the one
The high from the battle leaves you blind to my hidden gun
Fibers of the self, lonely and fading
A ghost of myself slowly cascading
See me, save me, not because it's what I need
But because this tortured soul has an endless healing bleed
Floating is the dichotomy of me
Made of earth and air, when will I be able to flee

What you choose to see compared to what I fully am
Both a wolf and a lamb

Knowing I need a dominant and a submissive
Knowing my gray is the recipe of command, curiosity and permissive

Not fitting in the structures of the invisible box
Morphed by experiences to live as a fox
You can't know what I need
If I am the one who is always in the lead

Don't just see what you want to believe
Choose to see the parts of me that grieve
Invisible while wearing a crown
Behind the smile lives an intuitive frown

Watch my embers slowly fade
Never really understanding the price I paid
By all standards I made it through
Achieved, accomplished, took off and flew

Did everything they said I couldn't
Designed the life they said I wouldn't
With armor of resilience
A story of perseverance

Knowing all I needed to do
A checkmate to win this battle with you
Yet this still remains a tortured souls plea
Tell me, in another lifetime who would I be

Hush Little Monster

This is a bedtime story just for you
Some sing their little ones lullabies but honey that's not for you

Hush little baby what you crying about
Your ass is staying in that crib so don't fuss or pout
What? You need a mom or dad
Don't waste your time wishing that's what you had

Little girl shut up before I whoop your butt
If you don't stop I'll throw you out on the highway like a mutt
Scared? Go tell someone who cares
Speak on our skeletons? No one dares

You're too much, you needy thing,
Hush hush now you need to be unseen
Make yourself small
Not talking about the opposite of tall

Don't ever think you have the key
That you are special or meant to be
Don't put pride on your name
Be grateful we've given you all that shame

Oh you whiny thing why are you here
Get out of my face, act like I care
Gone for days and don't leave a trace
Geeze, keep yourself up to pace

Hope is only an unwanted prayer
It's better to prepare to be the dragon slayer

Funny how all this starts to manifest
Not so perfect on your quest
Attention and validation whore
Honestly give it enough time they'll think you're a bore

Do you really know why they call you a tease
Hunny because it's best if you stay on your knees
There is no making love to someone like you
That's made for wifeys or someone pretty and new

You think someone special will stick by someone like you
That's the delusional borderline coming through

Put success in a box
Made you sly as a fox
Well whatever you think you've achieved
Jokes on you

It'll never be enough
To really break through

You worked so hard not to be like us
Prayed, did good, gave it all a fuss
You hear that epigenetic voice
Act like you really even had a choice

Deep inside you're empty and blue
All this pain that should be at us is actually spent with you
Hating you
All that energy we give is making you do

Caretake, responsible, strategic and bold
I'll continue to remind you the imposter syndrome you hold
Be invisible because you're not a star
Whether we are near or far

Your fate was determined when we laid eyes on you
We'd make you our puppet, never telling you anything true
We had all those secrets we knew you found out
You saw the chaos, pain, addiction and doubt

Don't worry we know you're not angry with us
We have you so busy blaming yourself
It left you longing for meaning
But we're bored over here feening

Don't dream of a world where maybe you can matter
It's not in this lifetime or the latter
funny funny little girl you're so naive
Because that will never be your truth, don't let yourself believe

You were born to a world where we couldn't even name you
You weren't the gender we were going for, shit what do we do

Parentify this inconvenience, make it have purpose
Otherwise you really are just worthless
You say you feel proud don't have room for that around
The gifts in you, you think you really found

You do big things, that actually makes you a traitor and snot
It's really annoying your perseverance and how hard you have fought
Act like you're better because you have a degree
Bought a house, made a life and created a family

Don't you know that doesn't mean shit with your history
Go to therapy, process it all and we'll still be your one mystery
Oh wait, you have a surprise, you want to show us love
Little one that's an inconvenience when that blunt has us flying high like a dove

That's the thing you always tried too hard
No matter what you did we had you barred
So you went on your journey of achieving it all
You sought out to do
Checked them boxes
Turned old into new
Nothing more to check, now what do you do?

Jokes on you when you thought you could be better than us
Again, why am I repeating myself, stop making a fuss
Immerse yourself as a mom no identity for you
Soon you'll realize those kids will also abandon you too

Shackled to our pain our story runs through
Can't escape the old for the new
Do that SEL shit to make it alright
But here we are still haunting you at night

Oh yes that's right we see you on TV
Don't worry we didn't watch, but just proud as can be
Think you made it big commanding that stage
Little girl we'll just keep turning the page

People only tell you what they think you need to hear
The reality is no one will keep you near
Popular on socials, add it to your cart
Bitch you know you were nothing from the start

Come up with those rules you really think that will help?
Shhh, hold you down no one can hear you yelp
Be a good little girl see if we care
Turns out, good or bad you're invisible here

Doesn't it feel good to hurt that bad
You'll need that chaos or you might go mad
Hahaha we are laughing at you
Here is the mic, do what you need to do
All this pain turned into purpose
All this past shit isn't my focus
Not that I'm trying to suppress
It's just that it's such a mess

Find a way forward, let it go
Concealed the cracks in the foundation, learned how to flow

But when that thing comes along that I actually really want
I'm thrown in this old shit that I thought I forgot

Can I trust what's meant to be, let go of what is and what's not
My fear is that you'll always continue to haunt

Can I lean in with no destiny, trying to be free
When control is what I've held onto in order to be
Longing starts to make you question your worth
It makes you hope for a new earth

Scared that it is not real
And what that would reveal
A girl who is longing for love,
A girl who believes in happy endings and Fairytales from above

A girl who desires and wants to be enough
A girl who no longer has to play tough

The ironic thing is, I can see all my influence, I can see my beauty and all of my light.
I can see I put up a really good fight
But I'm so tired being shackled to you
I need to let go, turn inward and love you know who

Crazy that even in this I feel the need to protect you
Save you from your trauma or feeling blue
Even in my pain, I'm fine I swear, I got it all together
I won't hate you, not now, not ever
I'll continue showing me who I want to be
I'm proud, filled with wonder, curious, someday free
honestly this monster is just a small part of me

What I can see and do—when the light embraces me...

Is nurture that monster, sing it a song
One of those lullabies that is soft and long
Because I'm not in a rush in loving that little one

Truth is her story is never really done
Her life will evolve, grow into anew
Give it time and patience, something borrowed, something blue
Lean in, open up, learn to receive
It starts with my ability to believe
That that monster is super worthy too
And in loving that monster I won't have to do
So sweet little monster, you can cry.
I'll actually be here to sing you a lullaby.
You are worthy
You are seen
You are enough
You are beautiful and wonderful and full of love

I Am From

I am from the yellow brick road and a duffle bag,
From a Velveeta box and wash rag.
I'm from Iowa winds and gypsy kin,
From rocks and stickers and scraped-up skin.

From the hollow—the pop-out camper adapts,
From the dustpan, where our labyrinth is a trap.
I am from the wild dandelion's seed,
Epigenetics producing an ornery weed.

A wish with roots in broken clay,
Needing to stand tall amongst the disarray.

I'm from camping fires and self-perpetuated storms,
From enmeshment's dance and shifting norms.
Where loneliness cracked like thunder skies,
And laughter lived between the lies.

From Betty, the sun-baked queen of ache,

And Alta, the shadow that abandonment makes.
I'm from chaos masked as love's disguise,
And numbing hearts with hollow cries.

From "You're too much," and also "not enough,"
To "Be a good girl, take care of our stuff."
From earth, air, water and fire,
Mary, did you know, Jesus is a liar.

From the jewelry box, the Germanic Europeans sway,
Where pot roast prayers and tuna helper stay.
From rocking them both to sleep at night,
While my own soul craved the light.

The family album? A mystery box,
Pippi tales through drunken talks.
In basements where secrets never kept,
Where grief and longing softly slept.

These parts—they hold a complex past,
A story stitched, both slow and fast.
Yet here I rise, soft and wild,
The mother now to my own inner child.

Rise Up

Hardships, struggle, and adversity
You are no stranger to me

Clouds coming and going
Darkness always showing
Energies ebb and flow
Yet nightmares never fully let go

Sadness, loneliness and pain

The devil inside cannot be tamed

You trick my mind, I want to rise high
But I can't tell if your voices are lies
Experiences, don't have to define me
Please let me be

Someone see beyond this outer shell
I don't want to stay stuck in my personal hell

I can sing, I can beam, say you can see
Just tell me you believe in me
Shackles releasing, breaking the mold
A new narrative about to unfold

The power of you
Help shine a light for me
The sun feels brighter
I feel so much lighter
Safety, connection helps me feel like I belong
For the first time you can hear my song

Meaning, purpose, and efficacy
My strengths I can now see
Deepening my understanding
Love and healing can soften my landing
A new level of awareness and regulation
I can now feel the sensation

Choices and rhythms are more healthy
I am evolving a new me

Enhancing and interconnecting
Rising and letting myself fly free…

TOOLS:
THE YOU INTERVENTION

Adult Attachment Inventory

What it is:

A reflection tool grounded in attachment theory that explores how early caregiving experiences shape your current relational patterns—secure, anxious, avoidant, or disorganized.

Why it helps:

Understanding your attachment pattern increases emotional intelligence and deepens awareness of how you relate, respond, and co-regulate with youth. It helps illuminate why certain behaviors trigger you and where your relational strengths naturally lie.

Tool:

Adult Attachment Inventory
https://traumasolutions.com/attachment-styles-quiz/

Activity:

Take the assessment using the link above. Review your results with curiosity—not judgment. Notice which patterns feel familiar and where they show up in your interactions with youth, colleagues, or loved ones.

Reflective prompts:

How do I typically respond when I feel rejected, criticized, or disconnected?
When my attachment wounds get triggered, how do my behaviors change?
What does my nervous system tend to do under relational stress—move toward, move away, or shut down?

Private Logic Reflection

What it is:

Private logic refers to the internal beliefs we form about ourselves, others, and the world—beliefs shaped by our lived experiences and attachment history.

Why it helps:

These beliefs often drive our reactions, expectations, and interpretations. Becoming aware of them allows us to respond more intentionally, rather than from old narratives or automatic assumptions.

Tool:

Private Logic Reflection Questions

- To be enough, I must/should…
- A good (parent/teacher/professional) should…
- I feel like a failure when…
- Youth should…Caregivers should…Professionals should…

Activity:

Choose several of the prompts above and write freely for each. Allow your answers to surface without censorship. Notice which beliefs feel inherited, which feel protective, and which feel outdated.

Reflective prompts:

What core messages do I tell myself when I'm stressed or overwhelmed?
Which of these beliefs strengthen who I want to be?
Which beliefs limit my capacity to show up with presence, compassion, or flexibility?

Parts Mapping (Internal Family Systems)

What it is:

A reflective process inspired by IFS (Schwartz, 1995) that helps you identify the different "parts" of yourself—Exiles (wounded parts), Managers (protective planners and controllers), and Firefighters (reactive protectors who step in when pain feels too close).

Why it helps:

Mapping your parts increases awareness of triggers as well as strengthens access to your calm, compassionate Self.

Tool:

Parts Mapping Templates (Google)

- **Exiles:** Parts that carry hurt, fear, shame, or unmet needs.
- **Managers:** Parts that try to prevent discomfort by controlling, pleasing, perfecting, or over-functioning.
- **Firefighters:** Parts that react quickly to protect—through anger, avoidance, shutting down, or numbing.

Activity:

Set aside time to identify parts in each category. Name what role each part plays, what it's protecting you from, and what it needs from your Self. Try approaching each part with curiosity and compassion.

Reflective prompts:

Which of my parts show up most often when engaging with youth?
When I feel triggered, which part usually takes over?
What does that part need—from me—to soften, relax, or step back?

Values Inventory

What it is:

A structured tool for naming your core values—the guiding principles that shape your choices, behaviors, and the way you engage.

Why it helps:

Values act like internal anchors. When we clarify our values, we become more consistent, grounded, and intentional—especially in moments of conflict or stress. Knowing our values also helps us create spaces that align with who we truly want to be.

Tool:

Personal Values Inventory
www.scottjeffrey.com/personal-core-values

Activity:

Take the assessment using the link above. Highlight your top five core values. Then reflect on how these values show up (or don't yet show up) in your daily interactions.

Reflective prompts:

How do my values shape the way I respond to challenging behaviors?
Where do my values support youth empowerment—and where might they unintentionally create pressure or expectation?
Am I creating an environment that reflects my values and invites others to discover their own?

Personality Priorities

What it is:

A framework from Adlerian psychology that identifies which internal motivation tends to drive your behavior—Comfort, Pleasing, Control, or Superiority (Kottman, 2001). Each priority brings strengths, vulnerabilities, and patterns that shape how you relate to others.

Why it helps:

Understanding your personality priorities offers insight into why certain youth feel easy to connect with while others feel more challenging. It also reveals what triggers your parts, what you tend to avoid, and how you may unintentionally communicate expectations in relationships.

Tool:

Descriptions of the Four Personality Priorities

- **Comfort:** Seeks ease, calm, predictability. Strengths include empathy and flexibility; vulnerabilities include procrastination or a tendency to avoid conflict.
- **Pleasing:** Seeks harmony and approval. Strengths include kindness and reliability; vulnerabilities include difficulty setting boundaries or overextending.
- **Control:** Seeks order, certainty, and predictability. Strengths include leadership and dependability; vulnerabilities include rigidity or difficulty with spontaneity.
- **Superiority:** Seeks competence, mastery, and usefulness. Strengths include high achievement and idealism; vulnerabilities include perfectionism or feeling "never enough."

Activity:

Identify which priority feels most like your primary mode of moving through the world—and which one might be secondary. Then reflect on how these tendencies show up in your relationships with youth.

Reflective prompts:

Who do I feel most naturally connected to or triggered by?

Am I interpreting a child's priority as defiance when it may simply be their way of navigating the world? *(e.g., a child seeking comfort avoiding stress; a child seeking superiority pursuing mastery)*

How might my dominant priority influence the expectations I place on young people? *(e.g., expecting children to "hurry" because I value efficiency, or expecting compliance because I value control)*

When do I overuse my primary priority in ways that may hinder connection? *(e.g., using control when co-regulation is needed, pleasing when boundaries are needed)*

What would it look like to honor a child's priority rather than trying to change it? *(e.g., offering choices to a control-priority youth)*

How can I lean into the strengths of my priority while staying aware of its blind spots?

Which priorities feel easy for me to connect with—and which priorities tend to trigger parts of me?

NERIS Type Explorer (16 Personalities)

What it is:

A personality assessment similar to the Myers-Briggs Type Indicator (MBTI). It explores how you take in information, make decisions, recharge your energy, and structure your daily life.

Why it helps:

This tool highlights your natural tendencies—whether you lead with intuition or detail, connection or logic, structure or flexibility. These preferences shape how you support and communicate, and what drains or energizes you.

Tool:

NERIS Type Explorer
www.16personalities.com

Activity:

Take the assessment using the link above. Read your full report with curiosity. Identify which parts feel like authentic strengths and which parts might lead to misunderstandings or misalignment in relationships.

Reflective prompts:

Which aspects of my personality type strengthen my ability to connect?
Which tendencies might inadvertently create distance, frustration, or misinterpretation?
How can I honor my natural style while staying flexible to meet the needs of others?

Enneagram

What it is:

A framework of nine core personality types that describe our internal motivations, fears, stress patterns, and pathways for growth. Unlike other tools, the Enneagram focuses on why we do what we do—not just what we do.

Why it helps:

The Enneagram offers profound insight into stress responses and protective patterns. It helps you understand what drives you, what overwhelms you, and what helps you return to your grounded, centered Self—all essential for attuned relationships.

Tool:

Enneagram Assessment
www.truity.com/test/enneagram-personality-test

Activity:

Take the Enneagram assessment and explore the type descriptions. Notice which traits resonate most deeply, especially around stress, conflict, and emotional triggers. Reflect on how this internal pattern shows up in your work with youth.

Reflective prompts:

Which Enneagram type do I most identify with, and what does that type tend to do under stress?
How does this insight guide my tendencies in relationships—such as withdrawing, overfunctioning, avoiding conflict, or becoming overly helpful?
What does my type need to feel grounded, compassionate, and present?

Temperament

What it is:

Temperament refers to the biologically rooted traits we are born with—patterns of energy, sensitivity, rhythm, adaptability, and emotional intensity that shape how we move through the world. These traits appear early in life and influence how we respond to people, environments, transitions, and stress.

Why it helps:

Understanding temperament increases both compassion and clarity. It allows us to honor our natural wiring rather than judge it, and it helps us recognize why certain youth feel effortless to connect with while others feel more challenging. When we understand our temperament, we can adjust our expectations, reduce shame, and create more attuned, balanced interactions—both with ourselves and with those we serve.

Tool:

You may explore your temperament by reflecting on the common categories used in temperament research. Most people fall somewhere along a spectrum of these traits:

- **Activity Level:** How much energy you naturally bring into daily tasks; whether you're more high-movement or calm and measured.
- **Regularity (Rhythmicity):** How predictable your sleeping, eating, and daily patterns tend to be.
- **First Reaction (Approach/Withdrawal):** Your initial response to new people, places, or situations—eager approach or cautious hesitation.
- **Adaptability:** How easily you adjust after the initial reaction; whether transitions come naturally or require time and support.
- **Sensory Sensitivity:** How strongly you react to sounds, textures, smells, lights, or environmental stimulation.

- **Intensity of Reaction:** The strength of your emotional expression—whether joy, frustration, excitement, or disappointment shows up subtly or powerfully.
- **Mood:** Your overall emotional tone—naturally positive and optimistic, more serious or reserved, or somewhere in between.
- **Distractibility:** How easily your attention shifts in response to external stimuli.
- **Persistence:** Your ability to stay with a task despite frustration, boredom,
or challenges.

Activity:

Reflect on your temperament using these categories. Notice how these patterns have shown up from childhood through adulthood—and how they influence your work with youth today.

Reflective prompts:

Am I expecting someone they biologically are not? *(e.g., asking a quiet child to be outgoing, or a sensitive child to "toughen up")*

Is my frustration more about a temperament mismatch than a true problem? Instead of trying to change them, how can I support their strengths and help them grow into who they already are?

How does my own natural temperament shape the way I connect, communicate, or set boundaries with youth?

How might my temperament influence the expectations I place on youth, especially those whose nervous systems operate differently from mine?

Authentic Happiness Assessments

The Authentic Happiness website (run by the University of Pennsylvania) offers a range of evidence-based tools that explore well-being, strengths, perseverance, compassion, and worldview. If you choose to explore these assessments, use them gently—not to judge yourself, but to better understand yourself.
www.authentichappiness.sas.upenn.edu/testcenter

Below are a few recommended tools and simple questions to help you reflect on what you discover.

VIA Character Strengths Survey

Your top character strengths (e.g., kindness, curiosity, fairness, leadership). Understanding your strengths helps you see what you naturally bring into relationships with others.

How often do I lead with my strengths in moments of stress or challenge?
Which of my strengths help me connect with youth most easily?
Which strengths do I underuse—and how might they support me in difficult interactions?

Grit Scale (Perseverance + Passion)

How you navigate long-term goals, frustration, and perseverance. Adults with low frustration tolerance often expect children to handle stress better than they can.

How do I respond when something is hard or progress is slow?
Do I expect people to persevere in ways that I struggle with myself?
How can I model healthy frustration tolerance for the young people I support?

PERMA Profiler (WellBeing Model)

Positive emotion, engagement, relationships, meaning, accomplishment. Low wellbeing in adults often shapes how we interpret behavior.

Which PERMA domains are thriving for me—and which feel depleted?
How does my current well-being influence my patience, attunement, or energy with youth?
What small shift could increase my capacity to show up with presence?

Compassionate Love Scale

Your capacity to extend care, empathy, and nurturance toward others. Working with youth requires compassion, especially when behavior is challenging.

When am I able to offer compassion easily—and when does it feel hard?
How do stress, exhaustion, or burnout impact my ability to stay compassionate?

Hope/Optimism Scale

Your overall worldview—hopeful, cautious, pessimistic, or resilient. Adults' belief systems deeply influence how they interpret youth behavior.

How do I tend to explain challenges—as temporary or permanent?
How might my worldview influence the expectations I set for youth?
Does my internal narrative lean toward "They will grow," or "This will never change"?

ACKNOWLEDGMENTS

The Chapter That Made Me a Mother

Micah—our firstborn. Our BB (you know what that means).
You move through this world with such tenderness. Such thoughtfulness. People always say, "Micah is so polite. He's such a good friend. He works so hard." And it's all so true. You care deeply about doing what is right. You give your whole heart to whatever you do and those in your circle. You are passionate and dedicated. You are attuned—to people, to tone, to fairness. You carry a quiet responsibility that sometimes feels heavier than it should. I know being the oldest isn't always easy. I know there are days that don't feel fair. But I hope—as you grow and stretch and become more of who you already are—that you never confuse responsibility with worth. You are wonderful not because you work so hard. Not because you do what is right. You are wonderful because you are you. The world is brighter because you are in it.

Kyler—our fierce, wandering, independent soul.
Everyone says you remind them of me when I was younger. I call you ornery—and I hope you always know that is a term of deep endearment. One of drippy aka pippy long stocking energy (you know what that means). You challenge molds. You question norms. You refuse to check boxes. You make people laugh louder and feel bigger. You make people feel special. You see needs and jump in to want to make a difference. You protect what matters to you with a ferocity that is breathtaking. But beneath that is the softest heart. You love deeply. You care in ways that are quiet and sacred. I hope you hold tightly to your energy. The world needs that spark. That courage. That refusal to be tamed. Forever our Nuggie.

Emalyn Gene—our youngest. We waited for your arrival, and you were the perfect addition.
Writing this book while you were a toddler felt like healing in motion. Raising you invited me to meet the little girl inside of me with more gentleness. More patience. More grace. Loving you taught me how to love her. You are brilliant. Sensitive in a way that is intuitive and wise. You sense what others miss. You ask questions that show that you see the world in such a unique way. You love deeply—and that will be your superpower. Even at four, you know what you want. You know what you deserve. I pray you never lose that voice. That steady knowing. I cannot wait to watch you continue to unfold, Pickle.

Elisha—you are one of the greatest gifts of my life.
You came into my world when I was searching for safety, for steadiness, for something that didn't feel like it might disappear. I remember seeing you for the first time—that smile. The warmth. The way you made a room feel softer just by being in it. Everyone who meets you feels it—that gentleness, that grounded kindness. When I dreamed about family—about the father of my children—I imagined patience. Loyalty. Love. Nurturing. Responsibility. Playful. You embody all of it. Building a family with you has been the greatest privilege of my life. Loving you—and being loved by you—gave me the security I needed to step fully into my light. I will spend the rest of my life grateful that you were a part of my journey.

Children of the Same Beginning

Tiffiney—I cannot imagine how heavy it must have been to be the oldest. Your memories stretch into years my little brain cannot even recall—years I know were not easy. You have carried weight in this world with a strength that is quiet and steady. You have persevered through barriers that would have broken many. You have raised two humans I am endlessly grateful for. Thank you for letting me be woven into their lives. Thank you for allowing me to become the auntie I always dreamed of being. Those memories—those ordinary, sacred moments—are some of my greatest sources of light. I was hard on you growing up. I carried judgment and anger that you did not deserve. You have taught me that life does not live in black and white—that there is gray, nuance, humanity in between. You have shown me that there is never only one right way to move through the world. Thank you for being my sister.

Sara—I am endlessly grateful you were born. The world said there were limits to what you could do—and you have quietly, steadily proven otherwise. You have overcome odds stacked against you with determination and grit that inspires me. As much as I wish I could remove every barrier from your path, I also know that the very things that make life harder have shaped you into someone rare and remarkable. You are special. Not despite your differences—but because of them. I am so proud of you.

Skyler—my very best buddy. In a childhood that often felt dark, you were light. There were days I felt like I was suffocating—and your presence gave me oxygen. You were the kindest soul I have ever known. Loving. Playful. Generous. Silly. Steady. You were everything I hoped to become in this world. You used to say you needed me growing up. But the truth is—it was me who needed you. In a world where love often felt confusing, your love was simple. Unconditional. Warm. It wrapped around me on the coldest days and reminded me that goodness was real. There are days grief that still catch me off guard. But there are more days where gratitude rises first. Your life mattered. Your life shaped me. I would not be who I am without you. You were—and always will be—one of the greatest gifts of my life.

Threads Woven along the Way

Bubba and Peanut—you two give my life so much joy. Seeing you born through adulthood has been one of the greatest experiences of my life. I am so proud of you. Every fiber of your being is beautiful and wonderful. I am so excited to continue to witness your lives evolve.

Journ and Syd—you two have not had it easy. You have fought and overcome so many obstacles. Still your hearts are filled with so much light and love. You possess so many gifts and are capable of endless possibilities. Your lives have been a blessing to me; I love you and always will.

Helen and Don—thank you for coming into my parents' lives when you did. For offering safety and steadiness. For loving them in ways that allow their later years to be softer, more peaceful, more whole. I am grateful my parents—and my children—have you. Don, you came into my life when I was in adolescence. Thank you for your ongoing patience and support of me.

Grandpa Larry—thank you for believing in restoration. For returning. For becoming a steady presence in my dad's life in adulthood. Your friendship to him has mattered more than you may ever know.

Great Grandma Alta—you showed me what resilience looks like across a lifetime. What legacy means. What strength wrapped in humility feels like. You were—and are—an inspiration.

Aunt Debbie, Uncle Barrett, Alexis, and Drake—thank you for being light in my childhood. For giving me spaces where I felt normalcy. For opening your home to Skyler—for being a safe harbor for him. He loved you deeply. He saw you as second parents, as siblings. Up until his final breath, he carried gratitude for the love you poured into him. Your family modeled something for me—something I tucked away quietly—and later built in my own life. Thank you.

To my extended family—shared DNA, shared history, shared traditions. Thank you for the holidays and stories and threads of heritage that shaped my becoming.

The Village That Grew With Me

To the many friends who have witnessed my evolution—Lauren, Kate, Amanda, Libby, Jaymie, Kim, Megan, Mel, Sara, Nicole, Abby V., Danielle and many more whose names live just as firmly in my heart—You have seen me in many versions of myself. Some of us found each other as high school girls laughing too loud. Some of us became college women trying to figure it out. Then Mothers. Businesswomen. Homeowners. Adults. Still, somehow, those same girls who have cried on bedroom floors and believed the world was both terrifying have also shown that life is also full of possibility. Some of the friendships distanced. Some carry on. Your love is warm. Your teasing is relentless. Your presence is steady. We have expanded our circle over the years, expanding our village, widening the table. The laughter has only grown louder. The stories deeper. The bonds stronger. Thank you for being my sisterhood.

Amanda—through thick and thin and we always seem to make it out the other side. Thank you for your unyielding loyalty.

Libby—making friends as adults is hard. Thanks for extending a hand and inviting me in. Your ongoing support and friendship have been invaluable.

Jaymie—you make me laugh and love deeper. Your compassion and warmth are often the blanket I need, thanks for being a vulnerable, loving friend.

Kate and Lauren—how did 14 year olds become 40 year olds. You've seen me in almost every chapter, thank you for being my friends.

Kim—regardless of distance you always think of me. Your thoughtfulness and care make my life better. Thank you.

Abigail—your soul sees me in a way I often go unseen. Your design is a gift to this world. Thank you for loving me.

To the Martelle crew—some of my greatest memories were formed running the streets of that small town. Sneaking out for late-night truth or dare. Pick-up football. Karaoke. Ghost in the graveyard. Simplicity that required imagination. Those friendships are etched into my bones.

Nelly—my childhood ride or die. Time and distance may have shifted the rhythm, but never the connection. Your friendship shaped me in ways that are permanent. I will love you—and feel tied to you—always.

To the Mount Vernon school crew—school dances. Sports. Slumber parties. Hallways filled with noise and belonging. I look back and feel lucky. Lucky to have walked those halls with you. Lucky to have grown up in a place filled with so many incredible humans.

To the Mount Vernon School District—you were safety. You were attachment figures when I needed them most. Teachers. Nurses. Coaches. You nurtured my strengths and gave me a haven when life felt unstable. Your belief in me allowed me to pour myself into passions that steadied me.

Years of Becoming

To my UNI crew—college was freedom and discovery. We were all learning who we were outside of everything we had known. Thank you for friendship and laughter and shared becoming.

To Camp Adventure—Europe expanded my world. It gave me experiences I may never have had otherwise. It widened my lens and my courage. Thank you to roommates, friends—that summer was one of the very best.

To Bremwood—working residential care while still so young taught me about vulnerability, mental health, and resilience in ways no classroom could. Those bonds will never fade. Your friendships felt like comfort and an anchor I needed during that time. Thank you.

Keki—a randomly assigned roommate who became sacred. You were the first to hear many of the stories written in this book. You listened with curiosity and kindness. You offered me your family—a model of love and steadiness. You were exactly what I needed at that stage of my life and you will always hold an incredibly special place in my heart.

Mount Mercy crew—grad school met me while I was starting my healing journey. Thank you for being my classmates and offering connection, reflection and learning. Many of you are now respected colleagues changing lives. I am grateful our paths crossed.

Dr. Lyle—your wisdom on systems, therapy, and the art of "it depends" shaped me profoundly. You modeled being—your lessons continue to guide me every day.

Dr. Kottman—your mentorship formed the play therapist I am today. Your legacy runs deep. Thank you for believing in me as a clinician, a mother, and a human.

Mollie—you saw something in me and truly believed in me. That belief was the warmth I needed to also believe in myself. Thank you for giving me opportunities to let my light shine.

To the therapists who have walked alongside my healing—thank you for helping me nurture myself. Your work changes lives. It helped change mine.

The Hands That Helped Shape This Becoming

Libby O'Donnell—you arrived at exactly the right time. Your editing, your insight, your steady encouragement shaped this manuscript in ways I could not have done alone.

James Freeman—you helped give structure to something that felt too big to begin. Your patience and belief allowed RISE to truly rise.

Mary Foreman—you took my heart and turned it into something tangible. Your gift is unmatched. Thank you for taking my wild art and illustrating this book with such care and being so patient with me, always.

Thank you to the Tanager team who read and offered feedback and edits along the way. Thank you for being in this with me.

Where We Rise Together

There is a word that found its way into our leadership language—carried in by Jennie, nurtured by many—Ubuntu. I am because we are.

It names what we have always known. That is the truth of this final section. This organization is where I grew up professionally. Where I learned. Where I failed and tried again. Where wild ideas were piloted and servant leadership was tested in real time.

School Based Program—You believed in me when I was still learning how to believe in myself. You saw the vision before it was fully formed and chose to build it with me. You were not just a team—you were courage in motion, steady hands at the beginning. What we created together changed the trajectory of my career. I carry that gratitude with me every day.

Jennie, Abby, Lindsey, Andy, Blake—Blood, sweat, tears, values, long conversations about leadership. I know you have moved on to the next chapters of your story, please know I will forever be grateful for our time together and what you gave to Tanager.

Maggie and Joella—Clinical directors in the thick of it beside me. Maggie, thank you for continuing to lead and advocate by my side year after year. You are a constant I've needed and I'll always feel grateful for you. Joella thank you for leaping into leadership with a service heart. You make us better. You both live RISE. You help me grow. You steady me. Words cannot capture what you mean.

Program Directors and Managers—Crystal, Emma, Tawny, Cassie, Lauren, Nicole, Tresa, Kenzie, Heather.
You are my village within these walls. You give so much of yourselves. You remind me of why. I've grown up in leadership with a lot of you, thank you for being my people and believing in me. Tawns I think we are twins separated at birth. Thanks for beliving in me and sharing parts of my soul.

Residential Managers—Amelia, Brooke, Tiffany
Residential services has wrapped their arms around RISE in ways I could not have imagined. You, programmatically, gave RISE life. It is so beautiful to see it woven into every piece of daily living for the youth we serve. Amelia

you might be one of the strongest advocates for this framework, thank you for embracing it the way you do.

Outpatient Program Supervisors—Nikki, Amy, Dawn, Robin, Maggie, Kelsey
You are in the trenches everyday supporting people who do the hardest work. You connect our values to direct work. Thank you for building bridges and supporting so many.

To all the staff, past and present—You show up for mission. You give yourself to a greater good. Thank you for being a part of the collective light.

To the Executive Team—Thank you for doing leadership with me every single day. For the hard conversations. The strategic pivots. The long meetings. The shared responsibility of stewarding an organization that holds so many vulnerable lives.

Jess—We stepped into executive leadership together. Two women learning how to hold vision while holding complexity. You did not have to embrace RISE the way you did—and yet you chose to learn it and live it. You breathe it in operations, in systems, in conversations where it would have been easier not to. You have been a friend in the trenches. A steady voice. A challenger when needed. A cheerleader always. I am deeply grateful we have walked this chapter side by side.

Mike—Thirty-five years of faithful leadership. That kind of legacy cannot be summarized—it can only be felt. Long before I understood executive systems or nonprofit complexity, you were shaping the culture I would one day grow inside of. Your steadiness, your commitment have left fingerprints across this organization. It has been a privilege to be supported by you.

Tanager Board—Thank you for believing in the work. For stewarding vision with trust.

To every youth and family past and present—Thank you for trusting me, for letting me witness your stories, for your courage. Each of you teaching me something about life, about love and about humanness. You will forever have a special place in my heart.

To our CEO, Okpara Rice—
There are people who manage. There are people who supervise. And then there are people who see.
Who influence. Impact. Lead.
You saw something in me long before I could see it in myself. You offered me a mirror—not one that reflected my doubt or my limits, but one that reflected possibility. Worth. Capacity. Greatness I had not yet claimed.
RISE—and this book—would not exist without your belief in me.
You have pushed me beyond the ceilings I quietly placed over my own head. You have challenged me to think bigger, lead braver, and trust deeper. Over and over again, you have nudged me to fly free—even when I was still gripping the edge. Your courage. Your advocacy. Your steady confidence in my voice and vision have been gifts I will never take lightly. Tanager is a place I call home—and that is in no small part because of the way you have supported every part of me. Not just the leader. Not just the clinician. But the whole human.
Thank you for being a mentor.
A brother in the work.
And one of the strongest supporters of my light.

Nonprofit leadership requires courage that often goes unseen. It requires balancing mission with margin, heart with sustainability, vision with reality. The altruism I witness daily humbles me. People who give their skills and hearts to a world that can never fully compensate them. The beauty of servant leadership—lived, not spoken.

To every colleague, partner, cohort, institute, and community voice who has influenced me—thank you. Growth, influence and accomplishment never happens in isolation.

This book—this life—is a tapestry.
And every one of you is a thread.
RISE is not mine.
It is ours.

It was born in conversation. In conflict. In courage. In collaboration. It lives because of every interaction, every relationship, and every human who has poured themselves into me and into a mission of empowering, inspiring and healing the lives of others.

Ubuntu. I am because we are.

A LETTER TO US

To me and to you.
For me. For you.

Being a child of trauma leaves wounds many will never see.
It wraps you in shadow and somehow teaches you how to find light inside it.

When the world keeps ticking, you float in the wind.
You flow in the water.
You burn with the fire.
You plant roots in the earth.

But this is not a letter about survival.
This is a letter about staying.

I see your soul.
I love you.
Always. Forever.

And if you forget, read this again and again—;

Reclaim the heart—it has been waiting.
Evolve like water—falling as a waterfall, floating as a lake, carving stone in ways that last long after you are gone.
Ground—even when you are blindfolded, even when the map disappears and you have to trust the soles of your feet in the sand.
Imagine yourself flying—not escaping, but rising—a bubble catching light, proof that we can still be held.

Nurture the fingerprint you leave on this world. There will never be another pattern like yours.
Amaze yourself with your own capacity to bend without breaking— like yoga at dusk, whispering 'Namaste' to the ache and meaning it.
Laugh—like Laffy Taffy, sticky-sweet and unapologetic—joy softens what tries to harden you.
Dance when the music feels far away. Your body remembers rhythms your mind forgot.
Dare to wash the mask away—like clay softening in a sauna—and let your real skin breathe.
Embrace the pauses—the red light glowing steady in the dark. Surrender in the stillness.
Wander. Take the long way home. Not all detours are mistakes—some reveal the road we could not yet see.
Anchor yourself when the current pulls. Hold tight—not to fear, but to hope.
Yearn. Want. Let yourself paint with no canvas.
Never forget that even when you feel alone, your soul connects beyond the knowing.
Exhale—and notice that you are still here, still breathing, still becoming, peace will find us.

This is not just a letter. It is an invitation.

There are journeys you have not yet taken.
Songs you have yet to sing.
Trees you have not yet climbed.
Stars you have yet to see.

There is still so much more ahead.

Stay.

REFERENCES

Ainsworth, M., & Bowlby, J. (1991). An ethological approach to personality development. *American Psychologist, 46*(4), 333–341.

Allen, B. (2023). The historical foundations of contemporary attachment theory: From John Bowlby to Mary Ainsworth. In B. Allen, *The science and clinical practice of attachment theory: A guide from infancy to adulthood* (pp. 13–35). American Psychological Association.

Bandura, A. (1997). *Self-efficacy: The exercise of control.* W. H. Freeman.

Bandura, A. (Ed.). (1997). *Self-efficacy in changing societies.* Cambridge University Press.

Bolton, K. (2022). *Restorative communities: From conflict to conversation.* Piper's Press.

Bowlby, J. (1988). *A secure base: Parent-child attachment and healthy human development.* Basic Books.

Boyes-Watson, C., & Pranis, K. (2020). *Circle forward: Building a restorative school community* (Rev. ed.). Living Justice Press.

Brown, B. (2010). *I thought it was just me (but it isn't): Making the journey from "what will people think?" to "I am enough"*. Gotham Books.

Brown, B. (2012). *Daring greatly: How the courage to be vulnerable transforms the way we live, love, parent, and lead.* Gotham Books.

Brown, B. (2015). *Rising strong.* Spiegel & Grau.

Brown, B. (2018). *Dare to lead: Brave work. Tough conversations. Whole hearts.* Random House.

Brown, B. (2020). *The gifts of imperfection* (10th anniversary ed.). Hazelden.

Chapman, G., & Campbell, R. (2016). *The five love languages of children: The secret to loving children effectively.* Northfield Publishing.

Clements, R., & Musker, J. (Directors). (2016). *Moana* [Film]. Walt Disney Animation Studios.

Colvin, G., & Sugai, G. (1989). *Managing escalated behavior.* Behavior Associates.

Dana, D. (2023). *Polyvagal practices: Anchoring the self in safety.* W. W. Norton & Company.

de Becker, G. (1997). *The gift of fear: Survival signals that protect us from violence.* Dell Publishing.

Docter, P. (Director), Del Carmen, R. (Co-director), Rivera, J. (Producer), & Lasseter, J. (Executive Producer). (2015). *Inside Out* [Film]. Walt Disney Pictures; Pixar Animation Studios.

Duschinsky, R., Granqvist, P., & Forslund, T. (2023). *The psychology of attachment.* Routledge.

Engler, B. (2022, September 2). Teaching your child to deal with conflict. *Connections Academy.* **https://www.connectionsacademy.com/support/resources/article/building-conflict-resolution-skills-in-children/**

Felitti, V. J., Anda, R. F., Nordenberg, D., Williamson, D. F., Spitz, A. M., Edwards, V., Koss, M. P., & Marks, J. S. (1998). Relationship of childhood abuse and household dysfunction to many of the leading causes of death in adults: The adverse childhood experiences (ACE) study. *American Journal of Preventive Medicine*, 14(4), 245–258.

Frankl, V. E. (2006). *Man's search for meaning*. Beacon Press. (Original work published 1946)

Gilovich, T., Savitsky, K., & Medvec, V. H. (1998). The illusion of transparency: Biased assessments of others' ability to read one's emotional states. *Journal of Personality and Social Psychology*, 75(2), 332–346. https://doi.org/10.1037/0022-3514.75.2.332

Goleman, D. (1995). *Emotional intelligence: Why it can matter more than IQ*. Bantam Books.

Goleman, D., Kaplan, R. S., David, S., & Eurich, T. (2018). *Self-awareness* (HBR Emotional Intelligence Series). Harvard Business Review Press.

Gold, C., & Tronick, E. (2020). *The power of discord: Why the ups and downs of relationships are the secret to building intimacy, resilience, and trust.* Little, Brown Spark.

Gottman, J. M., & Silver, N. (1999). *The seven principles for making marriage work.* Crown Publishers.

Green, H. (2013). *Using your brain to win in today's hyper-paced world.* Human Factor.

Greene, R. (2016). *Raising human beings: Creating a collaborative partnership with your child.* Scribner.

Han, J., Wong, I., Christensen, H., & Batterham, P. (2022). Resilience to suicidal behavior in young adults: A cross-sectional study. *Scientific Reports,* 12, 11419.

Hotchkin, T. (2020). RISE: Wellness and resilience framework. *Relational Child and Youth Care Practice,* 33(2), 40–49.

Hotchkin, T. (2024). *RISE: Together We Rise*. Tanager. https://tanagerplace.org/rise/

Kottman, T. (2011). *Play therapy: Basics and beyond*. American Counseling Association.

Kottman, T. (2015, December 4–6). *Introduction to Adlerian play therapy* [Training]. The Encouragement Zone.

Kralovansky, G., Taylor, H., & Margol, B. (Writers), & Crowell, J. (Director). (2011). *Remember this!* (Season 1, Episode 3) [TV series episode]. In J. Kolber (Producer), *Brain Games*. National Geographic. https://youtu.be/pHHREtLdwC8

Kuypers, L. (2011). *The zones of regulation*. Think Social Publishing.

Lambert, M. J. (1992). Implications of outcome research for psychotherapy integration. In J. C. Norcross & M. R. Goldfried (Eds.), *Handbook of psychotherapy integration* (pp. 94–129). Basic Books.

Landreth, G. L. (2012). *Play therapy: The art of the relationship* (3rd ed.). Routledge.

Latif, S. (2021, April 20). Attachment styles in children (& how to raise secure kids). *PositivePsychology.com*. **https://positivepsychology.com/attachment-styles-childhood**

Lew, A., & Bettner, B. (1996). A *parent's guide to understanding and motivating children*. Connexions Press.

Maslow, A. H. (1943). A theory of human motivation. *Psychological Review,* 50(4), 370–396. https://doi.org/10.1037/h0054346

Maslow, A. H. (1969). The farther reaches of human nature. *Journal of Transpersonal Psychology,* 1(1), 1–9.

Maté, G., & Maté, D. (2022). *The myth of normal: Trauma, illness, and healing in a toxic culture.* Avery.

McGill, J., Adler-Baeder, F., & Rodriguez, P. (2016). Mindfully in love: A meta-analysis of the association between mindfulness and relationship satisfaction. J*ournal of Human Sciences and Extension*, 4(1).

Nathanson, D. L. (1992). *Shame and pride: Affect, sex, and the birth of the self.* W. W. Norton & Company.

Nelsen, J. (2006). *Positive discipline: The classic guide to helping children develop self-discipline, responsibility, cooperation, and problem-solving skills.* Ballantine.

Nolen-Hoeksema, S. (2008). Rethinking rumination. *Perspectives on Psychological Science,* 3(5), 400–424.

Porges, S. W. (2022). Polyvagal theory: A science of safety. *Frontiers in Integrative Neuroscience,* 16, Article 871227. https://doi.org/10.3389/fnint.2022.871227.

Reichard, R., Avey, J., Lopez, S., & Dollwet, M. (2013). Having the will and finding the way: A review and meta-analysis of hope at work. *The Journal of Positive Psychology,* 8(4), 292–304.

Reivich, K., & Shatté, A. (2003). *The resilience factor: 7 keys to finding your inner strength and overcoming life's hurdles.* Harmony.

Rogers, F. (2003). *The world according to Mister Rogers: Important things to remember.* Hyperion.

Rosenberg, M. B. (2015). *Nonviolent communication: A language of life* (3rd ed.). PuddleDancer Press.

Ryan, R. M., & Deci, E. L. (2000). Self-determination theory and the facilitation of intrinsic motivation, social development, and well-being. *American Psychologist, 55*(1), 68–78.

Saltzberg, B. (2010). *Beautiful oops!.* Workman Publishing.

Siegel, D. J. (2020). *The developing mind: How relationships and the brain interact to shape who we are* (3rd ed.). Guilford Press.

Siegel, D. J., & Bryson, T. P. (2011). *The whole-brain child.* Delacorte Press.

Siegel, D. J., & Bryson, T. P. (2014). *No-drama discipline.* Ballantine Books.

Siegel, D. J., & Bryson, T. P. (2020). *The power of showing up: How parental presence shapes who our kids become and how their brains get wired.* Ballantine Books.

Siegel, D. J., & Hartzell, M. (2014). *Parenting from the inside out: How a deeper self-understanding can help you raise children who thrive* (2nd ed.). TarcherPerigee.

Sinek, S. (2018, January 5). *Choose falling over failure* [Video]. YouTube. **https://www.youtube.com/watch?v=TTMiILxqBSc**

Sinek, S. (2009). *Start with why: How great leaders inspire everyone to take action.* Portfolio.

van der Kolk, B. (2014). *The body keeps the score: Brain, mind, and body in the healing of trauma.* Viking.

Wachtel, T., & McCold, P. (2000). Restorative justice in everyday life. In J. Braithwaite & H. Strang (Eds.), *Restorative justice in civil society* (pp. 117–125). Cambridge University Press.

Wachtel, T. (2013). *Defining restorative.* International Institute for Restorative Practices.

www.ingramcontent.com/pod-product-compliance
Lightning Source LLC
LaVergne TN
LVHW010641110826
845149LV00014B/2910

* 9 7 9 8 9 9 5 1 7 9 6 0 3 *